THE FRENCH AND THE DARDANELLES

THE FRENCH
AND THE DARDANELLES

A Study of Failure in the Conduct of War

by George H. Cassar

London. George Allen & Unwin Ltd
Ruskin House   Museum Street

ISBN: 0 04 940034 7

Printed in Great Britain
in 11 point Plantin type
by the Aldine Press · Letchworth · Herts

Preface

It has been over half a century since the Anglo-French force withdrew from the blood-soaked beaches of Gallipoli. Many reasons combined to frustrate an enterprise the success of which would have marked a vital turning point in the history of the Great War. The narrow margin by which victory was missed makes this perhaps the most poignant tragedy of the conflict. No other episode during the war has been so widely discussed and none has aroused such fierce controversy.

About six months after the evacuation a Royal Commission was set up in London to inquire into the causes of the Allied defeat. The Commission report [1] came out the following year and concluded that the expedition had been ill-conceived and ineptly executed. But in 1917 the Commission was in no position to take a balanced view of the campaign and its relation to the total war effort. An additional year of slaughter in the trenches in France, the collapse of Russia and, after the war, the revelation by the Turks that they were on the verge of defeat on a number of occasions, all combined to shed new light on the subject. By the mid-1920s a battle of books was being waged and embers of the fire are still glowing. In recent years the trend has been to ascribe the Allied disaster to the higher direction of the war. The studies of Lord Hankey, *The Supreme Command: 1914–1918*; Trumbull Higgins, *Winston Churchill and the Dardanelles*; and Paul Guinn, *British Strategy and Politics, 1914 to 1918*, suggest that the setback was due not so much to the mistakes on the battlefield as to the failure of the politicians at home. But while these accounts give adequate attention to the English viewpoint there is too little on the French side. I have therefore tried to contribute towards filling the gap. In the light of fresh evidence and by reinterpreting where it seemed necessary facts already known, I have attempted to present a new focus on the process of decision-making which led directly to the Gallipoli catastrophe.

There is a wealth of literature on World War I, and doing research on an aspect of it requires consulting innumerable works. The principal books used are listed in the bibliography, but five proved of such help that they must be mentioned here. The voluminous memoirs of Raymond Poincaré, *Au service de la France*, are indispensable to any

[1] The report was never fully published and until 1965 was a classified document. A censored version of the first report was made public in 1917 and the final report, also heavily censored, became available in 1919.

subject dealing with war-time politics in France. These include not only day-to-day development on the political scene as witnessed by the French President, but also a summary of the results of the Cabinet meetings, especially valuable since official minutes were not kept. The published army documents relating to the Dardanelles Operation, *Les armées françaises dans la grande guerre*, tome 8, annexe, vol. 1, are very important for determining French military thought. The personal narratives of Joffre, *Personal Memoirs* and of Sarrail, *Mon commandement en Orient*, both of which relate conflicting testimony and so must be approached with caution, nonetheless provide the only comprehensible first-hand accounts in their heated controversy with the government during the summer and fall of 1915. J. C. King in *Generals and Politicians* vividly describes the relentless struggle between the soldiers and the civil authorities over control of the war.

The research for this project also involved examining an enormous amount of documentary material, ranging from service and personal records to recently declassified official papers. It has, unfortunately, not been possible to indicate several of the collections consulted in France. The literary executors did not wish to be besieged by calls from students and scholars and kindly granted me access to the papers in their possession on condition that I refrain from citing the source in the footnotes.

Ypsilanti, Michigan   G.H.C.

June 1970

Acknowledgments

Maps 2, 3 and 4 are reproduced from Alan Moorehead's *Gallipoli* (published 1956) by the kind permission of the publishers, Hamish Hamilton Ltd, London.

Contents

Maps

Introduction

'For armies can signify but little abroad unless there be counsel and wise management at home.'

Cicero

So much has been written on the causes of the First World War that any assertion of why the Powers went to war in 1914 inevitably would have to be qualified to such an extent that it would lose much of its importance. What emerges much more clearly, however, is the fact that the reasons for going to war were quickly submerged by the enormous effort which was required by all the belligerents to prevent the other side from winning a clear-cut military victory. As a result of this great exertion, perhaps the most basic aim of the Allies in 1914, namely the preservation of the *status quo ante bellum*, ceased to satisfy both sides as a legitimate political end for the war. This led to a vast confusion of war aims, again on both sides, but one that was to be more noticeable on the side of the Allies, possibly because they won and had to apply the aims which they professed and also because, within the Entente, there were several Powers of almost equal stature, all of which had Imperial as well as European ambitions.

The three main Allied Powers, Britain, France and Russia, were sometimes apt to confuse their Imperial with their European desires, and, in consequence, there was a tendency to revive old rivalries. These rivalries, however, were more often between themselves than with their common enemies, for the Allies controlled the seas around Europe and had quickly destroyed Germany's pretension of being anything but a Continental Power. This created many difficulties because in formulating their war aims the three Powers were constantly concerned more with each other than with Germany.

'The "war aims" of the Entente Powers sprang . . . from a

tangle of contradictory motives. Each wanted to improve its position – almost as much against its present partners as against Germany. Each came to accept the view that Germany should be destroyed as a Great Power, though each naturally emphasized the aspects of destruction which best suited its own need.' [1]

The campaign in the Dardanelles was to illustrate this confusion of aims and the way in which the Powers had become so limited in their wisdom that they could not bring themselves to discuss seriously the immediate political objectives of the campaign, as opposed to the long-range idea of the dismemberment of the Turkish Empire. The command of the seas, which the expedition tried to exploit, proved to be less of an asset precisely because the Allies were incapable of formulating exact political aims for their military actions.

The Alliance system was, in any case, weakened by the usual problems of priorities which have a tendency to disrupt joint operations – such as the Western front had come to be in practice, if not in theory, by the end of 1914. The Dardanelles campaign added to this strain. The two main partners in that operation, France and Britain, were not clear about the political ends – and they were even more confused about the place in the operation of the Russian Empire and the still-neutral Balkan states.

Another disruptive element in the enterprise was the continuous strife within each of the Governments between the military and civilian leadership. The civilian authorities sought to find in an Eastern strategy the solution to the stalemate on the Western front. But this Eastern strategy led them quickly into Imperial rivalries, so that they became more concerned with the possible gains to be achieved by the fall of the Turkish Empire than with the military and naval means for achieving that end. Moreover, they had to deal constantly with an army command reluctant to consider seriously a military alternative to the slaughter in the West. The soldiers were so obsessed with a military victory that they tried to prevent the civilian leaders from shaping the operation to suit whatever political ends they might envisage.

[1] A. J. P. Taylor, *The Struggle for Mastery in Europe* (Oxford, 1957), p. 537.

Much of the confusion can be traced to the misconceptions which nearly everyone had about the nature of the war when it started. Few believed that it could last very long, nearly all were convinced that it could be concluded without a major dislocation of the social and economic fabric of European civilization. It was to be a swift military campaign, not necessitating any major political or economic reorganization; 'business as usual' was the motto. And for this reason the soldiers and sailors could and should be given a free hand in running the war.

Toward the end of 1914, it was clear to the civilian authorities that their assumptions were fallacious, but this realization did not in any way solve the new and immensely complicated problems which were caused by the military stalemate. All the Powers began to reshape their economic and social policies in view of the necessity to fight a total war.

In the growing strain of harnessing a great nation for war, one of the major problems which emerged was the question of trying to find a structure of supreme command which would take into account the changing nature of the conflict. The campaign in the Dardanelles was an example of the divisions and the divergent interests which were not resolved by the existing command structure. This was particularly so in France, where the Governments prior to 1914 had made no provision for creating a body similar to the later War Council in England, that could serve as a link between civilian and military leadership. It was left to a series of laws dating back to 1875 to determine the relationship between the high command and the Government. In theory the President was in charge of the army, though in practice he always delegated the supreme command to the Chief of the General Staff. At all times the Minister of War remained responsible for the administration of the army. While the Cabinet or Council of Ministers [2] formulated the broad lines of strategy, the high command had complete freedom to carry out its orders. This principle appears cut and dried, but its application was difficult since there was no way to draw a line between policy and its execution. With no civilian-dominated body to co-ordinate Government and army power, it became difficult for the politicians to avoid interfering somehow

[2] *Conseil des ministres.*

in the conduct of operations, an interference which often seemed to the military to be misplaced. There were occasions when it was very tempting for a strong commander, because of his popularity, to try to influence or even to coerce the Government into accepting his views about grand strategy. The Dardanelles campaign illustrates the fatal weakness in the command structure of the Government, as the conflict between the advocates of a Western strategy, or the soldiers, and those of an Eastern strategy, or the politicians, was sharpened by the presence of the German army on French soil.

The French Government, like the other belligerent governments, did not try to solve the problems created by the stalemate in the most obvious way of seeking a political settlement for the European crisis; nor did it feel strong enough to wrest the control of the war on the main front from the hands of the soldiers. Instead the civil authorities welcomed the possibility of opening a new front, one over which they might exercise more direct control, and which might break the deadlock in the West.

The first suggestion for such a 'second front' was a plan for a landing in Salonika, which would serve to complicate the military situation of the Central Powers and also help Serbia. The French high command naturally opposed such an idea, which would weaken its over-all control of the war and draw troops away from what it considered to be the main theatre of war. And there can be no doubt that in this early stage, before the arrival of large numbers of British units, it would have been difficult to find sufficient French troops to make such an operation feasible. The civil authorities were, therefore, forced to abandon this project, but, at the same time, resented this clear impotence in the face of military opposition.

Soon after this incident, the French Government received an invitation from the British to co-operate in a naval enterprise which had a similar strategic aim, namely the forcing of the Dardanelles and the capture of Constantinople. It was at first thought that purely naval action would suffice so that no units would be diverted from France. The risks of course were great, but the stakes were far higher. Thus the French consented but without enthusiasm.

Early in 1915 the Anglo-French fleet, sent on a mission of death, proved a ghastly failure. Committed fully since the outbreak of war to land operations in France, the Government drifted into a military campaign in Gallipoli despite the strenuous opposition of the army that any reduction of strength on the main front would expose the Allies to a crushing defeat. Without sufficient resources for one theatre the country found itself engaged in two. For the better part of 1915 the civil authorities were unable to decide between the rival policies of attacking Germany at her strongest point, on the Western front, or at her weakest point by way of the Dardanelles. With the enemy firmly entrenched on French soil it was tempting not to defer to the army's wishes that the main effort be continued on the Western theatre. Ill-supported and often forced to improvise, the troops at Gallipoli were allowed to moulder until threatened with destruction.

The expensive and disappointing results of the attacks on the main front in the spring and early summer led to increasing discontent in the country and after the failure of the second offensive in Gallipoli, the French Government came forward with a proposal to send out a new army to bring the campaign in the East to a quick conclusion. The plan turned out to be as illusory as a mirage. Barely three weeks later the Government reversed its original offer and pressed instead for an expedition to Salonika. The English fought the idea, pleading for a renewed attempt on the Peninsula, but to no avail. Salonika closed the curtain on the Dardanelles. Already over-extended, the Allies could not meet the demands of two theatres in the Near East.

This account, then, proposes to investigate the reasons for French participation in the Dardanelles expedition; the question of war aims among the Allies as it relates to the operation; the sudden decision of the French to send troops to Salonika rather than to the Dardanelles and the subsequent manœuvring to force acceptance of this view upon the English; and the continuing struggle between civil and military leaders in France over what may be called grand strategy and the effects of this struggle on the military operations in Gallipoli.

Chapter 1

ARMY AND STATE BEFORE WORLD WAR I

'Wars are in reality . . . only the manifestations of policy itself. The subordination of the political point of view to the military would be unreasonable, for policy has created the war; policy is the intelligent faculty, war only the instrument, and not the reverse. The subordination of the military point of view to the political is, therefore, the only thing which is possible.'
Clausewitz

'The Republic exists; it is the legal government of the country. To want anything else would create a new revolution and the most formidable one of all. Let us not waste time proclaiming the Republic but use our time to stamp it with its desirable and necessary characteristics.'
Adolphe Thiers, 1872

'For the attack only two things are necessary; to know where the enemy is and to decide what to do. What the enemy intends to do is of no importance.'
Loiseau de Grandmaison, 1912

The outbreak of the First World War brought a great upsurge of patriotism in France (as it did in all the belligerent nations) that seemed to heal all the angry strife of the preceding years. Seldom in her long history had France known such complete unanimity. The people of the country were told that the war was a struggle to resist German aggression and to preserve national liberty and independence. With no thought for the state of preparedness or formidable strength of the enemy, the general conviction was expressed that France would easily win the war, recover the lost provinces of Alsace-Lorraine and regain the hegemony of Europe. If there were sceptics that viewed the outcome of the conflict with some alarm they were quietly submerged by the delirious enthu-

1

siasm of the public which found ample security in the Alliance. It was taken for granted that when the Russian 'steamroller' began to move and when Britain, unprepared for war, could bring her resources to bear, the Germans would be crushed within a matter of weeks. Reflecting the bellicose mood of the country, crowds filled the Paris streets with cries of 'To Berlin!' and 'Down with the Prussians!' Parents waved off their sons to war amidst the clamour of patriotic songs and warlike slogans, with every expectation of their return before Christmas. Swept by the war hysteria, political groups agreed to lay aside their grievances and rivalries and stand together in the hour of crisis. And in the 'national community created by war the Army became the highest and most perfect symbol of the *union sacrée*, reawakening the old fervour that had prevailed during the quarter century following the defeat of 1871'. The conduct of war demanded the closest cohesion between the political and military structures, but abdication of power, even temporarily, into the hands of the high command was an unprecedented act in light of the traditional distrust the state harboured for the army.

Since the emergence of a professional army in the seventeenth century, which created the problem of civil-military relations, French history records numerous clashes between political and army leaders. During the early reign of Louis XIV the army, professing loyalty to the monarch and ready to suppress internal rebellion or fight foreign wars if paid promptly and adequately, was nonetheless an undisciplined, semi-autonomous body within the state. The practice of venality and plurality of offices was rampant; the responsibilities of officers in various posts were vague and often overlapped; and finally there existed no supreme commander, with the result that local leaders acted as their own masters, frequently disregarding regulations and orders from the king, and even remaining inactive or refusing to co-ordinate their movements during battle. For decades the officer corps had endeavoured to preserve its traditional prerogatives and ideas and had tried to destroy any force that threatened its interests or aims. However, when Michel Le Tellier became Minister of War in the period of Mazarin's ascendancy, the military arm was gradually brought under the control of the state. Displaying tact and patience, but never excluding a firm hand, Le Tellier was able to pare away obsolete posts, terminate multiple appointments and create a military hierarchy with the duties of successive ranking officers clearly delineated and in which military authority was concentrated in the hands of a commander-in-chief who was responsible to the Minister of War. This programme of reform had a twofold effect. First it eliminated waste and confusion and promoted order. Second it compelled the officers to recognize that the real chief of the army was the king, upon whose favours they depended for advancement and wealth. Le Tellier's policy was continued by his successor and son, the Marquis de Louvois, who completed the transformation of the French army, the character of which remained unchanged until the revolution of 1789.

The overthrow of Louis XVI and the triumph of the radical Jacobins led to a war between France and her neighbours. The French, without adequate leadership, fared badly from the start, and as they fled before the advancing enemy armies panic seized the capital. The National Convention, therefore, voted dictatorial powers to a group of twelve called the Committee of Public Safety. On August 23, 1793 the Committee issued a decree of the *levée en masse* which called for the mobilization of the total human and material resources of the state. Under the direction of Lazare Carnot, warlord of the republic, the armies were equipped and disciplined, and competent officers were appointed to positions of command.

In order to maintain a close watch over the armed forces, as it was suspected that most high-ranking officers still harboured royalist sympathies, the Jacobins undertook to reshape the structure and command of the army. A series of laws made all male citizens eligible to enter the officer corps, forbade army leaders to use force or coercion against the populace unless at the request of government authorities, and required all soldiers to swear a new oath of allegiance to the republic. Contrary to sound military principles the Jacobins refused to set up a single system of command lest too much power in the hands of a general ultimately lead to the establishment of a military dictatorship. It now fell on the shoulders of the 'representatives on mission', usually chosen from the ranks of the National Convention, to control the army at the front. They inculcated the common soldiers with the new revolutionary ideas, arranged operational plans with divisional commanders, promoted or demoted officers and even executed generals who did not produce victory.

The changes in the army had an immediate and telling effect. The French resumed the initiative, defeated the armies of the coalition on every front and hurled them back. By 1794 the Jacobins could well afford to promise aid and fraternity to all peoples wishing to recover their liberty. National energies, unleashed by the revolution, carried the French armies to spectacular victories in the Netherlands, along the Rhine and across the Pyrenees. At home, meanwhile, the successive political groups were having difficulty in trying to realize the early goals of the revolution. What had appeared so easy in theory proved elusive in practice. Feeling that the revolution had betrayed their hopes, the people began to turn away from the Directors, the new men in control of government. The decline in the political prestige of the Directory left the army as the only organized and cohesive force capable of winning the support of the public.

The conduct of negotiations with enemy governments and the administration of conquered territories first drew military leaders into the game of politics. Once the means of entry was afforded, these senior officers refused to retire from political life. Between 1795 and 1799 the army sustained the incompetent and corrupt Directory by providing money extorted from subject states and by suppressing internal disturbances. As the 'arbiter' of power, the army became the most important institution in the state. What some radicals had feared and tried to prevent at the start of the European War now gradually occurred. The figure of one general, Napoleon Bonaparte, the brilliant and ambitious Corsican, forged to the front of the French political stage. France was drifting toward a military dictatorship.

First and foremost in Napoleon's mind was to secure undisputed control over the army. Having staged a *coup d'état* himself, Napoleon feared similar adventures on the part of other generals. Consequently he purged the army of officers suspected of harbouring political ambitions and shipped those that were dissatisfied to distant or diplomatic posts. He tried to manage his generals by keeping them divided and in a constant state of jealous rivalry for his favours. Napoleon considered that lavish rewards and honours to his generals were part of the price he had to pay to keep them out of politics. The surest way to soften their resentment was to knit their fortunes to the leader who alone had it in his power to gratify their expectations. As Napoleon foresaw, this policy worked brilliantly and even in later years when he faced defeat he continued to retain the loyalty of the army.

To cultivate the image of a child of the revolution, Napoleon pretended to dissociate himself from the army, proclaiming to the Council of State on May 4, 1802 that 'never should military government prevail in France' except if the nation be 'brutalized by fifty years of ignorance' and he added, 'the soldier knows no law but force. He considers nothing but himself. He sees nothing else'. While Napoleon may have found it convenient to assert the predominance of civilian leadership over the military, he had no intention of renouncing his ambition as a soldier in order to become entirely a statesman. Guided by romantic notions, love of glory and power as well as a thirst for fame that would make his name immortal, Napoleon charted a course which plunged Europe into a decade of devastating warfare. Centralizing in his own person the political and military direction of the war, the Corsican general planned both grand and military strategy. Rarely in history has a general equalled Napoleon's military genius or talent to inspire fervent devotion and patriotism in the men under his command. In his brief, active career, Napoleon trampled across half of Europe and left behind a legacy envied by later generations of dictators and professional soldiers.

The principle of the nation-in-arms, established by the Revolutionary Government in 1793, perished with Napoleon at Waterloo. Under the Constitutional Charter recruiting was carried on entirely by voluntary enlistment. This method failed to produce a sufficient force and in 1818 the Law Gouvion St Cyr supplemented it by the annual draft of a contingent of up to 40,000 men. The conscripts were selected by lot out of the age group eligible, though military exemptions were provided if individuals could find a substitute. The peace-time size of the army was fixed at 240,000 and the term of active service at six years. The main omission from this legislation was the provision for an effective trained reserve.

Reduced in size and influence the army came to recognize, especially after 1830, that its interests could best be served by confining itself to military matters and ignoring political disputes.

In this new role the army saw itself as an arm of the state, owing loyalties not to the existing regime but to the nation, with the duty to preserve social and political order. Should a crisis arise the soldiers would await orders from their immediate superior who in turn would refer to the man above him 'until finally the chain of command' reached the Minister of War. This attitude was reflected during the revolution of 1848 when local army commanders hesitated to act without explicit directives from their hierarchical superior. Meanwhile the king, rather than employ repressive measures and provoke further bloodshed, abdicated and left the country. News of the change of government shocked the officer corps, although they accepted it as a *fait accompli*. It is remarkable that in spite of the antipathy of military leaders towards republicans, none showed the slightest inclination to resist the new régime by force of arms.

From the time that he became President of the Republic, Louis Napoleon pursued policies calculated to enhance his personal prestige with the different elements in the nation, in particular with the army. Before his term was about to expire, Napoleon asked for a revision of the constitution that would extend his period of office from four to ten years. When the Assembly declined to co-operate he prepared a military *coup d'état*. Generals who could not be trusted were removed in favour of those known to be loyal to the President. At last on December 2, 1851 Napoleon sent army units to arrest his opponents and to disperse the Assembly. The coup was far from being a 'military revolution' as some historians have alleged. Army commanders had not planned nor been responsible for it, but as agents of the Government had merely obeyed the instructions of their constitutional chief.

Essentially a pacifist, Napoleon III had little of the personal craving for conquest and wars which had marked Napoleon I. But the memory of his uncle's romantic empire, added to his desire to raise the prestige of his dynasty, caused him to adopt an aggressive foreign policy for which he had neither heart nor skill. Time had dulled the recollection of the bloody reality of Bonapartism and sharpened the memory of its glories. Once again policy and strategy fell under the direction of the same person. During the 1850s and early 1860s the French army carried off the honours in the Crimean War, in Italy, as well as advancing the tricolour in

Africa and the Far East, and emerged from these adventures with greatly enhanced prestige both at home and abroad. 'In the glitter of the Second Empire the army, splendidly uniformed, its colours emblazoned with new battle honours' was looked upon as a model for many European countries. No one had the slightest notion at the time that behind this magnificent façade lay a crumbling structure. The French army was not only lacking in efficient organization and modern equipment but it was also led by 'drawing room generals'. Equally serious was the failure of political leaders after 1818 to revive nationwide conscription and to borrow from countries like Prussia those military ideas and institutions that had proved effective, especially a system of mass reservists and a highly-trained General Staff.

The rapid and overwhelming victory of Prussia in the war against Austria was regarded as a bad omen in France, and Napoleon III was moved to take steps to increase the size and quality of the French army. Through Marshal Niel, then Minister of War, the Imperial Government drew up a scheme of universal compulsory service. The recruits for the year were to be divided into two classes: the first was to serve five years in the active army and four in the reserve and the second four years in the reserve only. A *garde mobile* was to be formed, consisting of all those who had been exempt from military service, to be used for home defence. By this means it was hoped to obtain a total of 1,200,000 men. France could then match man for man the military power of Prussia. But the legislators raised strong objections to the plan. 'Do you want to turn France into a barracks?' exclaimed Jules Favre, pacifist and deputy of Paris. To which Niel retorted angrily: 'Take care that you don't turn it into a cemetery.' The Marshal's efforts were to little avail. In January 1868 a bill for the organization of the army was enacted into law but in such a mutilated form that its purpose was practically nullified. Niel died the following year and with him died any hope of modernizing the French army. The new Minister of War, General Lebœuf, abandoned most of his predecessor's proposals and even neglected to strengthen the defensive works along the eastern frontier. On the even of the Franco-Prussian war the *garde mobile*, on which Niel had depended to aid the regular army, was not actually organized, trained or equipped. Inferior to the Prussians in everything but small arms and possibly courage, the French army drifted toward defeat at Sedan.

The news that Napoleon III and over 100,000 troops were in Prussian hands brought the Imperial Régime crashing to the ground. The second phase of the war was led by Léon Gambetta, Minister of the Interior of the provisional Government of National Defence, whose fiery patriotism and indefatigable energy inspired the country to continue the war. He ordered a *levée en masse* of all men from the ages of twenty-one to forty; but the raw recruits which he enlisted could not possibly match the highly trained soldiers of von Moltke. And even if Gambetta's plan to relieve Paris had the slightest chance of succeeding, all was lost as a result of his undue interference in military matters and the premature surrender of Marshal Bazaine at Metz.

In the period between the suppression of the Paris Commune and the Dreyfus affair, the army played only a minor part in the events that shaped the destiny of the Third Republic. Burning for revenge, the army could only think of rebuilding itself for the next inevitable confrontation with Germany. This attitude was not felt by the politicians who, having witnessed the long power struggle with President MacMahon and the apparent conspiracy of General Boulanger, were ever mindful of a revival of Caesarism. They regarded the military structure as being composed largely of royalists and clerics, faithful to the old concepts of order, honour and glory, and opposed to a republican form of government. To defend French national security by conscription [1] and heavy military expenditures was also to undermine the republic by placing enormous influence and power in the hands of such men. It seemed to the politicians that the only way to neutralize the power of the army and so eliminate the perennial threat to the state was to republicanize the military command. But early attempts to accomplish this ended in failure.

Before the close of the nineteenth century the politicians had accepted an arrangement which would give the soldiers considerable autonomy within 'a specific military sphere'. The civilians would refrain from intervening in strictly military matters and, in turn, the soldiers would remain aloof from politics. The Dreyfus

[1] Military service was declared compulsory for five years in 1872. The term of duty was later reduced to three years.

affair, however, forced the army out of this position. The politicians reacted by 'reversing what had come to be the accepted assumptions of civil-military relations in France'. Many officers were removed for suspected royalism and more important the system of promotion was taken out of the hands of a military council and vested in the Ministry of War. This meant that a politically-minded Minister would be inclined to favour those officers whom he considered to be reliable republicans. Under General André, appointed to succeed Galliffet in 1900, this new power was flagrantly abused. As part of his policy, André used informers, especially freemasons and often from the non-commissioned ranks, to obtain information on members of the officers' corps. A great collection of files indicated the officers who attended mass, sent their children to Catholic schools and uttered anti-republican sentiments; and the Minister of War was frequently guided by the accumulated data on these index-cards when making promotions. This sordid practice eventually leaked out to the public in 1904 and caused such an uproar that André was obliged to resign.

The departure of André did not alleviate the bitterness that had been sown between the army and the republic. In 1905 the Government voted to reduce the period of active service from three years to two. The conscripts would serve a shorter term, after which they would pass into the reserves. The purpose of the law was to diminish the control of the professionals over the minds of French youth and create a civilian reserve that would offset the reactionary officers' corps. One supporter of the bill claimed that it would open for the army 'an era which I will dare to call . . . the era of civilianism'. The military officers viewed this measure as the culmination of a vengeful campaign directed against the army. The morale of the army fell to a low point: discipline grew lax, many officers resigned their commissions and even the applications for officer training schools declined.

A number of forces and circumstances combined to resolve the deepening hostility between the soldiers and the republic. In 1906 the Government was compelled to call upon the army to check the wave of internal disturbances. Each outbreak made the state increasingly dependent upon the army. As diplomatic tensions reached new heights in Europe, the politicians, mainly absorbed in matters of national defence, began the process of normalizing relations with the military hierarchy. Finally the emergence to political power of a group of nationalists ensured the rehabilitation of the 'Army's moral and material strength'. It was due largely to their efforts that a law was passed in 1913, extending the period of compulsory military service from two to three years.

The probability of a European war made it desirable to arrange a working balance between military autonomy and civilian control. Accordingly on October 28, 1913 the Government decreed that the Minister of War be empowered to direct and co-ordinate the war on the various fronts, while the actual planning and conduct of operations be left to local commanders.[2] By 1914 a new attitude toward the army had taken shape, but the old animosities lingered in the background and the military stalemate would once again bring them out in full bloom.

It becomes essential at this point to review separately the political and military developments of the Third Republic up to 1914. Only through this means can one obtain a complete picture and so place into proper perspective the intricate civil-military relations during the Great War.

The Second Empire came to an end on September 4, 1870, two days after the defeat of the French army at Sedan. A group of Parisian politicians, in true Jacobin tradition, overthrew the existing régime and proclaimed the establishment of a republic. A provisional Government of National Defence desperately sought to carry on the struggle but it was beyond hope. After the fall of Paris, moderates negotiated an armistice which permitted the election by universal manhood suffrage of a National Assembly to conclude the terms of peace and draft a new constitution for the nation. The outcome of the election was startling at first sight, for the monarchists captured more than 400 of the 600 seats in the new Assembly. But the French vote was more for peace than for restoration of the monarchy. Republicans had favoured continuing the war, whereas the royalists had called for immediate peace.

Having re-established peace and order, the National Assembly could not decide whether France would be a republic or a monarchy. The main problem was the division in the ranks of the

[2] Pierre Renouvin, *The Forms of War Government in France* (Paris, 1927), p. 27.

royalists between those who wanted the succession of the Bourbons and those who supported the Orleanist dynasty. As a measure of expediency they named Adolphe Thiers President of the Republic, but when he appeared to defend the republican principle they replaced him by Marshal MacMahon, a staunch royalist, who could be trusted to step aside as soon as a king was selected. Meanwhile after heated discussions the Assembly passed a series of laws in 1875 which served as the constitution of the Third Republic but could operate equally well under a monarchy. The new laws provided for a President, a two-chamber legislature and a Council of Ministers headed by a Premier (President of the Council).[3] The President was to be elected for a term of seven years by the Senate and Chamber of Deputies sitting in joint sessions; the Senate would be chosen indirectly; the Chamber was to be elected every four years by universal manhood suffrage and could be dissolved at any time by the President with the approval of the Senate.

Until 1875 a restoration of the monarchy was not inconceivable. But each attempt at a 'fusion' of the two branches of the royal family proved unsuccessful when, suddenly, the monarchists discovered that their opportunity had passed. As soon as its work was completed the Assembly dissolved itself. In the general elections of 1876 the republicans won a resounding victory. For partisan motives President MacMahon dissolved the Chamber the following year and sought to use the administrative machinery to obtain a conservative majority in the new house. Once again the voters returned a republican majority. Two years later when the royalists lost control of the Senate, MacMahon resigned and was succeeded by the republican Jules Grévy. Thereafter the 'presidency declined in authority, its powers falling into disuse'. The premier and his cabinet, requiring the confidence of the legislature in order to survive and function effectively, became the real executive of the state.

Although the royalists and conservatives were no longer in a position of strength they were loath to accept the republican régime. In the 1880s, when the country was wracked by factionalism, corruption and scandals, the anti-republican elements turned to General Boulanger, Minister of War in 1886–7, who appeared to

[3] To avoid confusion I will refer to the President of the Council as Premier or Prime Minister.

be a man of destiny. In 1889 Boulanger had a chance to lead a *coup d'état*, but lost his nerve at a crucial moment and fled to Brussels where he later committed suicide on the grave of his mistress. The Third Republic had withstood a second crisis; now its survival was assured.

Following the triumph of republicanism there came a period of political instability. The republicans split up into numerous factions according to the varying shades of republican thought, with the result that no political group was strong enough or sufficiently organized to assume the responsibility of forming a ministry and, therefore, each ministry had to be supported by coalitions subject to constant shifting in the play of personalities and principles. This system frequently produced cabinet crises, making it extremely difficult for governments to hold office long enough to carry out long-range policies. No sooner was a government formed than it became the target of violent attacks. The parties in opposition, especially pivotal centre groups, saw in the overthrow of a cabinet a possible way to promotion. Very often, however, a cabinet reversal did not mean a major change in personnel; most members of the old ministry would appear in the new one, only assigned to different portfolios. Between 1890 and 1914 the Third Republic had twenty-six ministries with an average existence of less than one year.

As the republic became more established it also became more radical. From the group that had loyally supported Gambetta's Republican Union and had stood foremost on the battle-line for the republic, there eventually developed the Radical Socialist party, the strongest and best organized group in the Chamber. Usually an indispensable part of every coalition government, the Radical Socialists were the dominating force in French politics from 1902 until the outbreak of the World War. The Radical Socialists were a 'grouping of the middle left' and liked to think of themselves as the party of the republic. They drew their support largely from the lower middle classes in the town and villages – small independent businessmen, farmers, professional men and minor civil servants. Party doctrine committed the Radical Socialists to anti-clericalism, anti-militarism and anti-Caesarism, while championing egalitarianism, private enterprise and private property. Although the Radical Socialists abhorred the principles of Marxism, they did not hesitate to join hands with the extreme left when a rightist threat appeared to be in the making.

The year 1914 saw the return of the Radical Socialist party to power after a brief interlude in the ranks of the opposition. The Cabinet was under the leadership of a nominal Prime Minister, Gaston Doumergue, the real power lying in the hands of Joseph Caillaux, Minister of Finance. Son of a former Finance Minister and member of a rich conservative family, Caillaux achieved brilliant academic results before entering politics. His untiring energy, aggressiveness and shrewd financial mind gained him nation-wide renown and allowed him independence of behaviour which he often pushed too far. Uncompromising, vain, arrogant and unscrupulous, Caillaux was regarded by his contemporaries with varying admiration and dislike. No one ignored either him or his influence. Caillaux might conceivably have become Prime Minister for the second time [4] had it not been for the fateful events of March 16, 1914. On that day Madame Caillaux shot and killed the editor of *Le Figaro*, Gaston Calmette, for publishing certain letters which had passed between herself and her husband prior to their marriage. Upon hearing the news, Caillaux resigned his cabinet post and rallied to the defence of his wife.

Strangely enough, the scandal did not affect the popularity of the Radical Socialists in the general elections in May 1914, for they captured 136 seats in the Chamber of Deputies, more than any other party. Nearly everyone in the country expected them to take over the new ministry. However, the French President, Raymond Poincaré, baulked at the verdict of the voters. Aware that the Radical Socialists were determined to repeal the three-year service law, Poincaré selected as head of the new cabinet René Viviani, a member of a small group which stood between the Radical Socialists and the Socialists. On June 16, 1914 Viviani assumed office.

Under normal circumstances the choice of Viviani as Prime Minister would not have been a logical one. It is true that Viviani was industrious, congenial, a gifted orator possessing an excellent memory, but he lacked strength of character, conviction, and experience in administration with the result that he had to place

[4] Caillaux became Prime Minister in 1911, but his pro-German attitude led to the downfall of his Government the following year.

13

too much reliance on his colleagues for guidance. Poincaré was aware of Viviani's shortcomings, but he was more interested in safeguarding the three-year service law. Moreover, he probably reasoned that since Viviani's mediocrity would excite no jealousy under which rival ambitions might unite, the Prime Minister could always depend on a working majority in the Chamber. It was generally expected that Viviani's ideals would find favour with the left; his acts with the right. As the prospect of a war with Germany appeared imminent, political harmony was deemed vital to the unity of the country.

The Viviani Ministry, which was represented by all sections of the Chamber including the Radical Socialists, consisted of a remarkable collection of personalities.[5] The commanding leader was Aristide Briand, a former Prime Minister, who came out of retirement to accept the portfolio of Justice. As a young man he had championed labour rights and anarcho-syndicalism, and in 1902 was elected as a socialist deputy. He first attracted public attention by his skilful handling of the law for separation of Church and State. Briand was not a strict doctrinaire and, after his break with the extreme left, refused to identify with any political group, though he maintained friends and connections in all camps. His dialectic power, flexibility and intuition, combined with his deep knowledge of politics and diplomacy, enabled him to move in and out of the premier's office on ten occasions, a distinction unmatched by any politician in the history of democratic France.

Alexandre Millerand, Minister of War, like Viviani and Briand,

---

[5] After the French setback at the Battle of the Frontiers in August 1914 the Minister of War, Adolphe Messimy, was forced to resign and subsequently Viviani reshaped his cabinet to include the leaders of all the major parties in the country. The new cabinet is listed as follows: René Viviani (Prime Minister), Aristide Briand (Minister of Justice), Alexandre Millerand (Minister of War), Théophile Delcassé (Minister of Foreign Affairs), Louis Malvy (Minister of the Interior), Victor Augagneur (Minister of Marine), Alexandre Ribot (Minister of Finance), Albert Sarraut (Minister of Public Instruction), Marcel Sembat (Minister of Public Works), Gaston Thompson (Minister of Commerce), Gaston Doumergue (Minister of the Colonies), Fernand David (Minister of Agriculture), Bienvenue-Martin (Minister of Labour) and Jules Guesde (Minister without Portfolio).

was an independent socialist at the start of the war. Having held the same Cabinet post in Poincaré's Ministry between 1912 and 1913, Millerand had done much to restore the army's image which had been tarnished in the wake of its scandalous behaviour in the Dreyfus affair. In many ways Millerand was an able politician and administrative officer, but his gifts in that direction were offset by stubbornness, arrogance and a cold personality. As a war leader he was badly miscast. Lacking imagination in the formulation and conduct of higher strategy, he too readily believed all that the army told him and allowed General Joffre, Commander-in-Chief of the French army in the West, to usurp his authority over the military forces, thus reducing him to a mere mouthpiece for *grand quartier général* (French high command).

Théophile Delcassé returned to the Ministry of Foreign Affairs, a post he had held at one time for seven consecutive years in five different cabinets. An excellent manager of men, shrewd and calculating, Delcassé had achieved amazing success in strengthening France's international position and in restoring the balance of power in Europe. In 1914, however, the 62-year-old Delcassé was in the twilight of his political career. As a central figure in French politics for more than twenty years, the strain of his burdensome responsibilities had sapped his vitality and spirit. The clearness of vision and sense of dexterity which had been so conspicuous in his earlier diplomatic career were no longer in evidence. Although Delcassé's last tenure of office was a complete failure, he was one of the most outstanding statesmen in the Third Republic.

These four men – Viviani, Briand, Millerand and Delcassé – together with President Poincaré, dominated the French political scene during the first year of the war. An old hand at politics, Poincaré had forsaken his law practice to enter the Chamber of Deputies in 1887. He earned a quick reputation as an expert on law and finance and in the ensuing years held various cabinet posts. In 1912 he was called upon to form a government to deal with the Agadir crisis. Fearful of German militarism Poincaré sought to forge closer links with Russia and England. Near the end of his term he decided to run for the office of President of the Republic and narrowly won the election. In his new role Poincaré presided over the work of the Cabinet and guided and influenced government action. Unlike his predecessors after 1879, he used the full powers of his office, but he was always careful not to overstep the narrow limits of his constitutional jurisdiction. As President of the Republic, he remained throughout the war a symbol of national unity.

On August 1, 1914 Poincaré ordered the mobilization of the French army. As the country was on the threshold of a decisive struggle there could be no room for political cleavages. On August 4 the President addressed the Chamber of Deputies and in a dramatic plea called for a 'Sacred Union', whereby the various political parties would join hands in a fraternal alliance of all Frenchmen.[6] The need for unity had already manifested itself the day after the mobilization decree when the President virtually turned over control of government to the army. Under the provisions of a law passed in 1878 the President could declare a state of siege in the event of 'imminent peril caused by a foreign war or armed aggression'.[7] In the face of common danger, the Chamber unanimously ratified Poincaré's act in the afternoon of August 4 and agreed to maintain the state of siege in France until the end of the war or until it was revoked by a decree of the President, acting on the recommendation of the Cabinet.[8]

The Government was so overwhelmed by external pressure that it was ready and eager to entrust itself into the hands of an army which it had previously regarded as a great political danger to itself and the republic. And it may have been true that politically the army had been dangerous, but its major preoccupation for many years had been the planning of a new clash with the Germans, which some viewed as unfortunately inevitable and some as a welcome opportunity to reverse the verdict of 1870. It becomes necessary, therefore, to examine the army, not so much from the point of view of its political ideas but from the point of its military efficiency and strategic outlook, and it was, in part, these which were to be tested in 1914–18.

.   .   .   .

[6] France, assemblée nationale, *Annales de la chambre des députés, débats parlementaires* (Paris, 1915), 4 août, II, p. 907.

[7] Pierre Renouvin, *The Forms of War Government in France*, p. 11.

[8] France, assemblée nationale, *Journal officiel de la république française* (Paris, 1915), 8 août 1914, p. 7126.

The events of the Franco-Prussian War dispelled popular belief in the French army's primacy in battle and pointed out the defects in its organization and system. After the French shook off the initial shock of defeat they began to reform their military structure with a view to regaining the leadership of Europe. As a start they adopted the principle of universal compulsory service, the duration of the military term was first fixed at five years but subsequently reduced to three. The General Staff was reorganized on the Prussian model in 1874. At the same time the National Assembly voted large sums of money to improve or build new fortifications, replenish military supplies and modernize army equipment. The *école militaire supérieure* was created in 1878 to train the officer corps in certain technical skills especially that of mastering the art of warfare. For the study of military theory old French practices were revised and adapted to conform to changing circumstances.

When French military analysts probed into the causes of the disaster of 1870–1, instead of relating the defeat to the many factors responsible for it, they singled out the aggressive tactics of the Prussian Commander, General von Moltke, as the principal one. Reaching out to consult the texts of Clausewitz and Jomini, the French theorists concluded that the basic ingredient of Napoleon's victories lay in the emphasis he placed in the doctrine of mass attack. The more they read the more they became convinced that by sheer dint of the will to conquer, an attacking force could break through the centre of an opposing army and fling its wings asunder. Thus victory was reserved for any army which seized the initiative and opened with a vigorous offensive, without due concern for strategic or tactical principles.

The crystallization of the doctrine of this new school was accelerated by the appearance of the writings of Colonel Charles Ardant du Picq, a French officer who died of wounds shortly after the outbreak of the Franco-Prussian war. Ardant du Picq's work entitled *Etudes sur le combat* was published in 1880 and attracted the attention of a very wide audience. His research, which involved questioning French soldiers who had taken part in the Crimean War and the Italian campaign of 1859, revealed that the collision of armies and hand-to-hand fighting was virtually unknown, since the defenders usually broke and fled before a mass of fired-up attackers. Therefore if the spirit of the attackers was developed to a point where it was superior to that of the defenders, the attackers would always win. He wrote:

'In battle, two moral forces, even more so than two material forces, are in conflict. The stronger conquers. . . . With equal or even inferior power of destruction he will win who has the resolution to advance, who . . . in a word has the moral ascendancy. Moral effect inspires fear. Fear must be changed to terror in order to vanquish. . . . Indeed the physical impulse is nothing. The moral impulse which estimates the attacker is everything. The moral impulse lies in the perception by the enemy of the resolution that animates you.' [9]

Ardant du Picq's views on war became the guiding principles of the school of attack, which found a champion in Lt-Col. Fernand Foch, a youthful instructor at the *école de guerre*. In a series of lectures on nineteenth-century warfare, later published in two volumes, *De la conduite de la guerre* and *Des principes de la guerre*, Foch elaborated a doctrine of massive attack which dominated France's military outlook prior to and during the Great War. He maintained that the basic formula for victory was Napoleonic audacity, engaging the enemy whenever possible, attacking with dash and boldness without thought of cost or practicability of a tactical manœuvre. Foch quoted the French philosopher Joseph de Maistre as saying, 'A battle lost is a battle one believes one has lost, for a battle is never lost materially.' He went on to say: 'And if battles are lost morally, they must also be won in the same way, so that we can add: "A battle won is a battle in which one refuses to acknowledge defeat."' [10]

Foch undoubtedly placed too much emphasis on the value of moral forces, but he did not lose sight of the fact that war also involved the use of material strength. He advanced the idea that any improvement of firearms was certain to redound to the advantage of the offensive. Foch proceeded to 'give a mathematical demonstration of that truth:

---

[9] Colonel Ardant du Picq, *Battle Studies* (New York, 1921), pp. 123–7.
[10] Marshal Foch, *The Principles of War* (New York, 1920), p. 286.

'Suppose you launch 2 battalions against	1
You then launch 2,000 men against	1,000
With a rifle fire of 1 shot to a minute, 1,000 defenders will fire	1,000 bullets
With the same rifle, 2,000 assailants will fire	2,000 bullets
Balance in favour of the attack	1,000 bullets
With a rifle firing 10 shots a minute, 1,000 defenders will fire within 1 minute	10,000 bullets
With the same rifle, 2,000 assailants will fire	20,000 bullets
Balance	10,000 bullets

'As you see, the material superiority of firearms quickly increases in favour of the attack as a result of improved firearms.' [11]

It is incredible that such reasoning could emanate from the mind of a soldier who was to show considerable skill in guiding the Entente to victory in 1918. Foch revealed himself to be completely ignorant of even the fundamentals of war. In the first place, assuming that the defenders are lying down and not in an entrenched position or firing from cover as they would almost always be, they would still offer only one-eighth as much target as the attackers. Despite the fact that in this instance the assailants hold a numerical superiority of two to one, the advantage clearly lies with the defenders. Second, the attackers are unable to take careful aim with the result that most of their bullets are wasted, whereas the defenders have time to be precise and are more likely to hit their target. Third, the attackers must rely only on the ammunition they are able to carry, while the defenders usually have an ample supply of reserve ammunition within reach.[12] Foch had obviously paid little heed to the defensive strength of the entrenched riflemen as shown in many memorable battles during the American Civil War, and, more recently, at Plevna during the Russo-Turkish conflict. If he relied entirely on the effects of a frenzied attack to unnerve the defenders, as seems to be the case, he

[11] *Ibid.*, p. 32.

[12] Major-General J. F. C. Fuller, *The Conduct of War, 1789–1961* (London, 1961), p. 123; Hoffman Nickerson, *The Armed Horde, 1793–1919* (New York, 1942), p. 203.

19

committed a grave error, for nearly always it is the attackers who became panic-stricken at the sight of their companions falling around them in droves. It would be foolish to deny that an offensive plays no part in winning a war; and Foch was right to preach the importance of attack, but he was wrong to negate all other strategic or tactical principles.

As might be expected, the revolution in French military thinking was enthusiastically supported by the young staff officers known as the 'Young Turks'. The few dissenters among high-ranking officers in the army were either retired or stripped of their power. In 1911 General Michel, French Commander-in-Chief designate, correctly predicted that the Germans would sweep through Belgium before invading France. He recommended, therefore, that the French deploy the bulk of their forces west and north toward Belgium and await the enemy.[13] This course was wholly at variance with that of the 'Young Turks', who succeeded in having him replaced by General Joffre. Left free, the 'Young Turks' turned their attention to developing the so-called Plan XVII. Ignoring the probability of a German encirclement through Belgium, the plan called for a massive drive across the common frontier to paralyse enemy communications in Lorraine and roll back both opposing wings.

The die was now cast. The 'Young Turks' intended to push on to the bitter end. Colonel Loiseau de Grandmaison,[14] the most ardent exponent of *l'offensive à outrance*, explained:

'The French Army, returning unto its traditions, no longer knows any law other than the offensive. . . . All attacks must be pushed to the limit . . . to charge the enemy with the bayonet, in order to destroy him . . . [even] at the price of bloody sacrifice. All other conceptions should be rejected as contrary to the very nature of war.' [15]

The time was close at hand when the French army could test its strategy. By 1914 the great Powers had split into two equally

---

[13] Major-General J. F. C. Fuller, *The Decisive Battles of the Western World* (London, 1956), vol. 3, p. 189.

[14] Chief of the Operations Branch of the General Staff.

[15] Hoffman Nickerson, *op. cit.*, p. 224.

balanced and hostile groups. Since 1905 a series of diplomatic crises had brought Europe to the brink of war. Each time the foreign ministers improvised temporary solutions and so the crisis passed. Nevertheless national rivalries continued, the Balkans remained a politically unstable area and everywhere tension mounted. Sooner or later a spark, whether by accident or design, was likely to set off a world-rocking explosion.

Such was the atmosphere in Europe when Archduke Ferdinand, heir to the throne of Austria-Hungary, and his morganatic wife were assassinated in the Bosnian town of Sarajevo on June 28, 1914. For this new incident no peaceful solution was improvised and all the nations began to prepare for the coming conflict more feverishly than ever. On July 28 Austria-Hungary shattered the uneasy peace by declaring war on Serbia. Within a week Serbia, Russia, Belgium, France and Britain stood ranged against Germany and Austria-Hungary. The first global war had started and in the words of Lord Grey, British Secretary of State for Foreign Affairs, 'the lamps are going out all over Europe; we shall not see them lit again in our lifetime'.

The war came as a shock to Europe. Despite the turbulent condition of European affairs during the preceding years, all evidence indicates that no nation desired war. In France the people had almost forgotten the nature of armed conflict, imagining that this phenomenon belonged to the past. They believed that even if the Kaiser tried to provoke war, the German people would not rally behind him. As late as the summer of 1914 the French socialists, who were committed to pacifism, at least in theory, urged workers not to participate in the event of the country being drawn into a capitalistic war. If the French had not been reconciled to the loss of Alsace-Lorraine, they thought less and less in terms of a recovery by force. In truth they could hardly welcome a conflict with Germany which, in recent times, had far surpassed their country in population and industrial strength. Yet overnight the mood of the public changed and the spirit of pacifism disappeared. It was evident that nationalism was the strongest sentiment in France as everyone, identifying their country's cause with righteousness, responded overwhelmingly to the call to arms. All the outstanding issues seemed forgotten; political groups buried the hatchet, there were no labour strikes or anti-war

21

demonstrations and volunteers matched the draftees in their eagerness to defend the homeland. Forged in crisis, army and state stood in unconquerable spirit before the supreme challenge that lay ahead.

Chapter 2

THE ORIGINS OF THE BALKAN EXPEDITION

'Sharing the opinion of their predecessors, the conferees, in common accord, assume that Germany will direct the greatest part of her forces against France, and will leave only a minimum of troops against Russia. . . . The Allied plan must therefore be to try to attack simultaneously both sides at once, in exercising the maximum combined effort . . .'.
The 1913 Military Protocol to the Franco-Russian Alliance

'The nature of war . . . tends to be governed by the motives which produce it.'
Clausewitz

'Why search elsewhere and far off for what I shall get here? I feel sure I shall break through and drive the Germans back home.'
General Joffre, 1914

The old adage 'Peace is at best a truce on the battlefield of time' sadly highlights all too clearly man's passion for violence and destruction. Since the earliest record of man, there have been only 227 years of peace.[1] The First World War, therefore, was not 'a historical abnormality; it represented, rather, an anticipated and recurrent norm'. But in its scope, horror and destruction it far transcended earlier conflicts.

The change in the nature of European armies and the application of the new technology to warfare accounted for the unprecedented slaughter and havoc of the Great War. In the latter part of the nineteenth century all the European Powers with the exception of Great Britain, following the example set by Prussia, adopted the principle of compulsory military training together with a reserve system. This meant that in any war which might develop all the

[1] Hanson W. Baldwin, *World War I* (New York, 1962), p. 1.

23

able-bodied men of a country could be transformed into a fighting force. Hitherto armies were limited in size, highly trained and frugally employed. Now manpower was cheapened and became expendable, as losses, however heavy, could always be made good. Mass production served to supply the new armies with destructive weapons that science invented or improved – machine guns, breech-loading rifles, poison gas, tanks, heavy explosives and long-range artillery. Large bodies of men could be hurried to the front by railways with the operation co-ordinated by telegraph. Warfare gained the dimensions of totality; it called for the entire material and human resources of a nation.

Europe stumbled into the Great War with only a partial appreciation of the forces soon to be unleashed. Moreover, none of the belligerents were seriously concerned about the purpose of the war. They saw the conflict as a climax to the traditional struggle for power, or as Clausewitz put it, 'a continuation of political intercourse . . . by other means'. The purpose was to disarm, rather than destroy, the hostile power so that it could submit to terms most advantageous to the victor. Such a policy would continue to preserve the fundamental structure of European politics as it had for over two centuries.

At the beginning of the conflict, each government sought to explain to its own people and to the world the validity of its national cause. In every case it was stated that the war was defensive. The combating nations had no definite aims except to win the war. The Central Powers came closest to an objective. Austria-Hungary, if nothing else, wanted to destroy the menace of South Slav nationalism. The German leaders originally had no fixed plans for territorial aggrandizement, but as their armies made conquests they contemplated the annexation of Belgium, and part of France in the West, and Poland in the East. The Allies were in a different position for they could not consider specific aims until they had turned back the tide of Germany's early victories. France had her sights on the recovery of the lost provinces of Alsace and Lorraine from the moment the first shots were fired, but she had not entered the war to conquer them. The immediate goal of the French was to drive the Germans from the homeland; that of the British to free Belgium and that of the Russians to protect Serbia and 'to survive as a great military Power'.

24

As the war progressed the goals of the belligerents tended to change. The enormous cost of the conflict in blood and treasure, and the need to give the people something for their sacrifices, led the civil leaders in Europe to modify the defensive, political objectives they had expressed in August 1914. Their subsequent policy was determined by the usual priorities and the arrangements that they arrived at in the period of the war.

Failure to anticipate at the start the gigantic proportions the war would assume, precluded an objective, clear assessment of war aims. Since 1866 the campaigns in Europe had been short, involving less than a twelve-month period of continuous fighting. The general expectation of political and military authorities was that the conflict would not last beyond six months.[2] This view was reinforced by the economists who maintained that owing to the high cost of modern armaments no nation could finance a long war. Both sides, therefore, looked forward to a quick victory by taking the offensive and inflicting a decisive defeat on the enemy.

In broad terms the French and Russian forces aimed to advance simultaneously from two directions. The French would advance rapidly through the Metz-Strasbourg area into Germany, while the Russians would execute an overpowering thrust into East Prussia. Germany's plan [3] called for a holding action against the slowly mobilizing Russians to permit her main armies to invade France in force. The Germans intended to wheel through Belgium and Luxembourg in order to outflank the heavily fortified French frontier. Sweeping like a scythe across northern France the Germans would encircle and occupy Paris and then turn east and fall behind the main French forces on the Alsatian frontier. This fatal blow having been delivered, German offensive power would then be directed against the Russians.

At first glance the Entente appeared to have a definite advantage over the Central Powers in manpower and economic resources. With respect to military strength, Germany was far ahead in the technical perfecting of her army. At the start of the war, Germany

[2] Lord Kitchener, British Secretary of State for War, stood practically alone in predicting that the war would drag on for three years.

[3] The Schlieffen plan – named after its author Count Alfred von Schlieffen, Chief of the German General Staff, 1891–1905.

placed 78 divisions in the field. The Austro-Hungarian army, considerably smaller and weaker, had a war-footing of 49 divisions. The second best army in Europe was that of France, which initially mustered 62 divisions. Russia had the largest standing army, some 114 divisions, in August; but her forces were inferior in every other respect. The British army during this period, though well-trained and disciplined, consisted of 6 divisions, trifling in size when compared with the conscript armies of the Continent. If her army was small, her predominance in naval power was unquestioned. Command of the seas would permit the Allies to trade with neutral countries and, at the same time, impose a blockade of the coast lines of the Central Powers and deny them access to world markets. If the war lasted long enough, the Allies, with a greater manpower potential and able to draw on greater resources, stood a better chance to win. Time worked to the advantage of the Allied Powers.

No one understood this better than General Joseph-Jacques Césaire Joffre, French Commander-in-Chief on the home front. Sixty-two years old at the start of the war, Joffre had been projected to the top of the military hierarchy after a less than spectacular career. Son of a village cooper, he had attended the *école polytechnique* and, despite an undistinguished academic record, had earned a commission in the engineers. Saddened by the loss of his wife, he applied for overseas duty and took part in the expedition to Indo-China in 1885. He remained three years at Hanoi as chief of engineers before returning to France. In 1892 he was sent to West Africa and two years later received his first battle command when, after a disaster to a French column, he was sent to pacify and occupy Timbuktu. After serving in the Madagascar campaign, Joffre was promoted general of a brigade in 1900 and five years later received command of a division, then of a corps. In 1911 he was appointed Chief of the General Staff, not on the basis of merit or ability, but simply because he was a sound republican with no party affiliations and because it was felt he would accept the military plans of the 'Young Turks' which other leading candidates were not prepared to do. Trained under a system which was no longer applicable in 1914, Joffre's slow wits, combined with his inexperience of actual warfare, did not ideally qualify him to lead the nation's army into battle. But while he lacked training and imagination he brought to his task energy, courage and an autocratic resolve. Radiating an air of almost infallible right and might he became in the minds of Frenchmen the great hero of the war and the indispensable symbol of their will to victory.

Whether Joffre was suited to a dragging defensive war is very much open to question. He was, however, far less committed than the Germans to a single formula for winning the war. At the beginning of the conflict he assumed that the Germans would advance through Lorraine and possibly attempt a feint invasion of Belgium. He did not believe that the enemy could muster sufficient troops to mount an offensive through Belgium. At any rate, Joffre was not overly concerned with what the Germans did in the north, reasoning that once Plan XVII was put into effect they would be forced to abandon their strategy in order to protect the Fatherland. Joffre was extremely late in appreciating the meaning of the Schlieffen plan. As the German scythe cut a wide swath through Belgium and north-eastern France, the futility of Plan XVII became apparent. At the Battle of the Frontiers – actually a series of engagements which extended from Belgium into Alsace-Lorraine – the French army was beaten back all along the line. His plan having collapsed, Joffre had no alternative but to give the word for a general retreat.

Meanwhile the German Commander-in-Chief, Helmuth von Moltke,[4] made a costly miscalculation. He reduced the striking power of his right wing in order to bolster the German forces in Lorraine and on the Eastern front. Consequently von Kluck, in charge of the First Army (on the right wing), lacked the strength to swing west of Paris as he was supposed to do and instead turned south-east to try to cut off the retreating French forces. In executing this manœuvre, von Kluck exposed his flank and left a gap of some thirty miles between his own army and von Bülow's Second Army. Joffre, who had been informed of the change in German strategy, stopped the retreat and prepared to make a stand near the Marne. The fate of France hinged on the outcome of this battle. After four days of fierce fighting the Germans were halted and compelled to withdraw. The French army was too exhausted

---

[4] Nephew and namesake of the great Helmuth von Moltke, he was by no means equal in character or ability. After the defeat of the Germans at the Marne he was replaced by Erich von Falkenhayn.

and disorganized to pursue the Germans and permitted them to take up positions along the Aisne River.

The first Battle of the Marne not only shattered Germany's hope for a quick triumph but also altered the whole character of the war. The war of movement gradually gave way to siege warfare as each side spread northward to outflank the other in a series of bloody but indecisive battles. The 'race to the sea' in all its blood and horror had created a front along a line extending over 450 miles, from the Swiss Alps to the North Sea. As the fighting ended in stalemate on reaching the Channel, both sides prepared their defences. What emerged was a different and unprecedented type of warfare. When the armies could no longer get around one another they tried to break through. On each occasion the line remained intact, although it might bend or stretch back, and always the attackers sustained far heavier casualties than the defenders. The Germans soon abandoned this strategy; but the French persisted despite the fact the invaders held the high ground and their improvised trench system grew increasingly elaborate.

The French High Command, or G.Q.G. as it was more commonly known, was slow to accept the novel conditions under which the war was being fought. It looked upon the system of trenches conceived by the Germans as 'a cowardly and unprofessional stratagem designed to trick the French army out of its just victory'. Unperturbed, G.Q.G. proposed to counter this invidious invention by using maximum manpower in concentrated attacks to create a break in the enemy line and permit passage of large numbers of troops and cavalry. The view held was that if the French, with their English allies, could kill Germans at a greater rate than they themselves were being killed, then they were bound to get through. And so began the cruel and senseless war of attrition. Battle-worn infantrymen were hurled repeatedly against impenetrable positions to be met in every instance by withering fire which would send the attackers reeling to the cover of their own line. The heavy artillery fire which preceded every attack rarely caused appreciable damage since enemy trenches were deep enough or provided with bomb-proof shelters. Once the barrage subsided and the signal 'over the top' was given, enemy machine-gunners could quickly get back into position and cut down the advancing columns as they picked their way through the entanglements. Increasing the number of attacks only meant an increase in the number of casualties. The solution lay, not in sending more men against machine-guns and barbed-wire but in establishing a new concept in military organization capable of dealing effectively with the new conditions of warfare.

This was the only alternative to mass slaughter. Yet Joffre applied to the new circumstances the same military principles governing the conduct of war that had long been accepted in the French army. Why was there no attempt to develop a military capability fashioned to suit the unique requirements of trench warfare? The answer is simple. Joffre and his staff were so fixed in their views that they were unable to stand away from their professional concern and realize that the French military system was outdated. Joffre may have been the product of a system, as was Pétain, but this is hardly an excuse for the way in which he conducted the war. It is no wonder that under such conditions progress on the main front was painfully slow; an advance of several hundred yards was heralded as a great victory and worth tens of thousands of lives. Whatever else may be said about the folly of G.Q.G. there was never any doubt of the heroism and grim determination of the French rank and file or of the officers who led them into battle.

In striking contrast to the deadlock that developed in the West, the war on the Eastern front retained its mobile character. At the start of the war the Russians, mobilizing with surprising speed, sent two converging armies into East Prussia to cut off the defenders and move up to the Vistula River. To meet this threat the German Government called from retirement the 67-year-old General Paul von Hindenburg, reputed to be an expert in the topography of East Prussia; and appointed as his Chief of Staff, Major-General Erich Ludendorff, a brilliant strategist who had won fame in the capture of Liège. Using a plan already prepared by the head of the operations department, Ludendorff hurled his forces between the two larger Russian armies and by a quick flanking movement annihilated one at Tannenberg. He then turned his men northward and two weeks later routed the other Russian army near the Masurian Lakes.

As the remnants of their two broken armies fell back in confusion, the Russians partially redressed the balance by scoring successes against the Austrians in Galicia. The tide turned, however, when Ludendorff shifted his attack to south-western Poland to relieve pressure on the Austrians. In a series of hard fought engagements the Russians were driven back to the gates of Warsaw. Here they rallied and stabilized the front as winter set in.

The results of the first four months of fighting on the Eastern front were not altogether unfavourable to the Allies. Russia's early invasion of East Prussia had compelled the Germans to transfer troops from the Western front. This had upset Germany's offensive plan and had enabled the French to win at the Marne. In the process Russia had weakened herself and needed time to rest. Her armies had suffered enormous casualities and her supplies of war material were nearly depleted. Moreover, there were indications that morale was declining and an increasing fear that victory was no longer within reach.

Toward the end of 1914 it was evident to British and French politicians that the strategy of their generals had failed to defeat the Germans. Two choices lay open to them: a political settlement or an extension of the war. The preferable alternative of a negotiated peace presupposed, in this case, France's willingness to renounce her claims to Alsace-Lorraine and Allied recognition of Germany's right to retain part of her newly acquired territories.[5] As such an arrangement was unthinkable, the civil authorities in both London and Paris began to explore the possibility of a flank attack somewhere in south-eastern Europe. In France, the pursuance of this policy brought to an end the brief era of harmony that had existed between the Government and its high command. While the politicians were anxious to break the stalemate by sending an expedition to the Balkans, the army leaders insisted that the war could only be won in France and that any withdrawal of troops from the main front would be an invitation to disaster. At first the conflict took on a mild form, but as the fortunes of the army declined, it would assume proportions reminiscent of the early struggles.

The global war, although triggered off by events at Sarajevo, had assumed from the start so overwhelming an importance elsewhere that the Balkan Peninsula quickly faded into relative

[5] A. J. P. Taylor, *The Struggle For Mastery In Europe, 1848–1918*, p. 538.

obscurity. The war was not expected to last long, negating the need to escalate the conflict and, in the process, of contracting additional obligations. The likelihood of a prolonged struggle, however, invariably drew the belligerent coalitions back to south-east Europe as each side burst into complex and conflicting diplomatic activity to gain new allies.

Of all the neutrals the far-flung Turkish Empire was one of the most important, offering a wide range of strategic possibilities. As masters of the vital Straits, the Turks could, at any moment, sever Russia's communications with the Mediterranean. The Asiatic provinces of the Ottoman Empire also provided a base from which to attack or threaten British power in Egypt and India. Equally important was the character of the sultan, who as spiritual leader of Islam, had the right to proclaim a holy war. Turkey was indeed an ally well worth having. The long-studied efforts of the Germans to cultivate the friendship of the Turks were on the verge of bearing fruit.

Germany's interest in Turkey began a generation before 1914 when she planned to secure economic control of Mesopotamia, an incredibly backward region but fertile and rich in mineral deposits. Before the Germans could extend their economic influence through Asia Minor, it appeared necessary to collaborate with Austria-Hungary to dominate the Balkans which lay in between. Such a *Mitteleuropa*, knit together into an economic federation under Teutonic leadership, would provide Germany with an empire equal to that of Britain and Russia. The foundation of this German edifice was the proposed construction of a railway line, linking Berlin, Constantinople and Baghdad and running thence to the Persian Gulf.

Gradually and inconspicuously the Germans contrived to usurp Britain's predominant position at the Ottoman capital. They provided loans to bolster the Turkish economy; advised the Turkish Government; abstained from taking part in Europe's ringing condemnation of Turkish atrocities in Armenia; and reorganized the Ottoman army. The Turks for their part believed that they had found a powerful friend willing to organize the finances of their nation, help to reconstruct their industrial system and provide moral and material support against the unfriendly encroachments of Petrograd.

The growing ascendancy of Germany at Constantinople found expression in a treaty of alliance on August 2, 1914. This was strengthened when two German cruisers, evading pursuit from the Anglo-French fleet in the Aegean, took refuge in the harbour at Constantinople and were then, together with their crews and commanders, formally incorporated into the Turkish navy. The *Goeben* and *Breslau* gave the Turks command of the Black Sea and tipped the scales in favour of the pro-German party in Constantinople. Late in October, without any declaration of war, the Turkish fleet entered the Black Sea and bombarded the Russian port of Odessa. The tsar replied by declaring war on Turkey and his allies promptly followed suit.

The entry of Turkey into the war was the first notable victory scored by the diplomats of either side. The case with the Balkans was much more delicate. These states occupied areas of great strategic value and controlled considerable resources, and naturally their friendship was eagerly sought. The main stumbling block to any positive line of action lay in the tense and confused state of politics growing out of the Second Balkan War. Split by conflicting interests and carefully fostered jealousies, there was not much possibility that the Balkans would unite in a common front against either the Entente or the Central Powers. They all craved an extension of their boundaries at the expense of their neighbours and imposed exorbitant terms as a condition for their active alliance. To satisfy the aspirations of one meant alienating the other. Each attempt at a negotiated settlement with any of these states involved tangled, complicated and tortuous diplomacy, usually accompanied by intrigue, deception and bribery.

In the opening days of the conflict Montenegro unhesitatingly went to the aid of Serbia. The remaining Balkan states all proclaimed their neutrality. Opinion within Greece was divided as to what course to pursue. Premier Venizelos had visions of a 'Greater Greece' extending to Asia Minor and including the islands of the Aegean with Constantinople as the capital. Only at the expense of Turkey could Greece fulfil her ambitions. In August the Greek Premier had favoured an immediate attack on Turkey (which was still at peace) but the Allies had reacted coolly to his offer.[6] By the

[6] This episode is also discussed in the next chapter.

time the Turks tipped their hand it was too late. King Constantine, a brother-in-law of the Kaiser, awed by the spectacle of Teutonic military efficiency and almost certain of a German victory, stubbornly resisted every move toward intervention.

After the death of the pro-German King Carol in October, the Entente built high hopes on Rumania's entry, holding out as an inducement Bukovina and Transylvania – the Rumanian-speaking parts of Austria-Hungary. The Rumanians, however, also cherished a grudge against Russia and wanted the liberation of their nationals in Bessarabia. The complete reunion of the Rumanian people involved the acquisition of all three provinces. The ideal solution was to achieve this through diplomatic channels, but in case of failure, war could not be excluded. Thus the new monarch advocated a policy of neutrality, at least until Rumania's interests could be more clearly ascertained.

When the war began in 1914 Bulgaria was inclined to lean toward Germany. Humiliated and reduced in size as a result of her defeat in the Second Balkan War, Bulgaria was determined to recover by whatever means possible the Macedonian territory held by Serbia and Greece. In vain the Entente tried to persuade the Serbs and Greeks to cede part of their recent conquests. It was evident that Bulgaria had ambitions far beyond what the Allies were able to satisfy. No such difficulty confronted the Germans, for they were in a position to meet her full demands. Anxiety began to develop in the Entente capitals of the West, that while Serbia was locked in a death struggle with Austria-Hungary, Bulgaria would seize the opportunity to fall upon her weakened rival.

The adhesion of Bulgaria to the Central Powers and the defeat of Serbia would lead to the establishment of a German political hegemony in the Balkans and the Near East. If and when the railroad line to Baghdad were completed, what was to prevent its extension to the Persian Gulf? It was less than a dozen years before that Dr Paul von Rohrbach, a fiery advocate of German imperialism, had observed in *Die Bagdadbahn* that should the Turks develop a railway system in Asia Minor and Syria, Egypt would be vulnerable to a land attack. The English had always been very sensitive to anything which threatened to destroy their power in Egypt. Without Egypt and the link to the East provided by the Suez Canal, England could conceivably lose India as well as her possessions in Central and East Africa. At first the idea of a Pan-German Empire that stretched from Hamburg to the Persian Gulf had been regarded by most statesmen in London as little more than a fantastic speculation of creative political writers. It was reasoned that Germany had too many insurmountable difficulties in her way. Now with Austria and Turkey under her control, the fate of Serbia hanging in the balance and the Balkan states hopelessly divided and helpless, what had hitherto appeared to be isolated and insignificant incidents began to take the shape of a calculated policy of expansion. Since the Germans had failed to crush the French armies in the West and for all practical purposes bring an end to the war 'they were going to hold what they had got, seize what remained to be seized, and then defy the Allies to break their hold'.

The French were even more alarmed, for their interests, far greater than any other Power in the Near East, were directly menaced. France's connections in this part of the world were centuries old, dating back, it was alleged, to the time of Charlemagne. In 1535 Francis I and Suleiman the Magnificent concluded a treaty in which the French were granted far-reaching rights and privileges. The accord, called thereafter Capitulations, provided the basis of a prolonged collaboration between France and Turkey that was to last until the start of the twentieth century. A treaty in 1740 confirmed the exclusive rights given to the French in the Near East. So sacred were they held in France that Napoleon III had defended them in the Crimean War and they became matters of agreement at the Congress of Berlin. A strong Ottoman Empire was a conscious aim of France, and the maintenance of its integrity became a cornerstone of French foreign policy decades before England gave serious thought to the Eastern Question.

Partly on account of historical precedents and partly on account of juridical rights under treaties with both sultans and popes, the French Government assumed the role of protector of Catholic Christians in the Ottoman Empire. Since the period of the crusades French religious orders had carried on missionary and educational work on an increasing scale and this activity was not the least bit hampered by the separation of Church and State after the establishment of the Third Republic. Government funds were still available to build Catholic missions, hospitals and educational institutions throughout the sultan's realm. Indeed it may be said that by 1914 French had become the language of culture and literature of all educated classes in the Levant.

France's economic and financial penetration was likewise strong and increased significantly in the latter stages of the nineteenth century. She held the bulk of Turkey's public debt, supplied experts to many posts, controlled the Imperial Ottoman Bank and administered the *régie des tabacs*. In Syria, the French obtained a monopoly on transport facilities and by 1914 controlled all but two railway lines. The cultivation of silk worms in Turkey and Syria was of special concern to the French textile manufacturers. French funds also flowed freely into public works programmes, harbours, factories for chemical products and scent, gas and electrical plants, big general businesses and practically every important concession or enterprise.

Over the years a number of organizations, interested in the affairs of the Near East, had sprouted in France. These groups actively supported the Government's Near Eastern policy and were constantly alert to anything that might undermine France's predominance in that area. They fervently believed that the wide diffusion of French capital, language, thought and influence in the Near East would indissolubly tie the people to France and create a bond of everlasting friendship. After the outbreak of the Great War they were joined by a segment of the press in urging that the Government take prompt and adequate means to safeguard French interests in the Eastern Mediterranean.

As if he was responding to the call, Aristide Briand, Minister of Justice, came out with a plan in November 1914 to send 400,000 Anglo-French troops to the Greek port of Salonika in order to protect Serbia, bring in the uncommitted Balkan states and develop an attack on the southern flank of Austria-Hungary.[7]

[7] Several prominent generals, Franchet d'Espèrey, Commander of the Fifth Army and Joseph Galliéni, Governor of Paris, were advocating a similar strategy as an alternative to the impasse that was taking shape in the West. See Paul Azan, *Franchet d'Espèrey* (Paris, 1949), pp. 42–3 and Marius-Ary Leblond, *Galliéni parle* (Paris, 1920), vol. 2, p. 57. Historical opinion as to which of the three men originally conceived the idea of a Balkan expedition is still very much divided. My own feeling is that it was Briand. This is based mostly on conversations Briand later had with Sir Francis Bertie, British Ambassador at Paris and Lord Esher, who acted

Opposition to the suggestion arose at once. Joffre asserted that the war could only be won by defeating Germany's main armies and that he could not spare the troops without seriously weakening his own line. The Cabinet, moreover, was inclined to side with Joffre, for it had not abandoned the hope of freeing France from the enemy.

Under the impact of this veto the idea of a Balkan operation was pushed into the background but it was not destined to remain dormant for long. Convinced that nothing more could be done in the West, Franchet d'Espèrey sought some other theatre to employ the newly raised armies. Working out the details of a plan at his headquarters, he proposed sending five army corps to Salonika where they would be transported to Belgrade as a preliminary move to a march upon Budapest.[8] The document was then submitted to President Poincaré on [about] December 1st through a Parliamentary deputy attached to the general staff of the Fifth Army.[9] The time was not propitious to contemplate action in the Balkans and for the present the matter was left in abeyance. Serbia had come under heavy attack near the end of November and its capital fell on December 2nd. Undaunted, the Serbs counter-attacked, recaptured Belgrade and before Christmas drove the

behind the scenes in the French capital, ostensibly on behalf of Kitchener. See Lord Bertie, *The Diary of Lord Bertie of Thame*, edited by Lady A. G. Lennox (London, 1924), vol. 1, p. 108 and Esher War Journals, February 21, 1915 (in the possession of his grandson Hon. Christopher Brett). Albert Pingaud in *Histoire diplomatique de la France pendant la grande guerre* (Paris, 1938), vol. 1, pp. 210–11 and 'Les origins de l'expédition de Salonique', *Revue historique*, vol. 176, juillet–décembre 1935, pp. 449–450, takes the position that Briand first hatched the scheme, after which both d'Espèrey and Galliéni gave their full endorsement. Georges Suarez, *Briand; sa vie – son œuvre* (Paris, 1939), vol. III, pp. 87–90, is of the same view. He suggests, however, that the Minister of Justice advanced his proposals on January 1, 1915. This seems to me to be highly improbable. Suarez was evidently thinking about the second time the Balkan project came up. As will be shown next it was d'Espèrey and not Briand who took the initiative.

[8] Part of the memorandum is reproduced in the appendix of M. Larcher, *La grande guerre dans les Balkans* (Paris, 1929). See also Alan Palmer, *The Gardeners of Salonika* (London, 1965), pp. 20–1.

[9] It was customary to have at least one deputy serving on the general staff of an army.

invaders back across the Austrian border. The startling resistance of Serbia rekindled Allied interest in the Balkans. On January 1, 1915 Poincaré discussed with Briand and Premier Viviani the prospect of creating a second front. Briand was all for it and Viviani, depressed by the recent setbacks in Champagne was no less enthusiastic. The three men agreed to invite Joffre's opinion on the advisability of this diversion in the Near East.[10]

Before the War no serious thought had been given to devise a supreme command structure adapted to cabinet government to co-ordinate or reconcile opposing views on strategy. The old *Conseil Supérieur de la guerre* had been founded as an advisory and consultative body. Its main function was to assist in preparing for war – to study the problems of recruitment and mobilization, to organize supply and to see to the manufacture of equipment and munitions. But this was a peace-time organization, not geared to war conditions, and after the outbreak of hostilities it was allowed to expire.[11]

Thus until the first days of August 1914, the higher direction of strategy was vested entirely in the hands of the Cabinet. The conduct of affairs in the Cabinet unhappily belied its immense responsibilities. For reasons of secrecy no proceedings were recorded and comparatively few departmental memoranda were circulated to the members. There was no prepared agenda or order of business. The Cabinet did not meet at regular intervals and often had to be summoned at rather short notice. Spur-of-the-moment action frequently resulted in confusion, with few having any clear notion of the decisions arrived at; cases arose when the matter was left so much in doubt that a Minister went away and acted upon what he thought was the accepted course only to be subsequently repudiated by his colleagues. In short, the chances appeared remote that the governmental machinery for the expected difficult task of controlling the war effort would reach a reasonably efficient standard.

It followed that the Ministers would be extremely reluctant to allow the power of decision on matters of policy to pass to any

[10] Raymond Poincaré, *Au service de la France* (Paris, 1930), vol. VI, pp. 1–3.

[11] Dean Pierre Renouvin was kind enough to provide me with this information.

group. But in the approaching hour of crisis the critical deficiency of the Cabinet system was never more apparent. This consideration and the belief that French arms would quickly carry the Germans, induced the Government to defer to the authority of G.Q.G. at the start of the conflict. To the horror of the French, the war took an ominous turn. The German sweep through Belgium and northern France, together with the collapse of Plan XVII, compelled the civil authorities to flee to Bordeaux. The existence of only one front already had reduced the role of the Minister of War. Now the absence of watchful politicians in Paris enabled the army to further increase its control and independence.[12] At Bordeaux during this period of turmoil and uncertainty it became almost impossible to know what was going on at the front, much less attempt to exercise some influence over the direction of the war. Angry demands for information from the High Command were ignored. Joffre refused to disclose the details of his future plans for he wanted to be left free of outside interference. His contempt for the Government can be inferred from a note which he sent to General Galliéni, then Governor of Paris: 'I should be obliged if you would send the Government no information concerning the operations. In the reports that I send them, I never make known the aim of current operations, nor my intentions.' [13]

When the political leaders returned to Paris at the end of 1914 they learned, much to their profound dismay, 'that power, once relinquished, is not so easily retrieved'. Permitted to set up a dictatorship in the early months of the war, Joffre had grown too fond of his freedom to want a return to a system where he would be constantly badgered by governmental questioning and hampered by ministerial restrictions. Since his victory at the Marne he had been transformed into a demi-god and worshipped both within France and abroad. He had a free hand in mapping strategy and exerted great influence over France's allies. Quite naturally he did not want to give up the benefits of his newly-won laurels and struck back at those who sought to curtail his authority or interfere in military affairs. Furthermore, Joffre would not tolerate the

[12] Pierre Renouvin, *The Forms of War Government in France*, pp. 81–2.
[13] Joseph Galliéni, *Mémoires* (Paris, 1920), p. 172.

inspection of Parliamentary Commissions [14] in war zones without the express approval of G.Q.G. and insisted that the Government rely entirely on the reports he submitted.[15] He conceded that 'the Commander-in-Chief is responsible only to the government, who can replace him if they do not approve of his action' [16] but knew too well that after the Marne his position was inviolable. Neither the existing government nor any other government for that matter could replace him without inviting its own demise and upsetting public confidence in the army. For those reasons Joffre was allowed to do almost everything that he pleased. Jean de Pierrefeu, an officer at G.Q.G., correctly summed up the situation when he wrote 'After the victory of the Marne there was in reality only one power in France, that of Joffre and his staff'.[17]

On January 7, 1915 when Joffre came to breakfast at the Elysée, he was asked about the possibility of sending an expedition to the Balkans. Viviani, together with Briand and Poincaré, argued that a diversion of this nature was the only means to offset the stalemate in France. Joffre impatiently rejected the proposal. His own plans included an attack in the spring against the enemy's defensive line in Artois and Champagne, for which he would require every available soldier. The French commander reasoned that it was senseless to divide his army by sending a force to fight in a remote corner of Europe and, in the process, endangering the safety of his position. The war could only be won by killing Germans on the main front and he felt confident that his projected attack would presage the defeat of the enemy.

Joffre appeared so resolute in his stand that the political authorities at the informal gathering thought it advisable to drop the subject. The military chief had always been given a free hand

[14] These were created in both the Chamber and Senate with a view to providing some measure of Parliamentary control over the war effort. Since the Commission's meetings were secret, the members were empowered by the legislators to inspect the front and to call in Ministers for questioning at any time.

[15] J. C. King, *Generals and Politicians*, chs. 1 and 2. See also Richard M. Watt, *Dare Call It Treason* (New York, 1963), ch. 7.

[16] Field-Marshal Joffre, *Personal Memoirs* (New York, 1932), vol. II, p. 397.

[17] Jean de Pierrefeu, *French Headquarters, 1915–1918* (London, 1924), p. 115.

in determining and executing the nation's war policies. To impose a strategic plan on him was certain to offend him and perhaps invite his resignation. For the present, then, nothing more could be done.[18]

This incident raised for the first time the whole issue of the right employment of the French forces and brought about a division between 'Westerners' and 'Easterners' – those who believed that every effort should be concentrated on the main front and those who sought to find a way around the entrenched line. The Westerners were clearly in the ascendancy at the beginning of 1915 and would remain so as long as the High Command exercised full control over the conduct of the war.

The original idea to send an expedition to the East had evolved in Paris; but the French soon forfeited their exclusive patent on revolutionary strategy. In London, at the turn of the year, other politicians were advancing schemes of a similar nature, but in a different atmosphere. One especially was taking definite shape; the man behind it was Winston Churchill; the project, the Dardanelles.

[18] Raymond Poincaré, *op. cit.*, vol. VI, p. 8; Marius-Ary Leblond, *op. cit.*, vol. 2, pp. 57–8; George Suarez, *op. cit.*, vol. 3, p. 91; A. Palmer, *op. cit.*, pp. 23–4.

Chapter 3

THE DARDANELLES AND THE FRENCH INVOLVEMENT

'It is said that the operation on the Dardanelles should have been planned from the first as a joint military and naval operation. . . . If this had been proposed the operation would never have been agreed to.'
Viscount Grey of Fallodon, *Twenty-Five Years*

'France cannot renounce . . . Alexandretta since . . . she needs a powerful base in the eastern Mediterranean to protect Syria.'
Senator Etienne Flandin, May 29, 1915

'The thing is going to be thoroughly done, but there is considerable risk and no great certainty of success. However, as there is to be no announcement, if the attempt does not come off it can be said out loud that there was no question of forcing the Dardanelles and that the only object was the bombardment of the forts.'
Raymond Poincaré, *Au service de la France*

The possibility of forcing a passage through the Dardanelles – the long tortuous channel linking the Aegean and the Sea of Marmora – had excited the imagination of naval and military strategists for more than a century before the start of the First World War. Stretching forty-one miles in length, from its mouth at Cape Helles to where it reaches the Sea of Marmora, the Dardanelles averages between three and four miles in width and closes to three-quarters of a mile at the Narrows. The strip of water is flanked on the west by the Gallipoli Peninsula and on the east by the hilly coast of Asia. Both sides were converted from early times into a formidable system of defences. A hostile fleet advancing into the Straits would thus be exposed to the enfilading fire from the batteries in Asia and the Gallipoli Peninsula. Even if some ships managed to break into the Sea of Marmora, as long as the shores were not occupied, not only would their communications be open to bombardment but the return journey would be extremely difficult and hazardous.

Since the days of Nelson there had persisted a belief in the British Navy that it was impractical for warships alone to attack coastal fortifications. In 1807 Admiral Duckworth, commanding a squadron, defied the odds and mastered the Hellespont. On the return trip Duckworth retained all his ships, but enemy gunners inflicted 150 casualties among his men. Technological changes in the nineteenth century made it unlikely that this exploit could be repeated. After the Turks multiplied and strengthened the fortifications along the Straits in 1885 naval experts took a discouraging view of the chances of even a combined operation. In 1906 a dispute between England and Turkey over the Sinai boundary led to a fresh examination of the problem. A joint military and naval report indicated that although a few ships might reach Constantinople, a purely maritime enterprise was 'much to be deprecated'. The General Staff went so far as to cast doubt on the feasibility of an amphibious attack. The Admiralty conceded, however, that while the cost would be heavy, a joint operation might succeed. The Committee of Imperial Defence then concluded that the risks were too great and that the operation should not be undertaken unless absolutely necessary. Here the issue was laid to rest until the start of the war.

In mid-August 1914 the Greek Government offered to place its entire naval and military resources at the disposal of the Entente. No action was taken until September 1st when Winston Churchill, First Lord of the Admiralty, arranged to have four naval and military officers examine and work out a plan for the seizure of the Gallipoli Peninsula by a Greek army and a British fleet. Two days later the Director of Military Operations, General Callwell, reported that since the General Staff survey of 1906, Turkish strength on the Peninsula had declined to a point where 60,000 troops might accomplish the task. Even then, he cautioned, the attack was 'likely to prove an extremely difficult operation of war'. Premier Venizelos was in favour of the proposed enterprise as long as Bulgarian neutrality could be assured. This was deemed insufficient by King Constantine, who stipulated that the Bulgarians must join Greece in a simultaneous attack on Turkey. As the latest demand could not be met, the Dardanelles project was shelved.[1]

Hostilities with Turkey broke out on October 31st. On November 3rd the Admiralty ordered Vice-Admiral Carden, Commander of an Allied Squadron in the Aegean, to bombard the forts at the entrance of the Dardanelles. The object of the demonstration was to discover the range of the Turkish guns. The action lasted about twenty minutes and, in compliance with Churchill's instructions, Carden gave the signal to withdraw before Turkish fire could damage the ships. The incident had unhappy results for it placed the enemy on the alert. Responding to the appeal of their German advisers, the Turks began to lay new minefields, strengthen the inner defences of the Straits, and re-arm the forts with modern Krupp guns.

When the War Council [2] convened for the first time on Novem-

[1] The genesis of the Dardanelles operation is drawn from the following sources: Brig.-Gen. C. F. Aspinall-Oglander, *Military Operations: Gallipoli* (London, 1929), vol. 1, chs. 2 and 3; *First Report of the Dardanelles Commission* (London, 1917), pp. 13–22, and *Supplement to First Report*, p. 1, the first of two heavily censored reports (the other being the *Final Report of the Dardanelles Commission*) based on testimony heard by a Royal Commission which was appointed to inquire into the 'origin, inception, and conduct of operations' in the Dardanelles. The full account was not published but it is now accessible to scholars. Evidence from this source is cited as Dardanelles Commission Report; Trumbull Higgins, *Winston Churchill and the Dardanelles* (London, 1963), chs. I–VII; Robert Rhodes James, *Gallipoli* (London, 1965), chs. 1 and 2; Lord Hankey, *The Supreme Command, 1914–1918* (London, 1961), vol. 1, chs. 23 and 24; Violet Bonham-Carter, *Winston Churchill as I Knew Him* (London, 1965), pp. 350–3; Winston S. Churchill, *The World Crisis: 1915* (London, 1968), vol. 2, ch. 5.

[2] Before the end of November, H. H. Asquith, the Prime Minister, decided to form a War Council, a special committee of the Cabinet charged with the control and direction of the war. The decisions taken in the War Council were not binding on the Cabinet and were liable to be thrashed out again in the presence of all the Ministers. The membership of the War Council consisted of the following Cabinet Ministers: H. H. Asquith (Prime Minister); Lord Kitchener (Secretary of State for War); David Lloyd George (Chancellor of the Exchequer); Sir Edward Grey (Secretary of State for Foreign Affairs); Winston Churchill (First Lord of the Admiralty); Lord Haldane (Lord Chancellor); and Lord Crewe (Secretary of State for India). Lt-Col. Hankey acted in the capacity of secretary; and A. J. Balfour, Lord Fisher, Sir Arthur Wilson and Sir James Wolfe

ber 25th to discuss the defence of Egypt and the Suez, Churchill suggested the possibility of employing a combined force to seize the Gallipoli Peninsula in order to dictate terms to Turkey. Kitchener dismissed Churchill's proposal by explaining that he had no troops available for secondary operations. Trained to think like a 'Westerner', Kitchener's eyes at this early stage were still focused on the vital front.

The slaughter in France, meanwhile, was surpassing all calculations. During the first three months of the war the mediocre and narrow-minded strategy of the Allies had netted no important gains but had cost them over one million casualties. At the end of December Hankey, Churchill and Lloyd George, each acting separately, produced papers in which they pointed out that the existence and probable continuation of the stalemate in the West imposed a need to find an alternative theatre of war. Lord Hankey suggested a flanking movement around the line through Turkey.[3] Churchill advocated an old plan conceived by Lord Fisher, First Sea Lord, for an invasion of Schleswig-Holstein. If the project succeeded, the entire Baltic Sea would be opened to the Royal Navy and a Russian army, under British protection, could land within ninety miles of Berlin.[4] Lloyd George in his paper stressed a landing either at Salonika or along the Syrian coast to cut communications with the Turkish Army threatening Egypt.[5]

Before the Prime Minister had time to revert to his normal practice of waiting upon events, there arrived at the Foreign Office on January 2, 1915 a telegram from the Grand Duke Nicholas, Russian Commander-in-Chief, requesting a demonstration against Turkey to relieve the pressure on his forces in the Caucasus. The appeal could not be ignored. The Russians were faltering and they were reportedly short of rifles and ammunition. Kitchener dis-

---

Murray regularly attended the meetings. If the occasion demanded, other ministers and officers were asked to attend. The War Council was largely dominated by three men – Asquith, Kitchener and Churchill – and of these Kitchener was by far the most powerful. See *First Report of the Dardanelles Commission*, pp. 3–4, 47.

[3] Lord Hankey, *op. cit.*, vol. 1, pp. 244–50.

[4] Winston S. Churchill, *op. cit.*, vol. 2, pp. 30–1.

[5] David Lloyd George, *War Memoirs* (Boston, 1933), vol. 1, pp. 322–30.

cussed the telegram with Churchill and wrote to him later in the day, 'We have no troops to land anywhere. . . . The only place that a demonstration might have some effect . . . would be the Dardanelles'.[6] Shortly afterwards Kitchener replied to the Russians, promising to stage a demonstration, but frankly admitting that its scope was unlikely to induce the Turks to divert sizeable detachments from the Caucasus.

The next morning (January 3rd) Lord Fisher, who had been informed of the Grand Duke's telegram, wrote to Churchill to urge an immediate combined attack on Turkey. He suggested that the Indian Corps and 75,000 seasoned troops be taken from France and placed ashore at Besika Bay. At the same time the Greeks were to be persuaded to attack the Gallipoli Peninsula, the Bulgarians to march upon Constantinople, the Russians to join the Serbs and Rumanians in an attack on Austria-Hungary; and a squadron of old British battleships would force a path through the Straits.[7]

The First Lord considered Fisher's plan impracticable. Kitchener had no men to spare and the order to divert even several divisions from the Western line would have been bitterly resisted by G.Q.G. and the British high command in France. In addition, the idea of a Balkan front did not take into view the deep-seated rivalry between Greece and Bulgaria. Churchill did, however, seize upon Fisher's concluding comment about the use of old battleships.

Even before the Turks sided with the Central Powers, Churchill had wanted to make a surprise attack on the Dardanelles. His imagination was now fired by the possibility of achieving a decisive victory with old battleships due to be scrapped at the end of the year. There were several other propelling factors. If the Germans using heavy howitzers of 5·9-inch and 8-inch calibre could reduce the Belgian strongholds, it seemed a reasonable deduction that the fire from the 12-inch and 15-inch guns of British ships would prove too much for the antiquated Turkish forts. Moreover, it was no secret that the Turks had only two divisions, some 27,000 men, guarding the Peninsula. These were

[6] *The First Report of the Dardanelles Commission*, p. 15.
[7] Winston S. Churchill, *op. cit.*, vol. 2, pp. 87–9.

further weakened by faulty equipment and organization, and the absence of a directive force was typical of the confusion and ineptitude which had led to the humiliation of Turkey in her recent wars.

On January 3rd, Churchill sent a 'purely exploratory' telegram to Carden: 'Do you consider the forcing of the Dardanelles by ships alone a practicable operation?' Carden replied that in his opinion the Straits could not be rushed but that 'they might be forced by extended operations with large number of ships'.[8] This was all that Churchill needed and he instructed Carden to prepare a detailed plan of operation.

On January 7th and 8th the War Council engaged in a thorough strategy review. Sir John French, Commander of the British forces in France, made an appearance to urge a gigantic assault along the coast of Flanders but received little encouragement.[9] Lord Kitchener then listed several theatres in which a new Allied offensive could succeed, expressing a preference for a combined attack on Turkey.[10] He estimated that such an operation would require 150,000 men but claimed he had no troops to spare. Kitchener expected the Germans to attack in France and, therefore, was unwilling to move troops from the Western front. The Council was inclined to believe that an operation against the Dardanelles deserved more study, but agreed that for the present the British should concentrate their entire resources on the main front 'as long as France was liable to successful invasion and required armed support'.[11]

Before the next meeting of the War Council, Vice-Admiral Carden forwarded his plan to the Admiralty. He proposed a four-staged attack on the Straits: (1) destruction of all entrance forts; (2) intense bombardment to clear the intermediary defences up to

[8] *First Report of the Dardanelles Commission*, p. 16.

[9] Unlike General Joffre, his French counterpart, Sir John French could not dictate war policy to the Government. He could make his views known when invited to do so, but all final strategic decisions rested with the civil leaders.

[10] Kitchener's first choice, an attack on Alexandretta, was abandoned after the navy reported that harbour facilities there were inadequate.

[11] Minutes of the War Council meeting of January 8, 1915; CAB 22/1 (London, P.R.O.).

Kephez; (3) reduction of the inner forts at the Narrows; (4) sweeping a channel through the minefield to enable the fleet to sail through the Narrows and into the Sea of Marmora. Carden estimated that the operations would require about a month.[12] Generally the scheme was well received by the naval experts. Fisher himself raised no objections and even proposed that the new battleship *Queen Elizabeth* carry out her final gunnery trials on the Dardanelles forts.

With a burst of enthusiasm Churchill put the plan before the War Council as it was about to adjourn on January 13th. 'The idea,' Lord Hankey later wrote, 'caught on at once.'[13] Exhausted after a long and unproductive session the Ministers were in a frame of mind to jump at anything that seemed to offer a solution to their problems. If the navy alone could get through, the Entente would reap tangible advantages: Turkey would be rendered helpless, the Balkans would probably be weaned from their neutrality and a supply route to Russia would be opened. On the other hand if the naval attack did not prove effective in the early stages it would be treated as a feint and broken off. Kitchener thought it was worth trying [14] and with the approval of the War

[12] *First Report of the Dardanelles Commission*, pp. 17–18; Winston S. Churchill, *op. cit.*, vol. 2, pp. 93–5.

[13] Lord Hankey, *op. cit.*, vol. 1, p. 265.

[14] Kitchener's role in the genesis is difficult to assess and may be greater than historians of the campaign have suggested. Lord Fisher was emphatic in his testimony to the Dardanelles Commission that the real moving spirit behind the naval attack was Kitchener and not Churchill. According to the First Sea Lord, when Kitchener could not find the means to fulfil his promise to the Russians he told Churchill: 'Look here we must do something for the Grand Duke; you do something at the Dardanelles, I have no army, I have no troops.' Dardanelles Commission Report, p. 191, CAB 19/33 (London, P.R.O.). This is the complete version of the proceedings.

It is strange that only a week before Kitchener contended that 150,000 troops would be required, yet at the meeting (on January 13th) made not the slightest allusion to military support. Violet Bonham-Carter recorded a conversation she had with Kitchener in February 1915 which would tend to give weight to Fisher's story. Violet Bonham-Carter: 'If the Dardanelles comes off W. will deserve full and almost sole credit.' Lord Kitchener: 'Not at all – I was always strongly in favour of it. No one who has seen as much of the East as I have could fail to appreciate its importance.' See *Winston Churchill as I Knew Him*, pp. 365–6.

Council authorized preparations 'for a naval expedition . . . to bombard and take the Gallipoli Peninsula with Constantinople as its objective . . .'. [15]

Upon receipt of the mandate from the War Council, the First Lord proceeded to open negotiations with the French Government to settle 'among other things the question of command in the Mediterranean . . .'. [16]

Since the beginning of the eighteenth century Britain had maintained a large fleet in the Mediterranean, except for a short period in 1796. Here was the centre of naval strategic gravity in Europe and the principal channel for the importation of Britain's foodstuff. Thus wrote the official British naval historian: 'It had become a canon of British policy – consecrated by repeated experience – that our Mediterranean Fleet was the measure of our influence in continental affairs, and the feeling had only increased since the road to India lay that way, and Egypt and Cyprus had become limbs of the Empire.' [17]

The increase in the strength of the German navy in the North Sea, which was expected to be the decisive naval theatre, had imposed a need on the British to concentrate their fleet in northern waters and to look to the French to take over the major role in other vital areas. By virtue of a convention signed on August 6, 1914 it was agreed that while the French fleet should assume general direction of naval operations in the Mediterranean and western part of the Channel, the British should look after the Atlantic, the Straits of Dover and the North Sea. There was also a clause which provided for the withdrawal of a portion of the British flotilla [18] in the Mediterranean as soon as the *Goeben* and *Breslau* were captured or destroyed.[19] The *Goeben* was faster and

[15] *First Report of the Dardanelles Commission*, pp. 18–23; Lord Hankey, *op. cit.*, vol. 1, pp. 265–7.

[16] Winston S. Churchill, *op. cit.*, vol. 2, p. 112.

[17] Julian S. Corbett, *Naval Operations* (London, 1920), vol. 1, p. 8.

[18] All the armoured ships except one.

[19] Anglo-French Naval Convention, August 6, 1914; E s 11, Marine archives (Paris, Historical section of the Ministry of Marine). See also A. P. Bienaimé, *La guerre navale, 1914–1915: fautes et responsabilités* (Paris, 1920), pp. 111–13.

more powerfully armed than any ship in the French navy, so only the British battle-cruisers had any hope of catching and sinking her. In principle, the French naval commander, Vice-Admiral Boué de Lapeyrère, was responsible for the entire Allied fleet in the Mediterranean; in practice, however, his jurisdiction never extended over the British naval division which acted separately and on the direct orders from London. On September 22nd, at the request of the Admiralty,[20] the French Minister of Marine, Victor Augagneur, ordered the dispatch of two ships under Rear-Admiral Guépratte to reinforce Vice-Admiral Carden's squadron in the vicinity of the Dardanelles.[21]

The intervention of Turkey created new problems and upset the pre-war view that the Mediterranean would not be the scene of major naval action. In the belief that an invasion of Egypt was now imminent, the Admiralty transferred Rear-Admiral Peirse to assume command of a fleet that was concentrating in the Egyptian zone to assist in the defence of the Canal.[22] The French did not need to be reminded of the importance London attached to the defence of Egypt and raised no objections when the British took charge of the eastern end of the inland lake. To keep an eye on the movements of Turkish troops southward and also with a view to future operations, British ships on patrol pushed well beyond Egyptian waters, seemingly on the way to take in the whole coastal road from El Arish to Alexandretta. Since the French had already acquiesced in the removal of the Egyptian areas from their general command of the Mediterranean, they were frankly alarmed at the prospect of further British encroachment. On December 28, 1914 the Minister of Marine sent a long memorandum to the Admiralty. He proposed that the Allied naval forces operating at the Dardanelles and on the coasts of Asia Minor and Syria as far as Jaffa in the south, fall within the sphere of Boué de Lapeyrère's responsibilities, while the Anglo-French ships on patrol in the Red Sea and on the coast of Asia Minor

---

[20] French Naval Attaché to Augagneur, September 20, 1914; X a 1, Marine archives.

[21] Augagneur to French Naval Attaché, September 22, 1914; X a 32, Marine archives.

[22] Julian S. Corbett, *op. cit.*, vol. 1, p. 402.

from El Arish to Jaffa be placed under the direction of Peirse, who would also enjoy an independent command.[23]

Churchill had his hands full with pressing Admiralty business at the turn of the year and it was not until the start of the second week in January 1915 that he got around to the French note. By then he had become absorbed in the brilliant prospects which were unfolding in the Mediterranean. When Churchill found that the proposed arrangements involved the transfer of the command at the Dardanelles from the British to the French Vice-Admiral, he declined to give the matter further consideration. He asked Sir Edward Grey to inform Paul Cambon, French Ambassador at London, that the 'Admiralty think the present arrangements had better stand for the time being'.[24]

Meanwhile the Comte de Saint-Seine, French Naval Attaché, reported to Paris that, in spite of daily visits to the Admiralty, he had been unable to elicit a commitment from the English.[25] Augagneur's annoyance turned to anger when he received a telegram from Boué de Lapeyrère the next day, explaining that Peirse was supposedly unaware of the recent understanding over the Mediterranean and had assumed that policing the coast of Syria was linked to his own duties as commander of the Egyptian naval zone.[26] Thereupon the Minister of Marine produced a second paper, much sharper in tone, insisting on prompt settlement of the respective spheres of action for the two navies in the Mediterranean along the lines indicated earlier.[27] This time Churchill reacted and promised a reply within several days.[28]

Now that the conflict in the Mediterranean had entered a new

[23] A memorandum, December 28, 1914; E s 11, Marine archives.

[24] Churchill to Grey, January 10, 1915; F.O. 800/88, Grey papers (London, P.R.O.).

[25] French Naval Attaché to Augagneur, January 8, 1915; X a 2, Marine archives.

[26] Boué de Lapeyrère to Augagneur, January 9, 1915; C a 20, Marine archives.

[27] Augagneur to Delcassé, January 10, 1915; Dardanelles operation, Box 4, fol. 1, Diplomatic archives (Paris, Ministry of Foreign Affairs). Cambon to Delcassé, January 13, 1915; E s 11, Marine archives.

[28] Cambon to Delcassé, January 16, 1915; E s 11, Marine archives.

phase and the English were contemplating a naval attack against Turkey, Churchill desired to modify the Anglo-French convention. This in itself might not have proven too difficult had Churchill been willing to confine himself to the problem of the Dardanelles. But the First Lord, with yet another scheme forming in his powerful mind, proposed to strike at Alexandretta at the same time as the attack on the Dardanelles. He explained to Kitchener that 'if we are checked at the Dardanelles we can represent that operation as a mere demonstration to cover the seizure of Alexandretta. I believe this aspect is important from an Oriental point of view'. [29]

Once Churchill obtained the approval of Asquith, Kitchener, Grey and Fisher for his subsidiary operation, he sent a note to the French Naval Attaché in London:

'The Admiralty have ... decided to attack the Dardanelles forts, and force, if possible, a passage into the Sea of Marmora. ... The Admiralty do not wish, in view of this very important operation, that any change in the local command in that portion of the Mediterranean should be made at the present time. ... They hope, however, that the squadron of French battleships ... will co-operate under a French rear-admiral. ... The War Office also considers it necessary during the month of February to occupy Alexandretta and the surrounding district in order to cut the Turkish railway communication at this most strategic point.' [30]

Attached to the memorandum when it arrived at the Ministry of Marine the next day (January 19th), were two letters from the Naval Attaché. The first told of a conversation with Paul Cambon who enthusiastically endorsed the idea of forcing the Straits, and urged that measures be taken not to discuss in public, or even in the Cabinet, the text of Churchill's proposals.[31] The other, cited

---

[29] Churchill to Kitchener, January 20, 1915; P.R.O. 30 /57 /72, Kitchener papers (London, P.R.O.).

[30] Churchill to French Naval Attaché, January 18, 1915; E s 11, Marine archives. See also Winston S. Churchill, *op. cit.*, vol. 2, pp. 112–13.

[31] French Naval Attaché to Augagneur, January 19, 1915; E s 11, Marine archives.

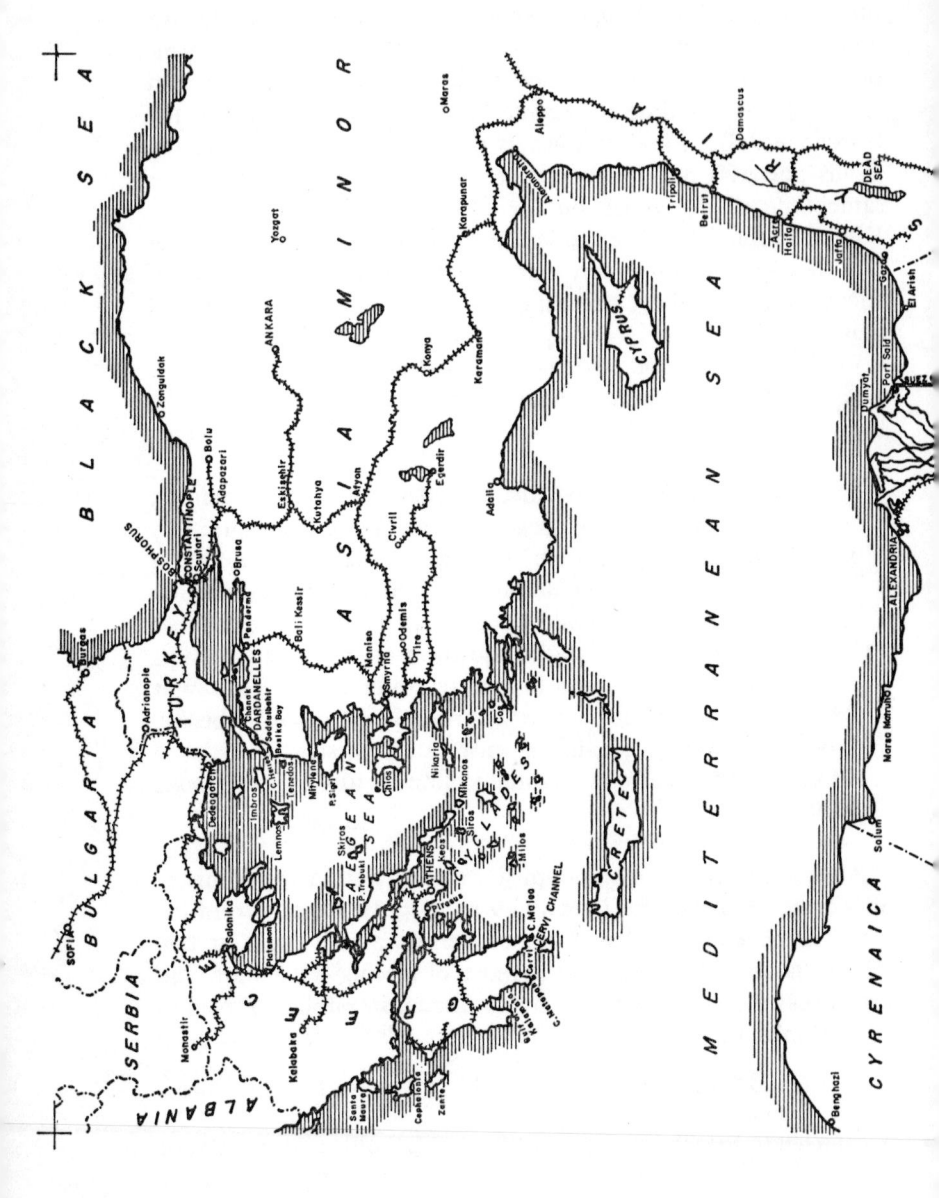

1. Eastern Mediterranean

immediately below, sought to justify the Admiralty's desire to readjust the naval zones in the Mediterranean and to allay French fears concerning British intentions in the Near East.

'As Mr Churchill was handing this document to me, he expressed the wish to have brought to your attention the tremendous military and political interest attached to an energetic and prompt action against the Turks. . . .

'The Admiralty hopes that the Russian Black Sea fleet will contribute to the success of the operation by guarding the exit of the Bosphorus in order to prevent the escape of the German-Turkish fleet and also by attacking simultaneously the defences of the northern part of the Bosphorus if conditions are favourable. Nevertheless the Admiralty wishes to communicate directly with the Russian Admiralty at a time thought to be appropriate and asks that you observe absolute discretion concerning this matter. This secret is, by the way, one of the most important ingredients of success. What makes the operation relatively simple is the absence of submarines in the area. The arrival of submarines would bring considerable danger. But information held to be of value by the Admiralty confirms that there are no shipyards on the shores of the Sea of Marmora able to assemble submarines sent by rail. Nevertheless these [submarines] could be sent by sea from Austria if the enemy suspected that there was a project under way to force the Dardanelles.

'The First Lord's answer emphasizes that the accords concluded on August 6 between the two Admiralties in order to divide the spheres of action in the Mediterranean had been drafted at a time when Germany and Austria were our only adversaries. The entry of Turkey in the coalition has rendered them obsolete as far as the Levant is concerned and necessitates their revision. . . .

'The First Lord has told me repeatedly and with insistence, that his greatest desire was to avoid doing anything that could offend the French Government and to remain loyally, sincerely and without questioning in complete harmony with it. He also told me, and authorized me to reveal to you, that the British Government considers that occupation of enemy territory by

British forces is essentially provisional and does not give exclusive territorial rights to Great Britain. All Allied conquests belong to the Allies.' [32]

The response to this in Paris was icy. Since January 7th the Minister of Marine had known that the Admiralty was thinking of forcing the Dardanelles by ships alone,[33] but he fully expected to be consulted before the scheme was agreed upon. He was, therefore, incensed when the project was presented as a *fait accompli*, especially as it ignored French privileges in the Mediterranean. Immediately he concluded that the English were trying to chip away at those rights in a bid to regain command of the lake. So vital for the French was control of the Mediterranean that it could not be left to a friendly power to secure it. Not only was it needed to protect their North African colonies, which the Germans obviously coveted, but also to cover the transport of their African armies to France.

A more serious consequence, perhaps, was Churchill's demand for control of Alexandretta, a seaport in south-western Turkey which the French had long regarded as being within their sphere of influence. It was the centre of the cotton growing belt; 'it was the end of the caravan routes from the desert' and the 'petrol-pipe line from Mosul terminated there'. Much of the seaborne trade of northern Syria, Persia and upper Mesopotamia passed through this port which had rail connections with the main Turkish system. Alexandretta was the gateway to Asia Minor and a vital link in France's strategy to dominate the Mediterranean.[34]

The French had no desire to cover up the decomposing Ottoman carcass, and in the past they had continually tried to check the rapid process of its disintegration. There lingered a genuine fear in Paris that should the Turkish Empire collapse, the relative strength of France in the Near East might be weakened rather than

[32] French Naval Attaché to Augagneur, January 19, 1915; E s 11, Marine archives.

[33] French Naval Attaché to Augagneur, January 7, 1915; X a 2, Marine archives.

[34] Stephen H. Roberts, *The History of French Colonial Policy, 1870–1925* (Hamden, 1963), pp. 591–2. See also Etienne Flandin, 'Nos droits en Syrie et en Palestine', *La revue hebdomadaire*, May 29, 1915, pp. 17–32.

strengthened.[35] For that reason the policy of the Third Republic remained unchanged, despite the fact that the Turks were now fighting on the side of the Central Powers. If it became impossible to save Turkey, then the French had arrogated to themselves Syria, Palestine, Cilicia and Alexandretta.[36]

When Churchill gave notice of an intended landing at Alexandretta, Augagneur concluded that the operation was not so much out of military necessity as it was for a desire to gain a foothold in Asia Minor.[37] To defer to English ambitions would be to provide the base for a future rival. It would also invite other European Powers to move into Ottoman territory and further threaten France's cultural and economic primacy in that part of the world. Determined to bar the intrusion of British power in the Levant, Augagneur issued a stiff rejoinder through the Naval Attaché:

'The Minister persists in claiming the execution of the convention of August 6, and the entire direction of the operations in the Mediterranean for the French Command. Under these conditions any operation must be planned and directed by us. The Admiralty cannot adopt a plan in which we would assume the role it would assign to us. Do insist firmly on this line of thought.' [38]

Churchill had anticipated some opposition from Paris but not an outright rebuke. He was bewildered and upset that Augagneur

[35] 'Note on the questions raised by the forcing of the Dardanelles', March 5, 1915; vol. 25, Delcassé papers (Paris, Ministry of Foreign Affairs).

[36] W. W. Gottlieb, *Studies in Secret Diplomacy during the First World War* (London, 1957), pp. 80–1; Maurice Paléologue, *An Ambassador's Memoirs* (London, 1924), vol. 1, p. 193; Lord Bertie, *The Diary of Lord Bertie of Thame*, edited by Lady A. G. Lennox, vol. 1, pp. 106, 120; A. J. P. Taylor, *Politics in Wartime* (London, 1964), pp. 180–1; C. J. Smith, *The Russian Struggle for Power, 1914–1917* (New York, 1956), ch. 4; A. Ribot, *Journal d'Alexandre Ribot et correspondances inédites, 1914–1922* (Paris, 1936), p. 58; Raymond Poincaré, *op. cit.*, vol. VI, p. 94.

[37] French suspicions, as will be shown in the next chapter, were not unfounded.

[38] Augagneur to French Naval Attaché, January 21, 1915; X a 37, Marine archives.

should choose this crucial moment to invoke the Anglo-French accord. Such an arrangement, he felt, was capable of being modified or cancelled by either signatory at any time and could not have any bearing on the new conditions created by the entry of Turkey into the war. In a mood of exasperation he poured his heart out to Grey:

> 'It is absurd for the French to claim that we are to make no movements into the Mediterranean except by their directives and under their command. That would be to inflict on Gr. Britain, as the forfeit for her services, conditions which could not be extorted from her by any power by war. The French ships placed under our direction have done little or nothing in the Channel and foreign waters and we are ready to release them at any time. The French Fleet moreover has itself done nothing in the Mediterranean. We are quite capable of conducting the Dardanelles operation without any assistance and I only suggested French co-operation out of loyalty and politeness.' [39]

Despite the temptation to discount the objections from Paris, Churchill must have realized that without French support he was in an impossible position. Accordingly, he arranged to have Augagneur join him at the Admiralty so that they could have the matter out. [40]

Before making any official pronouncement in London, Augagneur wanted his colleagues to endorse his mission. In these circumstances it became inpossible to remain silent on the intended operation in the Dardanelles as Churchill had requested. At a meeting of the Cabinet on January 23rd, the Minister of Marine revealed the British plan, taking time to explain that its execution was subject to French approval. Since precise and extensive information (as to what the English had in mind) was lacking, he had no difficulty in obtaining authorization to meet and make the necessary arrangements with the First Lord. [41] The next day

[39] Churchill to Grey, January 24, 1915; F.O. 800/88, Grey papers.

[40] Cambon to Delcassé, January 22, 1915; Journeys of Ministers and Personalities, Box 10, Diplomatic archives.

[41] Raymond Poincaré, *op. cit.*, vol. VI, pp. 29–30.

Augagneur communicated directly with Churchill to confirm his appointment set for January 26th and added:

> 'May I remind you that in my telegrams 52 and 53 [42] I recommended that you bring to the attention of the British Government the interest that we have in the region of Alexandretta, as well as in Syria itself. An operation in this region, similar to the one our Naval Attaché attributes to the thinking of the British Admiralty, could only take place with our agreement and co-operation.' [43]

On the afternoon of January 26th Augagneur arrived at the Admiralty, accompanied by his chief of cabinet, Commander Salaun. Churchill, on hand to greet the Minister of Marine, led him to a private room where they could talk more freely. Unfortunately no written record of the discussions has been preserved, although in the light of fresh evidence it is possible to piece together a synopsis of what took place.

Churchill began by outlining the reasons for the British Government's decision to send a naval force to attack the Dardanelles and how, in the view of Vice-Admiral Carden, this could be achieved. Augagneur remained dubious as to the ability of the navy to open a passage unassisted. To prove his point he alluded to a report recently conducted at his request by French naval intelligence which had concluded that a purely maritime operation to force the Dardanelles was unlikely to attain any useful purpose.[44] In his reply, Churchill endeavoured to calm the apprehensions of his French counterpart, observing that the vast improvement in gunnery had reshaped naval thinking on the problem of 'ships versus forts'. The potentialities of a ship like the *Queen Elizabeth* rendered a task hitherto impossible now comparatively easy or at any rate quite practicable. The First Lord felt certain that once the forts at the entrance of the Straits were demolished the Turks would abandon the struggle.[45] He indicated that in case the naval

[42] I was unable to find copies of these telegrams in the Marine archives.

[43] Augagneur to Churchill, January 24, 1915; X a 37, Marine archives.

[44] Augagneur before the Marine Commission, July 18, 1917; C7531 dossier 1022, pp. 44–5, National archives (Paris).

[45] *Ibid.*, p. 45.

assault did not prove effective it would be treated as a demonstration and broken off without serious loss of prestige.[46]

During the course of the conversation, Churchill apparently brought out a telegram he had just received from Petrograd which showed that the operation had Russia's 'entire good will and the Grand Duke attaches the greatest importance to its success'.[47] It was clear that if the Allies acted indifferently over the plight of Russia, the negative consequences would resound on the Western front.

The Minister of Marine was dazzled by Churchill's glowing pictures of the tremendous military and political results that would follow a successful naval attempt to breach the Dardanelles. A professor-turned-politician who had shown considerable skill as an administrator in various political offices prior to the war, Augagneur did not possess a clear understanding of what the navy needed nor the technical knowledge to shape a wise policy.[48] Without much imagination or initiative in the conduct of naval affairs and unable to draw on expert advice,[49] he must have sat uneasily in London in the presence of such an experienced and resourceful politician as Churchill. It is no wonder, then, that he succumbed to pressure from the First Lord.

Remarking later, Augagneur listed two reasons why he acquiesced in Churchill's proposals. First, Churchill's assurance that this was only an experimental attack, losses would be limited and ships could be withdrawn at any time. The Minister of Marine maintained that had he been kept informed of the fleet's inability to deal with the forts in the early stages, he would never have agreed to the naval attack on March 18th. Second, Augagneur was under the impression that Churchill had the unanimous backing of naval and civil authorities in England. The determination with which the First Lord tried to press the scheme upon his acceptance convinced him that failure to go along might open a rift in Anglo-French relations.[50]

[46] *Ibid.*, p. 48.

[47] Winston S. Churchill, *op. cit.*, vol. 2, p. 155.

[48] Léopold Marcellin, *Politique et politiciens pendant la guerre* (Paris, 1922), vol. 1, p. 25; A. P. Bienaimé, *op. cit.*, p. 181.

[49] The chief naval expert at the Ministry of Marine, Vice-Admiral Aubert, was not invited to make the trip to London.

[50] Augagneur before the Marine Commission, July 18, 1917; C7531,

To the two factors already cited by Augagneur, a third must be added. This involved readjustment of the naval spheres in the Mediterranean in accordance with the original French demands and Churchill's pledge to abandon, at least for the present, the idea of a landing at Alexandretta. Thus patrol of the Syrian coast including Alexandretta and as far south as Jaffa would be the affair of the French, while control of naval operations in Egyptian waters would remain in the hands of the British. As for Alexandretta, any future operation there would be undertaken jointly and in full co-operation.[51] Churchill was enough of a pragmatist to realize that he must dampen French speculation with regard to British aims in the Levant. In any event, the unlikelihood that he could get the necessary troops from Kitchener to capture Alexandretta [52] made it futile to create an incident when more serious matters, including the fate of the Dardanelles operation, rested on preserving friendly ties with the French. Well might Churchill declare to Grey after the meeting: 'I think it important to let the French have what they want ... even about Alexandretta. It will be fatal to cordial co-operation in the Mediterranean and perhaps elsewhere, if we arouse their suspicions ... in the region of Syria.' [53]

In return for these concessions, the British were left in control of the Dardanelles.[54] Churchill did not seek French participation

dossier 1022, p. 47, National archives; Augagneur to Lacaze (then Minister of Marine), February 26, 1917; E s 11, Marine archives. The letter is reproduced in full in the appendix. France, *Journal officiel, comité secret juin 1916 – octobre 1917* (Paris), séance du 28 novembre, 1916.

[51] Churchill to Augagneur, January 27, 1915; E s 11, Marine archives. This letter embodies the results of the conference held the previous day; Augagneur to Churchill, January 31, 1951; E s 11, Marine archives. This confirmed Churchill's observations and committed the French to support the British naval project. Both letters can be found in the appendix.

[52] Brig.-Gen. C. F. Aspinall-Oglander, *Military Operations: Gallipoli*, vol. 1, p. 60.

[53] Churchill to Grey, January 26, 1915, appended to Churchill's statement before the Dardanelles Commission; Dardanelles Commission Report, p. 251, CAB 19/28.

[54] Augagneur admitted to the Marine Commission that owing to insufficient naval strength the French could not under any circumstances have seized the initiative at the Dardanelles. Marine Commission Report, March 19, 1915; C 7532, dossier 1106, National archives.

in the projected naval enterprise but did not object to it.[55] Augagneur saw correctly that the French could not dissociate themselves from the venture. He told the Marine Commission in retrospect: 'Not to take part in the operation would have been, in case it succeeded, to witness the appearance of the English fleet alone before Constantinople. For us French who are deeply engaged in the Orient, [56] as you are aware, it would have been a very painful renunciation of our national pride and perilous for our interests.' [57] The extent of French commitment would be determined at a later date when the Minister of Marine could consult with the leading members of his Government.

The arrangements, having been concluded, gave Churchill everything he desired. To show his appreciation he provided Auganeur the next day with a tour of London and in the evening had him over to his home for dinner. After bidding farewell to his guest, Churchill must have breathed a sigh of relief. Failure to have arrived at an amicable settlement might have led to incalculable complications, especially now since there were signs that Lord Fisher was becoming increasingly restive over the idea of a purely naval attack on the Dardanelles.

Fisher's opposition was based, not so much on a conviction that the maritime operation would fail, as on a realization that it would prevent his own Baltic scheme from being carried out. Shortly before the War Council convened on January 28th he met Churchill and Asquith to talk things over. Churchill was under the impression when he came out of the room that all was well. But at the meeting of the War Council, as he started to give a report on the progress of preparations for the Dardanelles operation, Fisher left the table intending to resign. Kitchener rose also and overtook Fisher before he could make his exit, drew him aside and persuaded him to return. Fisher's objection was unmistakable, yet no one took notice. Lord Kitchener, who had just silenced the aged sailor's protest, echoed the general sentiment of the War Council when he declared that the operation was vitally important and that

[55] Churchill to Augagneur, January 27, 1915; E s 11, Marine archives.

[56] In this context it means Near East.

[57] Augagneur before the Marine Commission, July 18, 1917; C 7531, dossier 1022, p. 46, National archives.

'if satisfactory progress could not be made, the attack could be broken off'. During the recess Churchill had another long talk with Fisher and this time succeeded in converting him to his side. At the second session the First Lord announced that the Admiralty was now in agreement and that the plan would be put into action. 'This I took as the point of final decision. After it I never looked back,' wrote Churchill in *The World Crisis*.[58]

Quite apart from his optimistic prognostication about the outcome of the venture, Churchill could scarcely overlook the fact that the fleet would be embarking upon a task for which there was practically no precedent in naval warfare. A slight miscalculation or error of judgment might compromise the situation beyond repair. It is true that the fleet possessed the initiative but that advantage could be nullified by indiscretions at home. Secrecy was indeed the first essential if the fleet was to have the smallest chance of success. It would be easy enough to conceal the news from the British Cabinet until the last moment, but as regards the French Government similar precautions could not be guaranteed. While in London, Augagneur had refused to accept such a responsibility, insisting that it must be left to Premier Viviani to decide.[59]

Churchill was not content to leave such a question up in the air. He asked Paul Cambon to use his good offices to convince the Minister of Marine to withhold all information about the coming naval attack from the French Cabinet. To this end the Ambassador addressed a personal letter to Augagneur on January 29th in which he indicated that secrecy was vital if the fleet was to attain its objective and suggested that only those Ministers apt to be directly involved – Prime Minister, Minister of War and Minister of Foreign Affairs – should be told.[60]

[58] Winston S. Churchill, *op. cit.*, vol. 2, pp. 160–1; H. H. Asquith, *Memories and Reflections* (London, 1928), vol. 2, p. 59; Lord Fisher, *Memories and Records* (New York, 1920), vol. 1, pp. 89–90; *First Report of the Dardanelles Commission*, pp. 26–7; A. J. Marder, *From the Dreadnought to Scapa Flow* (London, 1965), vol. II, pp. 208–11.

[59] Augagneur before the Marine Commission, July 18, 1917; C7531, dossier 1022, pp. 45–6, National archives.

[60] Cambon to Augagneur, January 29, 1915; Allied Conferences, Box 10, Diplomatic archives.

Augagneur received the note as he was about to leave for the Prime Minister's office. With Viviani he discussed his arrangements in London and the two men agreed that only Delcassé should be taken into their full confidence. Millerand was to be kept out as there was no desire to arouse the high command. Both Viviani and Delcassé readily endorsed the idea of a naval assault on the Turkish forts, apparently because they were left with the impression that Augagneur was reflecting the considered opinion of the experts at the Ministry of Marine. This was, of course, not the case.

On January 30th Augagneur spoke briefly in the Cabinet about his trip to London. He appeared highly pleased with the results, pointing out that the question of command in the Mediterranean had been finally resolved.[61] As agreed in advance, no mention was made of the Admiralty's plan to force the Dardanelles or of the French intention to support it.

In the afternoon the Minister of Marine stopped by to see the President to acquaint him with more of the details. He turned over Churchill's memorandum [62] to Poincaré, who examined it with great interest. Poincaré considered that the naval attack involved considerable danger with no certainty of success but was comforted by the knowledge that it could not lead to disaster because the ships could be recalled at any moment. Augagneur confided that he personally had little faith in the success of the operation but as the English were prepared to assume nearly all the risks he did not feel he had the right to try to dissuade them.[63] Whatever may be said about Augagneur's conduct of naval affairs, there could be no question as to his political finesse. His apparent *volte-face* in the presence of Poincaré, after he had willingly agreed to the enterprise several days before, showed he was enough of a politician to take adequate means to protect himself against possible failure. If the Anglo-French fleet met with defeat, he could claim that he had been forced into the undertaking as a matter of political expediency and shift the entire blame on to Churchill.

If such an inference is correct it may explain why Augagneur did

[61] Raymond Poincaré, *op. cit.*, vol. VI, p. 33.
[62] See fn. 51.
[63] Raymond Poincaré, *op. cit.*, vol. VI, p. 34.

not invite the views of his naval authorities on the feasibility of the Dardanelles project. He was aware that the established opinion at the Ministry of Marine strongly deprecated unsupported naval action against forts. Some months ago when he had asked his leading experts to look into the problem of forcing the Dardanelles they had concluded that even a joint operation would prove a formidable task. He had not since requested an evaluation of the applicability of the Namur-Liège experience to a naval bombardment in the Dardanelles, but all evidence led him to believe that they would hold firm to their previous attitude. Apparently the Minister of Marine was convinced that he must see the Dardanelles business through. If he had sounded out his Admirals they were almost certain to stand in opposition to the idea of independent maritime action. To have acted contrary to the solicited advice of his naval staff would have been, in the event of the ships running into trouble, tantamount to committing political suicide. Thus by excluding the naval experts from the picture, Augagneur could always represent the expedition as having been an English scheme – conceived, planned and executed by them. Writing to the Admiralty on January 31st, the Minister of Marine concurred in the statements made by Churchill on the 27th and announced that the French Government would place four battleships at Carden's disposal.[64]

It is remarkable that even after he had arrived at an understanding with the First Lord, Augagneur elected to keep Vice-Admiral Boué de Lapeyrère, French Naval Commander in the Mediterranean, ignorant of the projected attack. Exactly what the Minister of Marine had in mind is not known. He may have feared that Boué de Lapeyrère would not take kindly to the news and possibly become a problem. If so, Augagneur could hardly hope to have kept him in the dark much longer. It was when Rear-Admiral Guépratte, in charge of the French squadron in the Dardanelles, made inquiries about munitions that Boué de Lapeyrère first suspected something was afoot. He sent Commander Docteur, deputy chief of his naval staff, to seek an explanation from Carden. The Commander had a long interview with Carden who, under orders to remain silent, spoke vaguely of a grandiose project

[64] Augagneur to Churchill, January 31, 1951; E s 11, Marine archives.

relating to the Dardanelles, regretting that he could not divulge specific details. Carden's immediate subordinates, however, talked more freely behind their chief's back and let word out that the Admiralty was laying plans for a naval attack on the Dardanelles. Boué de Lapeyrère was naturally furious when told of this, although he appeared unaware of the degree of French involvement. He cabled the Minister to inform him of the news and added:

'Your lordship probably is aware of this project, but in as much as it is very new to me and of great military importance, I would like Mr Herr [65] . . . to talk to you, in case you do not know its details. To my astonishment at not having been informed of the situation, while my subordinate Rear-Admiral Guépratte secretly knew of it, would be added a profound deception, if I saw this operation, quite tempting and quite feasible, take place outside my command and without having an opportunity to participate in it, with several of my battleships, at least as compensation for all the weariness we have been subjected to in the last six months.

'It truly appears to me that it would be very regrettable that a war operation of this importance should take place without the participation of the fleet which up to now, and after an understanding with England, has assumed all the responsibilities for what has happened in the Mediterranean.' [66]

Augagner replied immediately:

'I am pleased to enclose herein a copy of a letter which has been addressed to me by the First Lord of the Admiralty on January 27th.

'I have given in principle my adhesion to the proposals contained in this letter, and, in particular, to the co-operation of the French battleships operating in the Dardanelles to an action which will take place around February 15th in the Straits under the command of Vice-Admiral Carden.

'In the secret telegram sent to you today, I ask that you find out from Admiral Guépratte the main points of Admiral Carden's

[65] A naval officer on Boué de Lapeyrère's staff.
[66] Boué de Lapeyrère to Augagneur, January 31, 1915; E d 108, Marine archives.

project, and I would be thankful to receive your personal opinion on it.' [67]

In attempting to assuage the Naval Commander's anger, Augagneur did not scruple to practise deception. He did not communicate his note of January 31st, accepting the British venture as an independent operation. He wrote of adhesion in principle when in fact there was unequivocal support. Finally the inclusion of Churchill's proposals was designed not for their examination but for their execution.

Having finished with Boué de Lapeyrère, the Minister of Marine sent Rear-Admiral Guépratte a similar telegram in the course of which he stated: 'You undoubtedly must have had conversations with Admiral Hamilton Carden about the conditions under which this action can be undertaken: I would be grateful if you notified me immediately of the outline of your common plan of attack as well as your personal opinion on the matter.' [68] In his reply, Guépratte disclosed the plan of operation and concluded in optimistic terms: 'Am in complete agreement with V. A. Carden and have absolute confidence in success, the consequences of which will be incalculable.' [69]

The nature of Augagneur's instructions to the Admirals is clear proof that he had not seen the actual plan of operation, much less have had occasion to call upon his experts for their impressions, before formally consenting to collaborate with Churchill.[70] The

[67] Augagneur to Boué de Lapeyrère, January 31, 1915; E p 108, Marine archives.
[68] Augagneur to Guépratte, January 31, 1915; E d 108, Marine archives.
[69] Guépratte to Augagneur, February 2, 1915; E d 107, Marine archives.
[70] The Budget Commission which, through pre-war legislation, had a legal basis to investigate the services in the army and navy but not problems dealing with strategy, went beyond its constitutional jurisdiction when it asked Augagneur if there had been any discussion between the two naval staffs in order to concert a plan of operation. Augagneur's answer was not the least bit responsive to the question. Hence the conclusion drawn by the members of the Commission was that there had been no co-operation. But little did they know that not only had the Minister of Marine not taken part in preparing the naval plan but he had not got around to examining it until February 2nd, two days after he had agreed to allow French ships to participate in the attack. Augagneur before the Budget Commission, June 22, 1915; C7544, vol. 8, National archives.

fact that he personally had not examined the details of the plan could hardly have any bearing. The questions that had to be decided were of so technical a nature that only expert opinion rated consideration. The Minister of Marine had neither by long experience nor specialized study of naval warfare acquired instinctive knowledge of what might be done in a given situation. He had no way of foreseeing the technical difficulties involved in an attack on the Dardanelles, such as the value of naval guns with low trajectory against land defences, the danger from mines and the effect of mobile guns on mine-sweeping operations. Augagneur had agreed to the naval assault because he felt that the idea of gradual advance was feasible. For some reason he chose to think that he knew more about naval possibilities than the experts.

At about the same time that he heard from Guépratte, Augagneur received a memorandum from the Admiralty. At last Churchill exposed the complete plan of action and requested of the Minister of Marine two additional battleships,[71] small cruisers, destroyers, seaplanes and mine-sweepers. The First Lord did not anticipate much enemy resistance in the Straits and was confident that the appearance of the Allied fleet in the Sea of Marmora would provoke an uprising in Constantinople.[72]

Churchill's appreciation was forwarded to Vice-Admiral Aubert, chief of naval staff, for appraisal.[73] Although the Minister of Marine acknowledged Aubert's right to be heard (as was usual practice on all matters relating to naval strategy) he was, of course, not bound by his recommendations. It did not require clairvoyance to foresee the outcome. Charged several months before to head an investigation to determine the chances of a purely naval attack on the Dardanelles, Aubert had left no doubt that he considered this an impracticable undertaking.[74] To be effective, he had insisted, the way must first be cleared by land operations.[75] When Augagneur returned from London after his encounter with

[71] The French already had two ships under Guépratte attached to Carden's fleet.

[72] Churchill to Augagneur, February 2, 1915; E s 11, Marine archives.

[73] Aubert had hitherto seen several Admiralty reports on the Dardanelles, but these were of little importance.

[74] See pp. 57, 63 of this text.

[75] A. P. Bienaimé, op. cit., p. 182.

Churchill, Aubert had warned him that unless military assistance was available the fleet was unlikely to accomplish any lasting results. On both occasions the Minister of Marine had ignored or minimized the technical difficulties involved.

The British plan of attack, which was prepared by Carden, was in no danger of becoming a model for future naval operations. Apparently Carden assumed that his task entailed only the destruction of the Turkish forts along the defile. He did not contemplate possible means to deal with mobile howitzers or prevent the enemy from rebuilding their forts and replacing their damaged guns. Nor did he give thought, in the event of the ships getting through, as to how he expected to capture and hold Constantinople without an army. It was the failure to provide for the latter contingency that aroused the concern of Aubert. His comments to Augagneur on February 7th ran as follows:

'An important feature revealed by the reading of the diverse English memoranda is that in this expedition, which the English have initiated and will direct, the beginning can be seen but the end cannot.

'In most expeditions against cities, the attack and destruction of the defences comes first and are followed by the landing of the troops who take over the place and become its masters.

'In this case nothing similar happens.

'The destruction of the forts at Chanak and Kilid Bahr is expected to produce an effect on the morale [of the defenders]. Mr Churchill's last memorandum clearly indicates this.

'"It is believed that the slow and irresistible destruction of the forts by battleships that cannot be reached effectively by their fire will have a great influence on the morale of those in the forts that have not yet been attacked and might also have the effect of destroying the trust of the Turks in their Germanic advisers; and it is possible that the reversal of German domination in Constantinople will result from it."

'Here is what is clear.

'Politicians are qualified to know what they can attain from the start of military action. I am not qualified to so do. I can only state that Mr Churchill's memorandum stops with the destruction of the forts at Chanak and Kilid Bahr.

'What will be the ensuing military action?

'Let us suppose it to be as favourable as possible and let us admit that the Allied fleets arrive in view of Constantinople. The question is: What comes next?

'The Turkish government will probably be gone. We do not possess the necessary landing forces. What is to be done?

'Once more the problem seems to belong, at this time, in the domain of the politicians, since military action has not been determined.

'That is what we desire to establish.

'From a technical point of view, the general method of attack appears to be good.' [76]

It is significant to observe that Aubert was the first Allied naval expert to express misgivings over Carden's plan of operation, not on the basis of the 'ships versus forts' principle but because he perceived grave defects in it. He did not underrate the resistance that would be encountered at the Narrows but was more alarmed at the lack of adequate preparations in case the combined fleet broke into the Sea of Marmora. Without troops, he correctly reasoned, what would happen to the ships before Constantinople, even assuming that the Turkish Government had fled? The meaning was clear. Since a military force was needed to take and hold the Ottoman capital why not have it ready to co-operate in the naval attack?

As the report was unpalatable to Augagneur, he was careful not to show it to his colleagues. He obviously envisaged no problems and indicated this to Churchill: 'I have read the memorandum that you sent me on February 2. The provisions contained therein raise no objections on my part. They appear to me to have been conceived with prudence and foresight, permitting a withdrawal without suffering loss of prestige should the continuation of the operation present difficulties.' [77] The thought that the ships could be recalled at a given moment undoubtedly appeared to Augagneur to limit the danger to a justifiable risk.

[76] Aubert to Augagneur, February 7, 1915; E d 109, Marine archives.
[77] Augagneur to Churchill, February 9, 1915; E s 11, Marine archives.

But rarely in history have ships been able to stand up against forts. This was a lesson that the Minister of Marine had completely disregarded. Drawn in by political necessity and by the brilliant prospects as they seemed in the Mediterranean, he gave insufficient consideration to the disadvantages which would arise in case of failure. Augagneur had accepted too blindly Churchill's promise that the naval attack would be stopped if insurmountable obstacles were encountered. He had been carried away by the same enthusiasm and persuasiveness which had so impressed the War Council and had not reckoned on Churchill's determination once he had set his mind to the task.[78] For good or for ill the die had been cast. The matter now passed into the domain of action. From that point onward there could be no turning back.

[78] On January 19th Churchill had written to the Grand Duke about the projected naval operation, leaving no doubt that he intended to press the attack to a conclusion. F.O. 800/75, Grey papers. See also Winston S. Churchill, *op. cit.*, vol. 2, pp. 113–14.

Chapter 4

THE FIRST STEP TOWARD MILITARY CO-OPERATION

'We drifted into the big military attack.'
General C. E. Callwell, *First Report of the Dardanelles Commission*

'Having agreed for the sake of unity of command, and because of the superior strength of the British force, to place the French contingent under the supreme command of the British General, the French Government adhered most loyally to that arrangement. From first to last, too, the various commanders of the *Corps Expéditionnaire d'Orient* co-operated with the British Commander-in-Chief with unswerving loyalty; and it can here be acknowledged with warm gratitude that, thanks to their untiring efforts through the nine arduous months spent in the peninsula, there was never a single instance of friction.'
Brig.-Gen. C. F. Aspinall-Oglander, *Military Operations: Gallipoli*

At the beginning of February plans were being laid with the assumption that no troops could be spared for service in the Dardanelles. Churchill held firm to the notion that the navy alone could overwhelm the forts guarding the Straits and saw no reason for bringing pressure to bear on Kitchener for military assistance or even to send the entire Royal Naval Divisions as Admiral Oliver (Chief of Staff) and Captain Richmond (Assistant Director of Operations) had advocated. His only concession was to dispatch two battalions of marines on February 6th to enable small landing parties to complete the destruction of the Turkish guns at the Narrows.[1]

As preparations for the naval attack were moving ahead, a series of events suddenly liberated a number of British units in

[1] A. J. Marder, *op. cit.*, vol. II, p. 232; Brig.-Gen. C. F. Aspinall-Oglander, *Military Operations: Gallipoli*, vol. 1, p. 67; Julian S. Corbett, *op. cit.*, vol. II, p. 124; Trumbull Higgins, *op. cit.*, p. 136; Robert Rhodes James, *op. cit.*, p. 39; Winston S. Churchill, *op. cit.*, vol. 2, p. 170.

various quarters. A sub-committee of the War Council, appointed on January 8th to find an alternative theatre for the use of the New Armies, had recommended a landing at Salonika as the best means to help the Serbs. Kitchener was inclined to favour a show of force in the Balkans, hoping especially to induce the Greeks to abandon their neutral status. Premier Venizelos was apparently leaning towards intervention if Rumania could be persuaded to collaborate and if the Allies provided a sizeable contingent to guarantee against a flank attack from Bulgaria. On February 4th Lloyd George crossed the Channel to urge upon the political authorities in Paris the desirability of opening a new front in the Balkans. To his great satisfaction he found the French Government in a receptive mood. Sensitive to any threat to Serbia and anxious to win new allies, the French agreed to send a division to Salonika as soon as it could be spared from the main line. 'We ought not to dilly-dally any longer,' exclaimed Lloyd George upon his return to London. When the War Council met on February 9th, Sir Edward Grey announced that Bulgaria had accepted a loan from Germany and that her adhesion to the Central Powers now appeared imminent. The circumstances were so pressing that Kitchener proposed to dispatch a division at once to Salonika providing the French would do the same. The offer of two Anglo-French divisions was too meagre to satisfy the Greeks and they refused to plunge into the holocaust until a clear understanding had been reached with Rumania. Since the Russians had been driven back on the East Prussian front, and also forced to withdraw from Bukovina, it was not the moment to approach the Rumanians. Hence the Salonika project was dropped again.[2]

As soon as it became evident that troops would be available, naval opinion mounted increasingly in favour of a military landing on the Gallipoli Peninsula to coincide with the naval attack. If troops could be spared for operations in the Balkans, could they not be used against Turkey? Kitchener began to relent somewhat and promised at the War Council meeting on February

[2] Lord Hankey, *op. cit.*, vol. 1, pp. 272–9; David Lloyd George, *op. cit.*, vol. 1, pp. 349–60; Brig.-Gen. C. F. Aspinall-Oglander, *Military Operations: Gallipoli*, vol. 1, pp. 63–7; Winston S. Churchill, *op. cit.*, vol. 2, pp. 175–8; Raymond Poincaré, *op. cit.*, vol. VI, pp. 44–5; H. H. Asquith, *Memories and Reflections*, vol. 2, pp. 60–3; A. Palmer, *op. cit.*, pp. 25–7.

9th: 'If the Navy required the assistance of the land forces at a later stage, that assistance would be forthcoming.'[3] Despite signs of a possible change of policy, the absence of a specific commitment did little to alleviate the anxiety at the Admiralty. In a document presented to Lord Fisher, Captain Richmond emphatically stated that the 'bombardment of the Dardanelles, even if all the forts are destroyed, can be nothing but a local success, which, without an army to carry it on, can have no further effect'.[4] On February 15th Admiral Jackson, pleading for army aid, expounded along similar lines: 'The naval bombardment is not recommended as a sound military operation unless a strong military force is ready to assist in the operation, or, at least to follow it up immediately the forts are silenced.'[5]

The revolt among the junior naval experts had a sobering effect upon the civil authorities. On February 16th an informal but vital gathering of the upper echelon of the War Council took place. Jackson's memorandum together with the General Staff report of 1906–7 were passed around the table and created so favourable an impression that it was decided to send the 29th Division to the Greek island of Lemnos [6] and to direct General Maxwell, Commander-in-Chief of the British forces in Egypt, to prepare units of the Australian and New Zealand Army Corps for possible use at the Dardanelles. There was as yet no definite decision to employ these troops. They were emergency forces, ready to strike where opportunity might offer. Kitchener and his colleagues remained fairly confident, however, that the ships alone could master the Straits.

The next step was to communicate the news to the French Government: 'As the naval forces require the support of the army in their attack against the Dardanelles forts, we are preparing to

---

[3] *First Report of the Dardanelles Commission*, p. 30.

[4] 'Remarks on Present Strategy', February 14, 1915, A. J. Marder (ed.), *Portrait of an Admiral: The Life and Papers of Admiral Sir Herbert Richmond* (London, 1952), p. 144.

[5] *First Report of the Dardanelles Commission*, p. 30.

[6] By an informal arrangement with Venizelos, the English received permission to use Lemnos with its spacious harbour of Mudros, as a naval base for the operation.

send a division to Lemnos as soon as possible'.[7] A subsequent telegram from London indicated that there was no question of occupying the Gallipoli Peninsula, that the troops would be employed in mopping-up action only and that for this purpose a single British division would suffice.[8] French military co-operation was not invited, nor was it desired.[9] The imperialist-minded Kitchener had his sights fixed on Alexandretta which he hoped to link with the Persian Gulf and with the Euphrates after the Indian army had conquered Mesopotamia. He was convinced that if Russia moved into Constantinople, France into Syria and Italy into Rhodes, Britain's position in Egypt would be untenable without Alexandretta. He realized that the French also coveted the port [10] and had gone so far as to claim that it was part of Syria and thus within their sphere of interest.[11] But he believed that a British occupation of Alexandretta would ensure settlement of its possession in due time to the advantage of His Majesty's Government. Kitchener underestimated the degree of attachment of the French to Alexandretta and imagined that they could be persuaded to give it up if compensated with former German colonies.[12]

The announcement that the British intended to send military forces to the Dardanelles was not greeted with much enthusiasm in Paris. Convinced of the absolute priority of the Western front, the French did not have the means to figure in any capacity in

[7] Bertie to Delcassé, February 17, 1915; Dardanelles Operation, Box 4, fol. 1, Diplomatic archives.

[8] French Military Attaché to Millerand, February 20, 1915; France. Ministère de la Guerre. État-Major de l'armée. Service historique, *Les armées françaises dans la grande guerre* (Paris, 1924), tome 8, vol. 1, annexe no. 1, selected official documents relating to the Dardanelles operation. (Hereafter cited as *Les armées françaises dans la grande guerre*.)

[9] Kitchener to Churchill, February 20, 1915. 'I have just seen Grey and hope we shall not be saddled with a French contingent for the Dardanelles.' Winston S. Churchill, *op. cit.*, vol. 2, p. 182.

[10] Jukka Nevakivi, 'Lord Kitchener and the Partition of the Ottoman Empire' in *Studies in International History*, edited by K. Bourne and D. C. Watt (Longmans, 1967), pp. 321–6. Hereafter cited as *Studies in International History*.

[11] Lord Bertie, *The Diary of Lord Bertie of Thame*, edited by Lady A. G. Lennox, vol. 1, p. 135.

[12] *Studies in International History*, pp. 324–6.

secondary land operations. Yet it was feared that the absence of French troops in the Dardanelles would permit the British to establish themselves in the Levant. The subject was deliberated in the Cabinet on February 18th [13] and the Ministers deemed it indispensable to match the British division with one of their own. There could be little doubt that the position of the French Government was framed in response to political rather than military considerations. So urgent was the need to act quickly that Joffre had not been consulted [14] lest he raise objections and cause needless delays. Once the issue was settled it was imagined that the military chief could be persuaded to divert a token force from the Western front. If Joffre proved intractable the soldiers could, as a last resort, be taken from the depots. These troops were supposedly of inferior quality, lacking in training, discipline and equipment, and used to replace the casualties and sick on the main line. They were adequate as long as they were intermingled with regular troops but to send them alone against seasoned forces was unthinkable. Or so the professional experts believed. [15]

When Delcassé informed London of his Government's decision to concentrate a division at Lemnos, he raised the point whether

[13] There is no record of the precise date on which the entire Cabinet was told of the impending naval attack on the Dardanelles.

[14] J. H. Oehmichen, 'L'engagement de la coalition en Orient, 1914–1916,' *Review militaire française*, juillet 1923, p. 7.

[15] An Army Commission report presented to Poincaré on February 13, 1915 showed that there were 1,200,000 soldiers in the various depots, sufficient to keep the existing regular units up to strength for a period of at least six months and at the same time create a new army of manœuvre to be used to liberate the national soil. It was recommended that such an army be constituted in the immediate future and placed at the disposal of General Joffre. The civil authorities were quite amenable to the first proposal but not the second for they were anxious to play a role in the conduct of war. The idea of an army of manœuvre offered interesting possibilities in addition to providing men for a plan which they had under consideration. The General Staff at the Ministry of War had explored several ways in which to attack Turkey and had settled upon a police-type operation, involving landings at five key points in Cilicia, Lebanon and Syria. The plan called for 25,000 combatants in the initial stages, to be reinforced later by Syrian contingents. The object of this action was to secure the areas of particular interest to France in case the Ottoman Empire was broken up, afford a measure of protection to the Christian

the naval operations would be postponed until after the arrival of the military forces.[16] This was the first time that someone had suggested the possibility, now that troops were to be sent, of waiting for a combined attack. But Churchill, who was captivated by the mirage of success, persisted in ignoring every difficulty. He replied: 'Naval operations will proceed continuously to their conclusion, as every day we add to the dangers of the arrival of German or Austrian submarines and any lull in the attack would prejudice the moral effect on the Turkish capital.' [17]

At this moment the situation took a sudden turn. The Russian line was crumbling rapidly and it was thought that the Germans would transfer troops to mount a gigantic offensive against the Allies in France. In these circumstances G.Q.G. insisted that without the crack 29th Division it could not guarantee the inviolability of the main front. Under mounting pressure Kitchener cancelled his order to send the 29th Division to the Dardanelles and proposed instead to dispatch from Egypt the untried and ill-equipped Australian-New Zealand units. This elicited a sharp protest from Churchill who was becoming doubtful of the chances of success without the assistance of troops. Unable to sway Kitchener, the First Lord disclaimed all responsibility in case a disaster occurred in the Dardanelles owing to insufficient troops.[18]

Kitchener was persuaded that only minor military action would be necessary to support the ships in order to silence the concealed howitzers and complete the destruction of the forts. Beyond this

---

minorities, aid the Arab nationalists and cut off the army of Djemal Pasha from its main supply base. (Raymond Poincaré, *op. cit.*, vol. VI, pp. 60–1. 'General Considerations', February 1, 1915; Turkey, Box 2, fol. 5, Diplomatic archives.) Once the Government began to send troops to the Dardanelles it lost interest in the scheme.

[16] Delcassé to Cambon, February 18, 1915; Dardanelles operation, Box 4, fol. 1, Diplomatic archives.

[17] Churchill to Grey [?], February 18, 1915; P.R.O. 30/57/59, Kitchener papers.

[18] Brig.-Gen. C. F. Aspinall-Oglander, *Military Operations: Gallipoli*, vol. 1, pp. 71–2; Winston S. Churchill, *op. cit.*, vol. 2, pp. 181–2; Lord Hankey, *op. cit.*, vol. 1, pp. 281–2; Julius S. Corbett, *op. cit.*, vol. II, p. 143.

nothing was discussed. Thoughtful planning was sacrificed in the interest of haste. Would the troops disembark during the bombardment or after the forts had been reduced? Would they land at all if the naval assault failed? Would land operations subsequently be undertaken in the neighbourhood of Constantinople or confined to the Peninsula itself? The General Staff, which normally should have considered these questions, was not instructed to work out preliminary plans for the employment of the troops or even told until March 11th that military operations were to take place at the Dardanelles.

The threat of contending with a French force may have been partly responsible for the speed with which the operation was being organized. To be sure, Kitchener hoped that the retention of the 29th Division would lead the French Government, whose policy had always been maximum concentration on the main front, to abandon plans to send troops or at least to postpone their departure until after the fleet had cleared the passage through the Straits. The announcement to Cambon with regard to the 29th Division stipulated that it would not leave England before the effects of the naval bombardment on the Dardanelles forts could be determined.[19] No mention was made of the Australian-New Zealand contingents earmarked for the Near East. Apparently the idea was not so much to conceal their departure, for the French were bound to discover this sooner or later,[20] as it was to minimize their value and any part they might be expected to play in the operation. But Cambon was not so easily deceived and asked Grey why there had been no reference to the other units due to accompany the fleet.[21] The Secretary for Foreign Affairs was hard pressed to find an adequate explanation:

'I hear there is a misunderstanding as to what I said to you about sending troops to Lemnos.

'What I said was that the decision to send a division from England, which was communicated to the French Government

---

[19] Delcassé to Millerand, February 19, 1915; Great Britain, Box 1, fol. 1, Diplomatic archives.

[20] As it turned out the French Military Attaché found out the next day. See *Les armées françaises dans la grande guerre*, tome 8, vol. 1, annexe no. 1.

[21] Cambon to Grey, February 20, 1915; F.O. 800/57, Grey papers.

some days ago, had been suspended till it was seen how the naval operations which were to begin at once progressed.

'Subsequently I heard at the Admiralty that the naval brigade would go from here [22] and that this is entirely under Admiralty control. As the Admiral in charge of the operations may require early military assistance to make good his operations against the forts, 30,000 men of the Australian and New Zealand contingents now in Egypt have been placed at his disposal and will proceed as he requires them.

'If the French Government wish to send French troops, their presence and co-operation will be very welcomed.' [23]

The French were not convinced that it had been a 'misunderstanding' and, suspecting the worst, hastened to assemble a division for the Dardanelles. On February 22nd Alexandre Millerand, the Minister of War, approached Joffre to inquire if he could make up the required division. The army commander, who was not trained to consider political objectives as part of military strategy, had already decided that the enterprise was impractical [24] and thus declined to allow the levy of troops from the vital front.[25] In so doing he forfeited a chance to influence and possibly shape French war policy in the new theatre. Confronted by Joffre's refusal, Millerand instructed the General Staff at the Ministry of War to draw the troops from the depots in France and North Africa.[26] These soldiers were not subject to the jurisdiction of Joffre, who regarded them with politely concealed contempt.[27]

The new division, formed with amazing rapidity, was designated *Corps Expéditionnaire d'Orient* and consisted of Europeans,

---

[22] It was on February 9th, and not ten days later as Grey implied in the note, that Churchill declared in the War Council his intention to send marine detachments to the Dardanelles.

[23] Grey to Cambon, February 20, 1915; F.O. 800/57, Grey papers.

[24] Joffre to Henry Wilson (Chief Liaison Officers with G.Q.G.), February 25, 1915; Diary of Henry Wilson (in the possession of his nephew, Major C. J. Wilson).

[25] Field Marshall Joffre, *op. cit.*, vol. II, pp. 369–70.

[26] *Les armées françaises dans la grande guerre*, tome 8, vol. 1, annexe nos. 3–7.

[27] Joffre to Wilson, February 25, 1915, Diary of Henry Wilson.

French colonials, Foreign Legionnaires and Senegalese. Military opinion at the Ministry of War favoured giving command of the troops to General Lyautey,[28] the brilliant Resident-General of Morocco, but the unsettled conditions in that colony ruled out this consideration. Instead Millerand selected General Albert d'Amade, a man of personal charm, very cultured and a keen student of military history but one who had lost his taste for killing and perhaps his nerve, and as such was unsuited to exercise high command. The 59-year-old d'Amade had seen the usual service of French officers in Africa and had recorded his greatest triumph during the Shawia campaign in Morocco. In the opening days of the Great War he was placed in charge of the French Army of the Alps and upon Italy's notice of neutrality he was assigned to head a territorial group which had the difficult task of holding the line between Dunkirk and the British force. When the Schlieffen plan erupted, d'Amade wilted under the burden of his responsibility and suffered a form of personal collapse. He became comatose, was incapable of making positive decisions and completely lost confidence in himself and in his troops. Any notion of blocking the German advance fled from his mind and he could only think of retreating westward. Told by headquarters that he could fall back if his men proved incapable of holding the line, d'Amade decided not to wait for the enemy assault. Without any sort of direction the retreat turned into a *sauve-qui-peut* and for several days G.Q.G. lost all contact with d'Amade and his army. Joffre was so furious when he found out about d'Amade's precipitous withdrawal and of the mass confusion that followed that he promptly relieved him of his duties. Thereafter d'Amade was relegated to minor assignments until the creation of the Dardanelles Expeditionary Force presented a new opportunity for an active command.[29] While the Ministry of War had reservations

[28] Noted: February 25, 1915, Esher War Journals.

[29] This biographical sketch of d'Amade contrasts sharply with the one given in Edmond Delage's book, *The Tragedy of the Dardanelles* (London 1932), pp. 79–80. My information was obtained from the following sources: Emile Mayer, *Nos chefs de 1914* (Paris, 1930), pp. 201–46; Budget Commission, June 22, 1915; C7544, vol. 8, National archives; Field-Marshal Joffre, *op. cit.*, vol. I, pp. 116–17, 160, 183, 211, 220, 274; Raymond Poincaré, *op. cit.*, vol. V, pp. 261–2, 268, 289, 310.

about d'Amade, he was the most qualified and senior general who could be spared from France. Thus the circumstances of war had restored a career which, to all intents and purposes, was over.

On February 24th Delcassé asked Cambon to transmit an announcement to the Foreign Office that a French contingent of 400 officers and 18,000 men was being prepared for the Dardanelles; and to try to persuade His Majesty's Government to accept an arrangement which would place a French general in charge of land operations. Delcassé emphasized that the probable superior size of the British force should not have any bearing on the choice of a commander-in-chief. After all the French had renounced their claim to the Dardanelles despite the fact that they had more ships than the English in the Mediterranean. It was therefore only fitting that in this instance London defer to the wishes of the French Government.[30]

Cambon wrote back that several days before the French Military Attaché had sounded out Kitchener on the question of appointing a supreme commander in case troops were needed to support the fleet's action. Kitchener had replied curtly that since the operation was essentially naval in character and directed by a British Admiral, conduct of the land forces should be left up to the British Divisional Commander. The inference here was unmistakable. This was a British concern and it was their responsibility to see the matter through. To stress the point the Secretary of State for War alluded to the situation on the Western front where 350,000 British soldiers were under the orders of the French Generalissimo.[31] Cambon recognized that nothing further could be done and in his letter tried to dampen the irritation that was certain to develop in French governmental circles. If the authorities in Paris had relied on a reciprocal gesture from the English for their own unselfishness in yielding the naval command at the Dardanelles, Cambon questioned France's right to claim the entire Mediterranean, indicating that the accord of August 6, 1914

[30] Delcassé to Cambon, February 24, 1915; Dardanelles Operation, Box 4, fol. 1, Diplomatic archives.

[31] The circumstances were not exactly analogous. Sir John French, though usually framing his plans to coincide with those of Joffre, enjoyed a separate command.

had been concluded before the entry of Turkey into the conflict. He recommended that Vice-Admiral Carden be given provisional command of the Anglo-French troops until such time as military operations assume primary importance. If and when this occurred, the problem of determining a military chief could be raised again.[32]

Millerand, however, wanted a clear and definite understanding from the start. He abhorred a system of divided leadership which was apt to cause enormous delays, endless discussion, duplication of work and preclude the possibility of formulating or executing any consistent military policy. Reminded by the unfortunate precedent of the Crimean War as well as by the reigning situation on the Western front,[33] Millerand was convinced that the issue could not wait until the troops were in the midst of a major operation. If immediate acceptance of the principle of a single command for the Allied army meant that an Englishman would be assigned to the top post he was prepared to acquiesce. The fact that d'Amade, in whom he had little faith, was the other alternative undoubtedly made it easier for him to reach this decision. The Minister of War conveyed his views to Lord Esher,[34] who was often used as a go-between with the War Office.

Kitchener naturally recognized that dual control of strategy was contrary to every sound military dictum and he was glad to hear that Millerand was anxious to reach a mutual understanding over a supreme commander. It suited him even more that Millerand did not object to an English general, especially since he was not about to consider anyone who was not directly under his jurisdiction. His choice was a former subordinate, Lt-Gen. William Birdwood, currently commander of the Australian-New Zealand troops. Millerand accepted the selection, even though this officer was practically unknown in Paris. It was agreed that as long as the

[32] Cambon to Delcassé, February 24, 1915; Dardanelles Operation, Box 4, fol. 1, Diplomatic archives.

[33] There were periods when Sir John French and General Joffre could not agree on a strategic plan and this placed an unnecessary strain on their relationship.

[34] Esher to Kitchener, February 25, 1915; P.R.O. 30/57/59, Kitchener papers.

operations were primarily naval, the overall direction of the Allied armed forces would rest with Vice-Admiral Carden.[35]

Of greater consequence to Millerand than the haggling over an army commander for the Dardanelles, was the need to arrange a meeting with Kitchener, preferably in Paris so that Joffre could also attend, in order to consider common problems of which two required immediate attention. First, Kitchener had not yet pronounced on the future employment of the (British) New Armies and there was considerable apprehension in Paris that these units might be sent to the East instead of to France. Great and continuous pressure was being applied on the Secretary of State for War to induce him to agree to divert the 29th Division to France.[36] Apparently this last remaining division had become, in the eyes of G.Q.G., 'a symbol of Britain's future attitude with regard to the Western front'. Second, the exact nature of the operations to be undertaken at the Dardanelles had yet to be defined. There was not much point in accumulating troops on the spot until it was established how they would be used and where they would be disembarked.[37]

[35] Cambon to Delcassé, February 25, 1915; Dardanelles Operation, Box 4, fol. 1, Diplomatic archives; Cambon to Delcassé, February 26, 1915; E d 107, Marine archives; French Military Attaché to Millerand (copy of a note sent by Cambon to French Military Attaché), February 25, 1915; England, Box 70, War archives (Paris, Vincennes); Bertie to Grey, March 2, 1915; F.O. 800/167, Bertie papers (London, P.R.O.).

[36] Caught between 'Easterners' and 'Westerners', Kitchener adopted a policy of watchful waiting. It was not until March 10th when the situation on the Russian front had cleared and when military leaders in Egypt and the Dardanelles strongly urged a combined operation that Kitchener released the 29th Division for service in the East. In all likelihood the delay of three weeks, contrary to what Churchill later asserted, could not have affected the outcome of the first military attack. After the first week in March weather conditions made a landing almost impossible until the actual day of operation. The landings originally set for April 23rd were postponed for forty-eight hours owing to inclement weather. See Winston S. Churchill, *op. cit.*, vol. 2, pp. 182–9, 216; Brig.-Gen. C. F. Aspinall-Oglander, *Military Operations: Gallipoli*, vol. 1, p. 71, fn.; Sir Llewellyn Woodward, *Great Britain and the War of 1914–1918* (London, 1967), p. 76; Trumbull Higgins, *op. cit.*, p. 148.

[37] Delcassé to Cambon, March 7, 1915; Great Britain, Box 1, fol. 2, Diplomatic archives; Julian S. Corbett, *op. cit.*, vol. II, pp. 153–4; Brig.-Gen. C. F. Aspinall-Oglander, *Military Operations: Gallipoli*, vol. 1, p. 71, fn.

Kitchener announced that he would be happy to meet Millerand and Joffre but on condition that there be no discussion as to the disposal of the New Armies or with regard to the Dardanelles Operation.[38] Kitchener did not wish to commit himself lest he lay the ground for future entanglements. As he later explained to Cambon: 'I had promised you my 29th Division; I was unable to give it to you since it is en route to the East; you reproached me with it and I have no desire to expose myself to similar difficulties.'[39] The proviso was bound to deprive the conference of much of its value and the French were at a loss to understand why Kitchener refused to make his intentions clear.

There was a sense of urgency in the air. Joffre was complaining bitterly that without the New Armies he would have to interrupt plans for the next phase of his campaign; and Millerand was becoming increasingly uneasy about the whole Dardanelles adventure. The most disconcerting signal came from Lt-Col. Maucorps, Chief of the French Military Mission in Egypt. A former Military Attaché at Constantinople, Maucorps knew the Dardanelles and Turkish capabilities. He believed that there was practically no chance of the fleet being able to get through alone and that, even if it did, the transports would be exposed to severe fire from the concealed guns (which the ships could not be counted on to destroy). On February 25th Maucorps concluded a report which he made available to both English and French authorities. He pointed out that the fleet could not force the Dardanelles without military assistance and advocated a landing in the vicinity of Besika Bay on the Asiatic side as presenting the least difficulty. He considered that an attack against the Gallipoli Peninsula itself or even at the neck at Bulair would be extremely hazardous in view of the enemy's efficient system of defences. The garrison on the Peninsula numbered about 30,000 men and was led by Djevad Pasha, an energetic and resourceful officer.[40] Three

[38] Cambon to Delcassé, March 9, 1915; Great Britain, Box 1, fol. 2, Diplomatic archives.

[39] Cambon to Delcassé, March 22, 1915; Great Britain, Box 1, fol. 2, Diplomatic archives.

[40] A similar and more detailed appreciation was presented to d'Amade

days later Maucorps submitted a second paper in which he described, on the basis of information fed to him by Maxwell and his staff, the British units earmarked for the Dardanelles and concluded by insisting that, if a disaster was to be avoided, an Anglo-French force of close to 80,000 men would be required to help the Navy.[41]

Maucorps was a man whose judgment could not be discarded lightly, but Millerand took no action in the belief that the initiative rightfully belonged to the English. On March 11th Millerand received another prod from Maucorps. This time it was the gist of an appreciation by General Maxwell. In accordance with his pessimistic line this experienced British officer renounced the idea of an independent maritime effort and conceded that it might even become necessary to abandon the enterprise, for the arrival of sufficient army units on the scene appeared unlikely.[42] By then the scope of the intended operation was still very much in doubt. Kitchener had made no specific pronouncement and what little was known was contained in the following note sent by the French Naval Attaché on March 5th:

'The War Office having asked the Admiralty to deal directly with the French Government regarding the disposition of the troops to be used at the Dardanelles, the First Lord asks me to let you know that he considers it essential that from March 18th these troops should be in immediate readiness either to be disembarked at Bulair or sent through the Straits to Constantinople according to circumstances. The British military forces will be on that date in their transports near the scene of action. It is therefore indispensable that the French force should be there too, so that if necessary the most powerful effort can be made.

'It is of course not possible to predict the date at which the Straits will be opened, as the weather and the degree of Turkish

---

while he was in Alexandria. See *Les armées françaises dans la grande guerre*, tome 8, vol. 1, annexe no. 10.

[41] Maucorps to Millerand, February 28, 1915; Dardanelles Operation, Box 4, fol. 1, Diplomatic archives.

[42] Maucorps to Millerand, March 11, 1915; *Les armées françaises dans la grande guerre*, tome 8, vol. 1, annexe no. 25.

resistance are uncertain factors, but since the War Office is making all its preparations for the 18th, the day of embarkation of our troops should be calculated accordingly. . . . The order to embark could on the other hand be postponed if operations proceed less rapidly than expected.' [43]

The Admiralty was giving notice that it expected the troops massed by a certain date and ready for action but there was no detail as to their employment. It was obvious that the number of troops needed in the operation would depend on the plan that was adopted. Millerand was unwilling to become involved in a campaign, the extent of which would require diverting numerous units from the main front. With the Germans firmly entrenched on the national soil, it was no time to embark upon a new and serious military venture. Before proceeding any further, it was important that the English disclose what they had in mind. Did they envisage a landing in the north of the Peninsula to block the Bulair isthmus; or at Constantinople or in the neighbourhood? Did they propose any preliminary or later operations and, if so, what did these entail? To seek a solution of the Dardanelles problem without careful advance planning was to grope in the dark. On March 11th Millerand wrote despairingly to Delcassé, observing that the absence of information on vital questions, in addition to creating difficulties at the Ministry of War, was apt to have serious repercussions, and he insisted on the absolute need to break London's silence. [44]

The message was forwarded to Cambon on March 12th with instructions that he was to obtain satisfaction, but in a manner so as not to offend the English. [45] Cambon immediately headed in the direction of the Foreign Office on the assumption that Grey could fill him in on the details. Upon his arrival he discovered, much to his astonishment, that Kitchener had been unduly secretive about

---

[43] French Naval Attaché to Augagneur, March 5, 1915; X a 3, Marine archives.

[44] Millerand to Delcassé, March 11, 1915; *Les armées françaises dans la grande guerre*, tome 8, vol. 1, annexe no. 24.

[45] Delcassé to Cambon, March 12, 1915; Dardanelles Operation, Box 4, fol. 1, Diplomatic archives.

his plans [46] and had revealed nothing pertinent to Grey, not even Millerand's proposal for a conference. Grey appeared very concerned when told of what was happening and gave assurances that he would try to persuade Kitchener to remove his conditions and to parley with the French leaders. Less than forty-eight hours later at 10 Downing Street, the French chargé d'affaires was able to elicit a similar promise from Asquith. [47]

Both Asquith and Grey appealed independently to Kitchener to induce him to hold talks with the French. [48] Kitchener did not attempt to resist the pressure exerted by his two colleagues, perhaps because he now had a clearer vision of what course to pursue. He had finally made some important decisions and was in a more favourable position to answer questions put to him. On March 11th he had appointed Ian Hamilton, an accomplished professional with forty-two years of active service in the army, to replace Birdwood as Commander-in-Chief of the Allied force. The likelihood of Russian entry into the campaign [49] and the announcement that d'Amade would lead the French contingent, made it desirable that a general of greater reputation and seniority be given command. From the written orders given to Hamilton on March 13th it can be seen that there was still no intention of forcing the Dardanelles by a combined operation. The troops were to be used to occupy the Peninsula following an essentially uncontested landing [50] and perhaps for an assault on Constantinople. There were to be no operations of a serious nature until the fleet

[46] Kitchener had a tendency to be over-cautious and his mistrust of his colleagues caused him to keep information to himself.

[47] Cambon to Delcassé, March 12, 1915; Great Britain, Box 1, fol. 2, Diplomatic archives; French chargé d'affaires to Delcassé, March 15, 1915; Great Britain, Box 1, fol. 2, Diplomatic archives; Cambon to Delcassé, March 22, 1915; Great Britain, Box 1, fol. 2, Diplomatic archives. Noted; conversation between Bertie and Cambon, March 16, 1915; F.O. 800/167, Bertie papers.

[48] Delcassé to Cambon, March 14, 1915; Great Britain, Box 1, fol. 2, Diplomatic archives; Cambon to Delcassé, March 22, 1915; Great Britain, Box 1, fol. 2, Diplomatic archives.

[49] The details surrounding this event will be examined in the next chapter.

[50] Kitchener expected that the Turks would lose heart and evacuate the Peninsula once their sea communications were cut.

85

had exhausted every effort to penetrate the Straits. If a major landing became unavoidable, none should be attempted before the entire force available had assembled. The military occupation of the Asian shore was to be strongly deprecated, the orders concluded. On the last point, Kitchener left no room for discretion. He had warned Hamilton on the previous day not to become involved in any extensive campaign in Asia which he felt would place an unjustifiable strain on the resources of the country.[51]

On March 15th Kitchener received the visit of the French Military Attaché and brought him up to date on what actual decisions had been taken. Later in the day the chargé d'affaires, who had carried out an investigation on his own, conferred briefly with the Military Attaché [52] and then sent a telegram to the Quai d'Orsay.

'Lord Kitchener has not yet arrived at a plan in regard to the operations against Turkey. He considers that the action of the Allied forces has not yet progressed far enough to take a decision on what should be done after the forcing of the Dardanelles.

'At the present time Admiral Carden feels that the Straits cannot be forced by the unaided effort of the fleet.[53] The Turks have constructed numerous defences which cannot be destroyed by naval guns and which it will be necessary to take with the co-operation of the Expeditionary Force.

'Therefore, for the moment, the problem is to seize the Gallipoli Peninsula, to establish the force there strongly, and from there to bombard the defences on the Asiatic shore. As for the means to be employed to obtain this end, it is for Admiral Carden, Sir Ian Hamilton and General d'Amade to choose them.

'It will be only after opening the Straits to admit the fleet that

---

[51] First Report of the Dardanelles Commission, pp. 34–5; Brig.-Gen. C. F. Aspinall-Oglander, Military Operations: Gallipoli, vol. 1, pp. 89–90; Trumbull Higgins, op. cit., pp. 159–60; Robert Rhodes James, op. cit., p. 54.

[52] Chargé d'affaires to Delcassé, March 15, 1915; Great Britain, Box 1, fol. 2, Diplomatic archives.

[53] This did not reflect the true opinion of Carden at the time.

it will be possible to think about subsequent operations, the nature and importance of which will depend above all on the attitude of the Ottoman Government and the movements of the Turkish Army.

'Lord Kitchener will discuss willingly all these questions, as well as those concerning the operations in France, with you and General Joffre. He hopes, if the British Government consents, to be able to go to Chantilly next Monday, March 22nd or Tuesday 23rd; he could be away only for 24 hours, owing to pressing obligations here.' [54]

Contrary to what Kitchener had expressed earlier, the note suggested that the army would co-operate with the fleet in the attack on the Dardanelles. Here was another example of the muddle which was rapidly enveloping the entire project. Apparently it was still unclear in certain quarters of London that this was to be a purely naval attack.

Millerand was quite pleased by the report. Admittedly it was vague and some obvious questions remained unanswered, but these deficiencies were overshadowed by the announcement of Kitchener's imminent visit to Paris. Until the arrival of the British war lord, Millerand expected to gain a clearer knowledge of the situation from d'Amade who had just arrived on the scene.

D'Amade's appointment as Commander-in-Chief of the French contingent was an unexpected advancement and he was naturally excited. On March 2nd he reported to the Ministry of War to receive his instructions. He was to co-operate with the Allied fleet and the British troops in forcing the Dardanelles, in keeping the waterway open, and in any subsequent action directed against Constantinople and the Bosphorus. Moreover, he was to take his orders from Vice-Admiral Carden who would be in supreme command of the operations in the Near East.[55] For unknown reasons, Millerand made no mention of the fact that the British

[54] Chargé d'affaires to Delcassé, March 15, 1915; *Les armées françaises dans la grande guerre*, tome 8, vol. 1, annexe no. 29.
[55] 'Orders concerning the mission of the *Corps Expéditionnaire d'Orient*,' March 2, 1915; *Les armées françaises dans la grande guerre*, tome 8, vol. 1. annexe no. 17.

General would be in charge of land operations. With an inadequate description of his responsibilities and with practically no information of any kind, d'Amade and his staff left for Bizerte [56] where the French division was assembling.

The greatest problems facing d'Amade at Bizerte were not in connection with the preparations for battle but with the uncertainties of the operation. All he knew was that he must have his troops in readiness before March 18th to seize any advantage that might be gained. In the absence of specific instructions from Paris, d'Amade turned to General Birdwood who was still in Egypt, in the hope that he might shed some light on relevant questions:

'Admiral Carden, having the direction of operations and knowing the general goal to be attained, I consider that the plan of operations of the land forces which I am charged to concert with you is directly linked to the instructions of the Admiral.

'I beg you to inform me

(1) What you know of these instructions
(2) What military measures do you expect to take to prepare for them
(3) What assistance were you hoping the French contingent would bring to the joint operations
(4) What point of debarkation have you reserved for your troops?' [57]

Back came Birdwood's answer:

'There is up to now no order from Admiral Carden and the only instructions that I have received are to stand ready to leave when told to do so; neither one of us can do anything for the moment – I might receive my instructions from Lord Kitchener when all the plans are finished.' [58]

All preparations for the expedition having proceeded smoothly, d'Amade set sail for Lemnos on the first convoy on March 10th;

[56] Tunisian port.

[57] The telegram was sent through Maucorps on March 5, 1915; C.E.O.–C.E.D., Box 6, War archives.

[58] Maucorps to d'Amade, March 8, 1915; C.E.O.-C.E.D., Box 8, War archives.

the second convoy, already stocked and self-supporting, was due to leave three days later and wait at the entrance of the Dardanelles.[59] On arrival at Mudros d'Amade sent word to Carden asking if he had any plans for the employment of the French force.[60] Carden replied that it was up to General Ian Hamilton to decide when the troops would be thrown into action.[61] In the meantime d'Amade learned from Rear-Admiral Wemyss, Commandant of the base at Lemnos, that Hamilton had been appointed to take charge of the Allied army. Until this moment d'Amade had been under the impression that, being senior to Birdwood, the task was to devolve upon him and, accordingly, was preparing detailed plans for a landing in the Bay of Adramyti, to be followed by an advance into Asia.[62] These plans were near completion when he heard from Wemyss that the command of the Anglo-French troops had been given to Hamilton and this was subsequently confirmed by Millerand.[63] Apart from any personal considerations the immediate effect was to negate all the administrative work that d'Amade and his staff had undertaken.

Hamilton arrived at Tenedos in the afternoon of March 17th and hurried over to a meeting aboard the *Queen Elizabeth*. In attendance, besides Hamilton, were Vice-Admiral de Robeck, the new Naval Commander,[64] Guépratte, Wemyss, Commodore Keyes,[65] and d'Amade. De Robeck explained that while he was confident that the battleships could deal with the heavy guns inside the forts, the mobile howitzers, firing from hidden positions, were certain to hamper mine-sweeping operations. And in case the

---

[59] Millerand to French Military Attaché, March 8, 1915; England, Box 70, War archives.

[60] D'Amade to Millerand, March 15, 1915; C.E.O.-C.E.D., Box 6, War archives.

[61] Carden to d'Amade, March 16, 1915; C.E.O.-C.E.D., Box 8, War archives.

[62] Albert d'Amade, 'Constantinople et les détroits', *Revue des questions historiques*, 1 janvier, 1923, p. 24.

[63] Millerand to d'Amade, March 16, 1915; *Les armées françaises dans la grande guerre*, tome 8, vol. 1, annexe no. 31.

[64] Carden collapsed from the strain and worry on March 16th, leaving his immediate subordinate in command.

[65] Chief of Naval Staff.

fleet got through, these same guns would harass the supply transports that would follow. At any rate he intended to have a 'really good try' first.[66] No one stood up to voice opposition to de Robeck's arguments. D'Amade had secretly and for some time harboured serious doubts as to the wisdom of a purely naval attack. He was now apparently won over by de Robeck's generally optimistic attitude.[67] Hamilton may have had reservations but he remained silent.

Shortly after the meeting adjourned, d'Amade notified Millerand that Hamilton had received written instructions from Lord Kitchener to avoid any major military operation until the fleet had made every effort to break through the Straits and failed; and until the assembly of his full force.[68] Led to believe that the attack would be undertaken jointly by the army and navy, Millerand was surprised about what he thought was a sudden change in plans. By this time Millerand had come to accept the proposition that the fleet was not strong enough to ensure the success of the enterprise. If he objected to the idea of independent maritime action there is no evidence to support it. In truth, it was not only too late but hardly his place to do so. More probably he kept his views to himself, sat back and hoped for the best.

The hour was at hand when the power of the fleet to overcome the forts guarding the Narrows was to be put to the final test. Attention in Paris and in London was momentarily diverted from the main area of combat on the Western front to the gleaming water of the Dardanelles.

---

[66] A. J. Marder, *op. cit.*, vol. II, p. 245.

[67] Albert d'Amade, *op. cit.*, p. 25.

[68] D'Amade to Millerand, March 18, 1915; *Les armées françaises dans la grande guerre*, tome 8, vol. 1, annexe no. 35.

Chapter 5

A DIALOGUE IN ENDS

'I could not admit my right to impose on my people the terrible sacrifices of this war if I did not reward them with the realization of their time-honoured ambition.'
Tsar Nicholas II, March 3, 1915

'In the attainment of such an important goal, disregarding comparatively small losses, the enemy should have repeated his attacks with great force, and in all probability he would have succeeded in forcing the Straits by sea. . . .'
The Turkish War in the World War (Official Turkish History)

'From whatever standpoint the naval attack on the Dardanelles fortress is viewed, whether of the hopeful plans it supplanted, or of its very speculative character, or of the misuse of naval power, or of the risks involved and the losses entailed, or, not least, of its false objective, as a strategical conception it stands self-condemned.'
Sir Gerald Ellison, *The Perils of Amateur Strategy*

By mid February the Allies had concentrated a powerful fleet in the Mediterranean in view of the operations that were to take place. Never before had so many ships been seen at one time in these waters. In addition to the auxiliary vessels, the fleet comprised the *Queen Elizabeth*, *Inflexible*, twelve semi-dreadnoughts, including the *Lord Nelson* and *Agamemnon* and four French battleships under Rear-Admiral Guépratte.

The attack was planned in three stages: first, a long-range bombardment out of reach of enemy guns; second, a bombardment at medium range; and finally, an overwhelming fire at short range. Under cover of this attack, mine-sweepers were to sweep the channel toward the entrance of the Straits. On February 19th Carden opened his attack on the outer forts. The results of the first day's bombardment were inconclusive for, as long as the ships were moving, marksmanship was inaccurate. The only way the Straits would be cleared was by short-range individual engagement with each of the Turkish guns. Carden intended to renew the assault the next day but the bad weather caused a delay.

As the naval guns pounded away at the Turkish fortifications, the French were already thinking about the future guardianship of Constantinople and the Straits. Although the two problems could not be treated separately, the French were more interested in Constantinople where their financial stakes were enormous, and could not afford to remain indifferent to its fate. The Quai d'Orsay was definitely convinced that London had designs on the entire region and that Churchill's drive to the Dardanelles was, in fact, a cover to 'bid for the last link in the British power chain encircling the future Levantine Empire from Cyprus and Suez to Aden and the Persian Gulf'.[1] This naturally raised the question of a serious conflict of interest with Whitehall. The English could argue that, having borne the brunt of the fighting against the Turks, they were entitled to fashion the peace terms. In so doing they were certain to oppose some of the French claims in the Levant, particularly those they coveted.

To offset the preponderant strength of the British in the Dardanelles and in the process to neutralize their bargaining power, Delcassé sought to induce Russia's active participation. On February 20th he sent a note to Alexander Isvolsky, Russian Ambassador at Paris, announcing the start of the naval bombardment in the Dardanelles and the conviction that the operations would be over in three or four weeks. He requested that the Russian navy undertake operations at the mouth of the Bosphorus to coincide with Anglo-French action in the Straits. Delcassé stressed the desirability, 'particularly from the political point of view', of the simultaneous appearance of the three Allied fleets before Constantinople.[2] Several days later the invitation was extended to include army support as well.[3]

---

[1] W. W. Gottlieb, *op. cit.*, p. 103.

[2] Isvolsky to Sazanov, February 20, 1915; *Constantinople et les détroits*: secret documents belonging to the former Foreign Minister of Russia; translated by S. Volski, G. Gaussel and V. Paris; edited and annotated by G. Chklaver (Paris, 1932), vol. 2, pp. 44–5. Hereafter cited as *Constantinople et les détroits*.

[3] Isvolsky to Sazanov, February 24 [?], 1915; *ibid.*, p. 49.

It will be remembered that the Grand Duke had asked the British on January 2nd to arrange a demonstration to force the Turks to withdraw troops from the Caucasus. The appeal turned out to be unnecessary. On January 4th the Turks suffered a crushing defeat at Sarikamish and the handful that survived began the long march back home. The relaxation of Turkish pressure had radically altered the situation, but the Grand Duke kept the news of his victory from the English.

It is now known that the Russian military chief deliberately exaggerated the dangers to which he was exposed. His purpose for doing so was entirely political. A. J. P. Taylor writes: 'The danger in the Caucasus was imaginary. The Grand Duke wished to distract attention from his own inability to take the offensive against Germany; more important he wished to compel Sazanov [4] to acquire Constantinople by diplomacy, since he could not do it himself by force of arms.' [5]

Since the days of Catherine the Great, Russia had been striving for an outlet to the Mediterranean. On several occasions in the nineteenth century she made a determined bid to acquire Constantinople and the Straits, but England and France collaborated to arrest her advance lest she grow too strong and interfere with their own designs for development in Asia. It was not surprising therefore, that Sazanov would view with jealousy and suspicion the proposed intrusion of his western allies towards Russia's own goal. He recalled in his memoirs: 'I was very much in sympathy with the idea of the French and English troops driving a wedge between Turkey and the Central Powers, but I intensely disliked the thought that the Straits and Constantinople might be taken by our Allies and not by the Russian forces.' [6] The Russians could have averted any danger to foreign control of the Straits simply by seizing them. In fact, Sazanov had advocated this course in December 1914, but the Stavka (Russian High Command) had refused to weaken the main effort against Germany and Austria.[7]

---

[4] Russian Foreign Minister.

[5] A. J. P. Taylor, *The Struggle for Mastery in Europe, 1848–1918*, p. 540.

[6] Serge Sazanov, *Fateful Years, 1909–1916* (London, 1927), p. 255.

[7] Bazili to Sazanov, December 28, 1914; *Constantinople et les détroits*, vol. 2, pp. 8–12.

Sazanov would have preferred an Anglo-French landing in Macedonia in order to isolate Turkey from the Central Powers and he tried to prevail upon the High Command to raise objections to the Dardanelles venture in case troops were unavailable to take part in the occupation of Constantinople.[8] The Grand Duke, however, ignored the plea, for his military situation was still unstable. He felt that any attack against Turkey would dissipate Ottoman strength and ease the pressure on the Russian forces in the Caucasus, as well as determine the attitude of the Balkan states. On the other hand, because he had no surplus troops and because of the weakness of the Black Sea fleet, he definitely could not render any support.[9] It was not, at any rate, deemed advisable to become embroiled in a hazardous adventure. The High Command had regarded the forcing of the Dardanelles by the Allied navy to be an almost impossible task; and that 'even if they succeeded in capturing the Straits, annihilating the Turkish fleet and intimidating the capital of the Ottoman Empire, they will not be able to take possession of it: no landing force they might be able to send would be capable of defeating the Turkish Army . . .'. But from a military viewpoint the operation would be useful and 'very desirable' and 'we risk nothing . . . by encouraging the English to realize their projects'.[10]

This is how matters stood when Sazanov received Delcassé's telegram, urging Russian entry into the Dardanelles operation. During the next week Grey and Churchill, unaware of the French proposal, made a similar suggestion to Petrograd.[11] Sazanov probably discerned the depth of Anglo-French rivalry over certain portions of the Sultan's realm and saw a golden opportunity to play off one power against the other. Already the Allied fleet had demolished the outer forts (February 25th) and entered the Straits, causing Sazanov to dance with impatience lest Russia

[8] Sazanov to Koudachev, January 21, 1915; *ibid.*, pp. 26–7.

[9] Grand Duke to Kitchener around January 25, 1915; *ibid.*, pp. 30–3. See also Winston S. Churchill, *op. cit.*, vol. 2, pp. 155–6.

[10] Koudachev to Sazanov, January 25, 1915; *Constantinope et les détroits*, vol. 2, pp. 27–30.

[11] Benckendorff (Russian Ambassador at London) to Sazanov, February 25, 1915; *Ibid.*, pp. 50–1; Sazanov to Koudachev (copy of Churchill's telegram), February 28, 1915; *ibid.*, p. 52.

should forfeit her historic ambition. Unable to make much headway with the Stavka, the Foreign Minister tried to get Tsar Nicholas to intercede on his behalf.[12] The Tsar, who did not need to be reminded of the prize at stake, apparently coerced the Grand Duke into changing his views, for the Stavka suddenly announced on March 1st that it would provide troops and initiate naval operations in the Bosphorus.[13] Sazanov's persistence had paid off. Jubilantly he notified Paris and London that his Government would soon mount an attack against Turkey from the East.[14] Before taking a moment for respite, the Russian Foreign Minister was driven into diplomatic action by the news that the Greek Government had offered three divisions for use at Gallipoli (March 1st).

Spurred on by the naval success on February 25th, the Greeks were now ready to move.[15] In return for their co-operation they were promised Smyrna and a substantial portion of the hinterland. In addition to this the Greeks hoped to acquire Constantinople or at least wanted to ensure neutralization of that city, for such 'an arrangement would give them a focal position by virtue of a large, rich, close-knit and zealously Hellenic community of their co-nationals among the local residents'.[16]

The first link in the chain in the Entente's grand strategy of uniting the Balkan states was on the verge of being forged. However, Sazanov was convinced that Constantinople would fall without the need of outside arms and he was not keen on allowing the Greeks to join the expedition. Since the Russians had not received any assurance that Constantinople would be assigned to them as part of the peace settlement, they were unwilling, in view of the known pretensions of Athens, to entertain the thought of King

---

[12] Sazanov to Koudachev (copy of the note sent to the Tsar), March 1, 1915; *ibid.*, pp. 53–4.

[13] Mouraviev to Sazanov, March 1, 1915; *ibid.*, p. 55.

[14] Sazanov to Isvolsky and Benckendorff, March 3, 1915; *ibid.*, p. 57.

[15] For a detailed account of the diplomacy between Greece and the Entente see G. F. Abbot, *Greece and the Allies, 1914–1922* (London, 1922); S. Cosmin, *L'Entente et la Grèce pendant la grande guerre, 1914–1915* (Paris, 1926), 2 vols.; A. Frangulis, *La Grèce et la crise mondiale* (Paris, 1926), vol. 1.

[16] W. W. Gottlieb, *op. cit.*, p. 95.

Constantine entering Constantinople in triumph at the head of his troops. It was feared that once the Greeks had installed themselves there, no amount of Russian pressure could compel them to leave. Sazanov had put much significance on the long and friendly negotiations between London and Athens prior to the latest Greek bid for intervention. He suspected that the English were bent on placing the Greeks at the Golden Horn to act as an offset to Russian claims and to buttress their arguments for internationalizing Constantinople and the Straits. The consequence of any such agreement, as clearly shown by the Suez Canal experiment, would give control of the Straits region to the strongest naval power – the Royal Navy.[17] Therefore on March 2nd Sazanov indicated to the Foreign Office and to the Quai d'Orsay that Russia was determined to resist the presence of Greek forces at Constantinople.[18]

London hastened to appeal against the decision. Sir George Buchanan, the British Ambassador at Petrograd, redoubled his efforts to induce Sazanov to withdraw his objections. Although a man of long experience in foreign affairs, courageous, able and high-minded, Buchanan was not of a grasping or aggressive nature and in this he was like the policy he represented.[19] Nonetheless Buchanan later reported that he had persuaded Sazanov to reconsider when the French Ambassador, Maurice Paléologue, took it upon himself to intervene. Acting before the arrival of instructions from the Quai d'Orsay, Paléologue told the Russian Foreign Minister that in his opinion it would be a grave mistake to permit the Greeks to take part in the expedition. Paléologue had clearly exceeded his authority even though he probably believed he was anticipating the official French line. Any competent diplomat would have, as Bertie subsequently pointed out to Delcassé, 'held his peace if he had not received instructions to support his British colleague'.[20] This diplomatic blunder was typical of Paléologue's

---

[17] Serge Sazanov, *op. cit.*, p. 253.

[18] Sazanov to Isvolsky and to Benckendorff, March 2, 1915; *Documents diplomatiques secrets russes, 1914–1917*, translated by J. Polonsky (Paris, 1928), p. 266. Select documents from the Russian Foreign Ministry.

[19] See p. 101 of this text.

[20] Buchanan to Grey, March 14, 1915; F.O. 800/75, Grey papers; Bertie to Grey, March 9, 1915; F.O. 800/57, Grey papers. When Bertie

style of statesmanship. Sazanov was reported to have remarked once, 'Mr Paléologue is not a diplomat; he is a disaster.' As events turned out the conduct of Paléologue over the proposed inclusion of Greece was not sharply at variance with the policy of the Quai d'Orsay.

To all appearances it would seem natural that the French would abet any movement designed to frustrate Petrograd's ambitions in an area where they were so deeply engaged.[21] To be sure, Delcassé did not minimize the value of Greek arms though he could not overlook the complications that their participation would create. The Russians were reeling backwards under the German cannonade and to override their veto would have dampened their fighting spirit and possibly have led them to negotiate a separate peace with the enemy. Above all the whole-hearted effort and the entire strength of Russia were essential in order to avoid defeat in France. Then too, Delcassé could scarcely appreciate the prospect of Anglo-Greek domination in Constantinople. Finally, since the Greeks did not intend to wage war against Germany herself,[22] the Quai d'Orsay attached greater importance to Bulgarian co-operation.[23] Any hope of enlisting Bulgaria as an ally would disappear if an understanding was reached with Athens. The Bulgarians coveted a strip of land in the possession of the Greeks and it was evident that they would never consent to fight on the same side.

Posed in this way the Greek offer of help became a very delicate

---

reported the incident to Delcassé he was told that 'it was not by a long way the first stupidity that M. Paléologue had committed'. Delcassé offered to recall the French Ambassador if the Foreign Office desired to have him removed. Tempting as it may have been, London did not react to the proposal.

[21] W. W. Gottlieb, *op. cit.*, p. 96.

[22] King Constantine's dynastic ties with the Kaiser and his conviction of Teutonic invincibility had ruled out a conflict with Germany, but for the sake of national aspirations he was not averse to taking the field against Turkey.

[23] Bulgaria was the pivot of Delcassé's Balkan policy. He saw that her adhesion to the Entente would cut off Turkey from her allies, safeguard Serbia and open Russia's communications with the Mediterranean. C. W. Porter, *The Career of Théophile Delcassé* (University of Pennsylvania, 1936), p. 331.

97

matter. On March 4th Delcassé directed the attention of the Foreign Office to the idea that 'progress of Anglo-French fleet may be such as to appear before Constantinople without necessity of landing troops, except a small body to hold the Bulair lines. There might consequently not be any occasion for military co-operation with Greece. . . . If the Greek Government offer co-operation in the Dardanelles expedition they should be told that co-operation of Greece in the war must be entire and she must give active support to Serbia.' [24] At the same time Delcassé cautioned Sazanov against taking a negative posture in the event that Greece decided to enter the war without imposing any conditions. He strongly hinted that the Greek forces would be used mainly in support of Serbia and not in the Dardanelles. This concession was intended to make Greek intervention less objectionable to the Russian Foreign Minister.[25]

Delcassé could not have been more mistaken. Already emboldened by Paléologue's statement, Sazanov correctly gauged the weak protest from Paris as a sign that the French would not risk a confrontation over the issue. And, left in isolation, the English would almost cease to press upon Russia the acceptance of an unwanted ally. On March 5th Sazanov gave his reply to Paléologue who immediately relayed the message to the Quai d'Orsay:

'This idea [Greek participation] provokes strong objections from Mr Sazanov which I summarize as follows.

> (1) For political and religious reasons the appearance of the Greek flag in Constantinople would produce a deep impression of anxiety and irritation in Russia.
> (2) The Bulgarians would no doubt find an excuse to occupy Rodosto.
> (3) The Rumanians would also attempt to get involved in our action.
> (4) Finally Italy would probably seek to impose her assistance.

[24] Delcassé to Grey, March 4, 1915; Winston S. Churchill, *op. cit.*, vol. 2, p. 203.
[25] Delcassé to Paléologue, March 4, 1915; Greece, 1914–1918, vol. 1, Diplomatic archives; Isvolsky to Sazanov, March 4, 1915; *Constantinople et les détroits*, vol. 2, p. 107.

'But Mr Sazanov attaches the greatest importance to the fact that no one should intervene in such an intimate and trusting trio as the Allied Powers: "Between the three of us," he said, "there is certainty of complete understanding on any matter. What would happen if foreign elements should mingle with us? German diplomacy would quickly take advantage of the situation. Do not forget that there are Hohenzollerns on the thrones of Greece and Rumania."' [26]

It was apparent that Sazanov had made up his mind not to yield an inch. And Delcassé did not think that he could exert additional pressure lest he offend the Russians. He therefore excluded threats or coercive measures and contented himself with ineffectual general remonstrations.[27] The events of this period revealed that in Paris there was more political than military interest in the Dardanelles campaign. Strangely enough Delcassé did not seek to establish a common position with the English, or for that matter, even bother to keep them informed of his plans. The same cannot be said about Sir Edward Grey who had supplied the Quai d'Orsay with copies of his telegrams to Petrograd and had urged greater French co-operation. It was conceivable that Sazanov would have retreated from his hard line in the face of a determined bid by the two Western Powers acting in unison. But as long as one of his allies hesitated to push too far, he could manœuvre his way out of the diplomatic tangle. By the time Sazanov's fears were assuaged by the formal recognition of Russia's historic desire, the Entente's opportunity had passed.

The menacing echo from Petrograd had reinforced King Constantine's conviction against driving his country into so dubious a war. On March 3rd and again on the 5th, the Crown Council in Athens rejected all thoughts of Greek involvement in the campaign. In view of this rebuke, Venizelos submitted his resignation on March 6th and was succeeded by a new premier, who was committed to a policy of benevolent neutrality.

[26] Paléologue to Delcassé, March 5, 1915; Dardanelles Operation, Box 4, fol. 1, Diplomatic archives.
[27] Isvolsky to Sazanov, March 6, 1915; *Documents diplomatiques secrets russes, 1914–1917*, p. 255.

The episode with the Greeks, arriving on the heels of the demolition of the Turkish outer forts, hastened to crystallize Russian opinion in favour of a final settlement of Constantinople and the Straits.[28] When the question was initially brought up at the start of the war, the British had conceded that a solution in the interests of Russia was necessary. On November 9, 1914 Grey indicated that, if the war was fought to a successful conclusion, he would support an arrangement which was in accordance with the wishes of the Tsarist Government. King George V was more specific in his remarks to Benckendorff: 'As far as Constantinople is concerned, it is clear that the city must be yours.' At the time Sazanov gave the impression that Russia would be content with possession of the Bosphorus and neutralization of Constantinople. Diplomatic dialogues between Petrograd and the Western Entente capitals ran a zig-zag course until March 4, 1915 when Sazanov, under increasing pressure from groups in governing circles and in the Duma to put forward a precise statement of demands, laid claim not only to Constantinople and the Straits, but also to Imbros, Tenedos and southern Thrace up to the Enos–Midia line. The endorsement of those terms by France and England would transform Russia into a Mediterranean Power and lead her to predominance in the Near East. Apart from the political significance there was the fear that Russia, having obtained all that she desired, would lose interest in the war. Seen in this context the Russian note chilled the diplomatic atmosphere on both sides of the Channel. There was unquestionably a strong preference in Paris to demilitarize the Straits region and to ensure free access to the sea

---

[28] The convention concerning Constantinople and the Straits, known as the Straits Agreement, was decided after an exchange of notes between Petrograd, London and Paris over a period of five weeks. Many of the official documents can be found in *Constantinople et les détroits*, 2 vols., and *Documents diplomatiques secrets russes, 1914–1917*. As for the accounts dealing with the subject, there are A. Pingaud, *Histoire diplomatique de la France pendant la grande guerre*, vol. 1; C. J. Smith, *op. cit.*, and 'Great Britain and the 1914–1915 Straits Agreement with Russia: The British Promise of November 1914', *American Historical Review* (1965), vol. 70, pp. 1015–34; W. W. Gottlieb, *op. cit.*; Harry Howard, *The Partition of Turkey, 1913–1923* (Norman, 1931); and R. Kermer, 'Russia, the Straits and Constantinople, 1914–1915', *Journal of Modern History* (1929), vol. 1, pp. 400–15.

through the establishment of an international regime along the lines of the Danube Commission. Replying to Sazanov on March 8th, Delcassé made no definite commitment, suggesting a postponement of the whole question until the treaty of peace.

The response from the Foreign Office gave Petrograd more reason to rejoice. The British Government had no intention of establishing a permanent foothold in the area and the opposition in recent years to the fulfilment of Russia's historic dream was to some extent for the sake of public opinion.[29] Grey was now convinced that continued objection on the part of Whitehall would have such a disastrous effect on the Russians that even the loyalty of the Tsar might not suffice to keep them in the war. The policy of Grey at the time was to find every point at which Britain's interests clashed with those of a friendly nation and to work out an arrangement which would eliminate that cause of friction. The price was normally high since Britain had to make most of the concessions. In this case it was evident from the way in which Grey conducted the negotiations, prior to and after March 4th, that he never met Sazanov's demands with the immense resistance that they called for, and his pliant attitude undercut tendencies for compromise. Surely it was possible to keep Russian aspirations within certain bounds even while supporting them. It goes without saying that only a diplomat blind to elementary realities would agree to conditions in which his country's hopes, once the war had come to a favourable end, could be frustrated by a former ally. On March 12th, two days after eliciting the go-ahead from the British Cabinet and the leaders of the Conservative opposition sitting together, Grey officially agreed to the Russian desiderata, asking in return for a number of counter-concessions. The British conditions did not affect Russian domination over the coveted area and were promptly accepted.

Grey's surrender touched off a violent outcry in Paris where feeling in certain influential circles ran high against acceding to the aspirations of Petrograd.[30] Considering that the issue was of mutual concern it was remiss of Grey not to have invited and considered the views of the Quai d'Orsay in advance. The reversal of

[29] A. J. P. Taylor, *The Struggle for Mastery in Europe, 1848–1918*, p. 540.
[30] There are those who allude to the diary of Georges Louis, *Les carnets de Georges Louis* (Paris, 1926), vol. II, former Ambassador at Petrograd, as

Britain's traditional anti-Russian policy in the Near East placed Delcassé in an awkward position. In the past Britain and France, though pursuing their special aims in the sultan's realm, had enough in common to jointly resist the expansion of Tsarism to the Mediterranean. Now without that vital support, Delcassé understood, if no one else did in the Government, that France could not hold out alone. On March 15th Sazanov warned Paléologue that France's intransigence would force him to resign and possibly make way for an adherent of the League of Three Emperors. Nothing could meet the exigencies of the hour so well as an abandonment of France's long-standing obstructive policy. For that reason Delcassé was willing to wage a terrific fight on behalf of the Russian demands against powerful and well-entrenched opponents. These included all those who had financial interests in Turkey as well as Bombard, former Ambassador at Constantinople, Briand and Poincaré. The latter, perhaps the most fervent exponent of France's traditional Eastern policy was especially implacable: 'Russia has not yet participated in the Dardanelles operations. The promised troops are nowhere in sight. If Constantinople falls, Russia will not have had a hand in it. Nor must she lose sight that Rumania would never allow herself to be bottled up and that the Greeks would rather see the Turks than the Russians in Constantinople. . . . Lastly if Russia is assured that she will have Constantinople she will disinterest herself . . . wholly from the war against Germany.' [31] On March 9th Poincaré had shattered political precedent when he sent a personal letter to Paléologue, imploring him not to make any concessions to the Russians.[32] Despite everything the opponents of appeasement could do, the grim 'force of circumstances was irresistible'. Delcassé argued with conviction in the Cabinet that the precipitous action of the English, lamentable as it was, had left them with no

---

proof of a pre-war settlement based on France's recognition of Russian rights to annex Constantinople and the Straits. As compensation Russia was to take a kind attitude toward French desires to recover Alsace-Lorraine. The official documentary evidence would tend to refute this assumption.

[31] Raymond Poincaré, vol. VI, p. 88.

[32] *Ibid.*, pp. 92–5.

alternative but to follow their example. If England, for many years the principal adversary of the Tsarist Government, had seen fit to give way, it would be hypocritical of the French, who professed to be Russia's sincerest friends, to endeavour to upset the applecart. And in the process Paris would almost certainly estrange the Russians and drive them into the arms of Germany.[33] For three weeks the Cabinet deliberated, explored different approaches to the question and in the end arrived at the only possible conclusion. On April 10th Paris formally consented to the Russian demands subject to the ultimate victory of the Entente and to the 'realization by France and England of their plans in the East and elsewhere'.

The Straits Agreement was a resounding diplomatic triumph for Sazanov. He had made no commitments except to undertake an attack in the Bosphorus. Even then the absence of Russian naval superiority in the Black Sea practically annulled any chance of important results. It can hardly be disputed that the Russians extorted concessions in excess of what their strength justified. For a minimal effort they had assured themselves of vast territorial gains. The real losers were the French and the English whose blood would serve to pay for that prize.

When de Robeck replaced Carden on March 17th he promised an impatient First Lord that, weather permitting, he would attack the following day. And so on March 18th de Robeck deployed his fleet and around 11.50 gave the signal to start the action. As the fleet moved steadily up the Straits, enemy batteries responded with a heavy and accurate volley but caused little damage. The ships on the other hand made good progress and by 13.45 the forts were practically silent. Thereupon the minesweepers were sent to clear the channel. At this point tragedy struck. The French squadron, in the rear, withdrew temporarily as it was relieved by British ships, and as it passed into Eren Keui Bay a violent explosion rocked the *Bouvet*. Inside two minutes the old French warship heeled over, capsized and vanished with almost all her 600-man

[33] Noted, conversation between Bertie and Ribot, June 22, 1915; F.O. 800/172, Bertie papers; Bertie to Grey (reports the gist of a discussion with Poincaré) August 26, 1915; F.O. 800/172, Bertie papers. See also Alexandre Ribot, *Lettres à un ami: souvenirs de ma vie politique* (Paris, 1924), p. 130.

crew. To those present it seemed that the *Bouvet* had received a direct hit on her magazine. Action was momentarily renewed as both battleships and forts intensified their fire. The *Inflexible* suddenly left the line, reporting that she had hit a mine in a spot where the *Bouvet* had gone down. Several minutes later the *Irresistible*, immediately ahead, suffered a similar fate and drifted toward the Asiatic shore. In each case the cause of the disasters was not positively known. The sea had been checked by both mine-sweepers and seaplanes and the only explanation was that the Turks had fired torpedoes from undetected tubes across the Straits, or released floating mines down the rapid current. It was not known until after the war that during the night of March 7th–8th a small Turkish steamer had laid a fresh row of mines, not across the Straits as was the habit, but parallel to the shore in Eren Keui Bay. This line had escaped notice mainly because the area had been swept clean prior to the fleet's earlier bombardment.

The extensive damage incurred, and the uncertainty as to what had caused the losses, led de Robeck to break off the engagement. Now the *Ocean*, in an attempt to assist the *Irresistible*, was herself struck and both ships foundered in the night. Out of eighteen battleships [34] three had been sunk and three (two as a result of gun-fire) had been disabled.[35]

The danger of additional losses by persisting in the attack was apparently not as great as de Robeck anticipated.[36] The Turks had

[34] Actually only sixteen warships took part in the attack.

[35] For accounts on the naval operations see Julian S. Corbett, *op. cit.*, vols. II, III; E. K. Chatterton, *Dardanelles Dilemma: the Story of the Naval Operations* (London, 1935); Sir Roger Keyes, *Naval Memoirs of Admiral of the Fleet: 1905–1915* (New York, 1934), vol. 1; Lord Wester-Wemyss, *The Navy in the Dardanelles* (London, 1924); and P. E. Gué-pratte, *L'expédition des Dardanelles, 1914–1915* (Paris, 1935).

[36] On this controversial issue the best testimony is supplied by those who were on the scene. Hans Kannengiesser, *The Campaign in Gallipoli* (London, 1928), p. 82; Dr C. Mühlmann, *Der Kampf um die Dardanellen* (Berlin, 1927), p. 74; and Raymond Swing, '*Good Evening!*' (New York, 1964), pp. 73–4. In addition the U.S. Ambassador at Constaninople, Henry Morgenthau in *Ambassador Morgenthau's Story* (New York, 1919), p. 225, has recorded a meeting with an American war correspondent, George A. Schreiner, who disclosed after an interview with General Mertens, Chief Technical Officer at the Dardenelles, that the Turks had used up practically all their big shells.

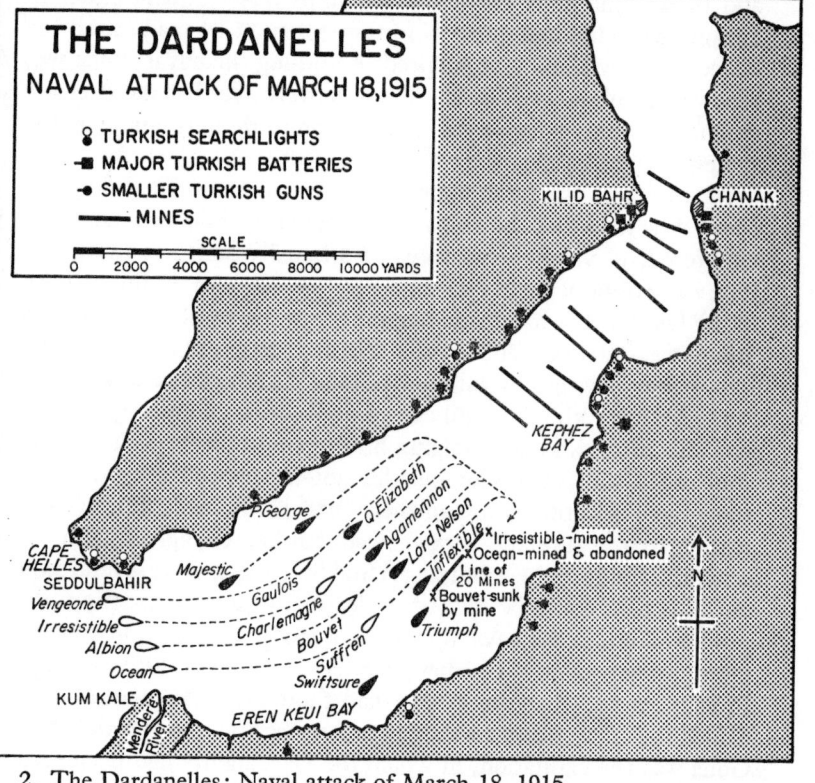

2. The Dardanelles: Naval attack of March 18, 1915

a reserve of only twenty mines and most of their long-range shells, which alone were effective against the ships' armour, had been expended. Morale among the gun crews was correspondingly very low. Enver Pasha, the Turkish War Minister, was reported to have said in retrospect: 'If the English had only had the courage to rush more ships through the Dardanelles they could have got to Constantinople . . .'.[37]

The key to the Turkish defence system was the minefield. The naval axiom that it was folly to pit ships against forts had been dashed to the ground. It was the mines and not the forts that had proven to be the main obstacle. The Straits could not be swept until the hidden guns protecting the minefield were destroyed;

[37] *First Report of the Dardanelles Commission*, p. 40.

and these same guns prevented the ships from moving closer to engage the individual guns. No progress could be made until the concealed howitzers were silenced. Assuming the naval attack was renewed within a week or so, it was conceivable that the enemy's defences would collapse for want of ammunition, enabling the mine-sweepers to clear the way for the fleet.

At first there was no thought of calling a halt to the naval operations. The idea that the ships would desist if difficulties were encountered, on which the venture had originally been approved, had long since disappeared. The concentration of troops in the vicinity of the Dardanelles had made it apparent to the world that a serious attack was intended and it was felt in London that it would be impossible to withdraw without running the risk of loss of prestige.

On March 20th Churchill cabled de Robeck, promising to make good his losses and encouraging him to continue the fight. Churchill urged the Naval Commander not to suspend operations or allow the Turks time to repair their forts. De Robeck, in telegrams sent on March 19th and 20th showed that he, too, agreed with the general attitude of the Admiralty. He expected a delay of several days until his plan could be revised to deal with the floating mines.[38]

The failure of the naval attack left a much deeper impression in Paris. It was over a German wireless on March 19th that the French learned that the *Bouvet* had foundered. Augagneur confirmed the announcement shortly before the Cabinet met that day. Gone was the exultation, in which the Dardanelles had been seen as the key to a new Eastern strategy. The gloom which overshadowed the Cabinet was reflected in Poincaré's memoirs: 'Viviani tells me that a feverish anxiety seems to prevail. Strange rumours are being circulated; and a group of alarmists, looking frightened, are predicting all sorts of catastrophes.'[39] Augagneur was told that the naval assault would start again as soon as the mines were cleared[40] and, at the request of Churchill,[41] rallied to the assistance of the fleet by sending the *Henri IV*.

---

[38] Winston S. Churchill, *op. cit.*, vol. 2, pp. 233–5.

[39] Raymond Poincaré, *op. cit.*, vol. VI, p. 119.

[40] French Naval Attaché to Augagneur, March 19, 1915; X a 3, Marine archives.

[41] French Naval Attaché to Augagneur, March 19, 1915, X a 3, Marine archives.

But the favourable moment for action was allowed to lapse. That mood of resolution which de Robeck manifested in the wake of the naval defeat evaporated within forty-eight hours. The presence of an available military force and the fear of removal from command in case of another setback sufficed to dispel it. De Robeck debated the entire situation in his mind and apparently as a delayed reaction to Wemyss' advice on March 19th to await 'any main operations . . . until such time as preparations for a combined attack could be made',[42] suddenly announced at a conference with the generals on the 22nd that he could not get through without the assistance of the army. Hamilton was of the same opinion and there was no further discussion. On March 23rd de Robeck signalled Churchill of his change in plans and added that the army would not be ready to land until the middle of April.[43]

Churchill was astounded by the message. He drew up a reply ordering de Robeck to resume the naval attack at the first favourable opportunity. But Lord Fisher, backed by Sir Arthur Wilson [44] and Sir Henry Jackson, declined to comply with the First Lord's request, arguing that it was not feasible to overrule the considered judgment of the Admiral and General on the spot. Thus Churchill bowed to the wishes of his professional advisers, at least for the moment.

The decision not to pursue the unaided effort by the fleet, like all the other decisions regarding the enterprise, was reached independently of the French. Churchill had been careful to keep Augagneur posted on the daily conduct of operations but he had not been willing to go so far as to allow him a voice in the formulation of naval strategy. It was perhaps his opinion that to associate the French with high-level policy would seriously hamper executive action or maybe he felt that as their contribution to the venture was minimal, they were not entitled to it. At any rate Churchill had no reason to suspect that Augagneur was unhappy with the present arrangements. His proposals were accepted with scarcely a murmur at the Ministry of Marine, as were his requests for ships and technical aid. The naval failure on March 18th appears to have shaken Augagneur from his lethargy. But if he was

[42] Lord Wester-Wemyss, op. cit., p. 237.
[43] Winston S. Churchill, op. cit., vol. 2, pp. 236–7.
[44] Admiral of the Fleet.

anxious to impose his views in the councils of war he was deterred from doing so by the knowledge that he had an inadequate grasp of the situation.

Still in a state of defeated helplessness, the Minister of Marine welcomed the news that the English planned a serious siege operation of a combined nature to be mounted around April 15th.[45] The announcement in the Cabinet on March 25th aroused no dissent. A disgruntled Poincaré wrote: 'The whole scheme is faulty, having been insufficiently thought out in London. It was the conception of the Admiralty too rapidly put into effect without due regard for military difficulties or diplomatic repercussions.' [46]

No sooner had thoughts on the subject begun to recede than the French Naval Attaché in London exploded a bombshell. He revealed to his superior that Churchill had appealed personally to de Robeck for an immediate return of the fleet to the Narrows. De Robeck's reply, which coincided with the opinion of the English Sea Lords, had strongly advised against such action.[47] On March 30th a telegram from General d'Amade lent credence to the report: 'The British Government and the English Commander-in-Chief request that the fleet pursue its effort, without regard for the defeat of March 18th, and maintain land forces ready to take advantage of an eventual success of the fleet in ensuring the freedom of passage of ships. Apparently no closely co-ordinated action of naval and land forces has been thoroughly established as of now in the minds of Lord Kitchener and General Hamilton.' [48] In the face of this evidence the Cabinet concluded that despite the negative expert advice Winston Churchill, with the possible consent of the British Government, was contriving to force a resumption of the naval attack. Anxious to get to the bottom of the matter the Quai d'Orsay cabled Cambon:

---

[45] French Naval Attaché to Augagneur, March 24, 1915; X a 3, Marine archives.

[46] Raymond Poincaré, op. cit., vol. VI, p. 130.

[47] French Naval Attaché to Augagneur. The date inscribed on the document is March 27, 1915, but it is incorrect. The letter was probably sent on March 28th or 29th; E d 109, Marine archives.

[48] D'Amade to Millerand, March 30, 1915; Dardanelles Operation, Box 4, fol. 2, Diplomatic archives. The telegram is worded a little differently in Les armées françaises dans la grande guerre, tome 8, vol. 1, annexe no. 50.

'Following the operation of March 18th it was apparently understood that the co-operation of land and sea forces was essential in order to obtain more important results and achieve the aim of the campaign. However, it appears that the First Lord of the Admiralty, in a personal telegram, urged Admiral de Robeck to pursue vigorously operations against forts by naval means only, without waiting for the assistance of the land forces.

'To this Admiral de Robeck allegedly replied that an immediate attack by the fleet on the Straits fortifications would be committing an error which might endanger the execution of a better and more ambitious plan.

'The Government believes that what must be avoided above all is running the risk of a defeat which could have deplorable repercussions on current events – it would be better to wait a few more days and attack in force and with complete co-operation when we are sure of ourselves. It is impossible that this could not be the British Government's opinion.' [49]

The French Ambassador forwarded the text of the telegram to Asquith and asked him to verify the information with Churchill.[50] Sensing that Churchill was perhaps intriguing behind his back, Asquith decided to pay a visit to the Admiralty. When shown the French note, the First Lord denied there was any substance to the allegation, insisting that a week ago he had accepted de Robeck's suggestion for a combined operation.[51] It is true that on March 27th Churchill had reluctantly sent de Robeck a telegram in which he had agreed to a discontinuation of independent maritime action in favour of a joint enterprise, but subsequently he had changed his mind and secretly began to press for another naval attack on the Turkish forts.[52] Churchill must have felt ill at ease in

[49] Delcassé to Cambon, April 3, 1915; Dardanelles Operation, Box 4, fol. 2, Diplomatic archives.

[50] Noted, April 3, 1915; F.O. 371 no. 2480, Foreign Office archives (London, P.R.O.).

[51] Ibid.

[52] This episode has been ignored by all the writers of the campaign except Mr Ian Hamilton who mentions it in passing in the fascinating biography of his uncle and namesake, The Happy Warrior: A Life of General Sir Ian Hamilton (London, 1966), p. 288.

the presence of the Prime Minister. If the full details came out it would serve as excellent ammunition for his numerous political enemies. Quite understandably Churchill wanted to bury the story before it started to circulate and so offered to set the facts 'straight' for the French.[53]

Churchill wasted no time in calling upon the French Naval Attaché and, invoking his formidable powers of persuasion, convinced him that it had been an unfortunate misunderstanding. Late in the day Cambon stopped by to see the Naval Attaché who told him in the light of de Robeck's refusal, the First Lord had abandoned the idea of pursuing purely naval operations. Cambon thereupon transmitted the message to Paris.[54]

The first phase of the great adventure was over. Instead of the navy clearing the way for the army as was originally envisaged, the soldiers had now to take the Gallipoli Peninsula in order to permit the fleet's passage through the Narrows.

To recapitulate this part of the operation, the British Sea Lords had stood firm against continuing the naval assault at a time when the defenders in the forts appeared ready to concede defeat. Churchill was compelled to knuckle under but not before he made a last-ditch effort to get de Robeck to reconsider. The First Lord did not possess the authority to overrule the Admirals, sack de Robeck and appoint a naval commander who would not shirk at the prospect of sacrificing several obsolete battleships to attain the desired results. Churchill later lamented that it was really at the end of March that the campaign in the Dardanelles was lost. He wrote with bitterness: 'Not to persevere – that was the crime.'[55]

There is some merit in what Churchill says but he carries this point too far. A campaign should have a clearly defined political as well as a definite military end. Indeed, forcing the Dardanelles could be but a preliminary step in the operation. But neither Churchill, Augagneur nor any of the other politicians in both countries gave serious thought as to what would follow. They and their Russian allies appear to have been more concerned with

[53] Cambon to Asquith, April 3, 1915; F.O. 371 no. 2480, Foreign Office archives.
[54] Cambon to Delcassé, April 3, 1915; Dardanelles Operation, Box 4, fol. 2, Diplomatic archives.
[55] Winston S. Churchill, *op. cit.*, vol. 2, p. 168.

laying rival claims to Turkish territory than with finding an appropriate solution to the enterprise. The alternatives were either total dismemberment of the Turkish Empire, which would entail a very ambitious military campaign and prior agreements amongst the Powers, or a demonstration, which it was hoped would bring about the overthrow of the pro-German administration and a separate peace. The second option might have proved more effective as an operation designed to help the Allied war effort against Germany, but it would not have fulfilled the Imperial ambitions of the Powers. In any event the divergent political ends envisaged by each Power called for a different type of action.

Given that the fleet had succeeded in anchoring before the Golden Horn, it is questionable whether anything would have been gained without an adequate landing force. The whole plan was contingent on a revolution occurring in Constantinople [56] and on the establishment of a friendly government which would seek peace. Let us examine the credibility of this assumption.

From the date the Young Turks deposed the depraved Sultan Abdul Hamid in 1909 they had been plagued by intermittent warfare and internal crises. The democratic ideas and progressive reforms which they had professed to espouse were quickly forgotten as their energies became dissipated in a desperate struggle for their own survival. By 1915 Turkey was in a chaotic situation. Apart from the military defeats recently suffered in the Caucasus and in Egypt, the state was almost bankrupt, living conditions were deplorable and the Young Turk regime was badly divided, corrupt and extremely unpopular. To western political observers,[57] who were on the scene and steeped in Turkish affairs, the climate seemed ideal for another revolution.[58] Assuming that

---

[56] Churchill had based this estimate on reports from naval intelligence.

[57] See especially, Henry Morgenthau, *Ambassador Morgenthau's Story*, pp. 227–8; Lewis Einstein, *Inside Constantinople* (London, 1917), p. xiv.

[58] The majority of writers on the campaign have maintained that even if Constantinople had fallen the Turks could still have held out. They point to the fact that plans were under way to transfer the seat of Government to the hinterland of Anatolia. From there the Young Turks were expected to rule and continue the struggle. My own impression is that Constantinople was the key to Turkish resistance and that without it they would have been reduced to impotence. The Ottoman capital had

their appraisal was valid, it is one thing for a revolution to begin, another for it to succeed. A successful revolution could have been achieved only if the Turkish army had been withdrawn into the interior or mutinied and refused to obey orders. Neither condition appeared to be present. Enver Pasha had made it quite clear that he intended to use every available soldier to defend the capital.[59] The likelihood of a breakdown of military discipline before an enemy was unlikely when the very existence of the nation was at stake. Enver had been careful to weed out all the undesirables from the army and to officer it with zealous and nationalistic Young Turks.

It has been argued that the fleet could have taken the extreme step of compelling the Turks to surrender by a bombardment of Constantinople. But thinking along these lines is unrealistic. It was against international law to bombard an undefended city. If the army had remained in Constantinople, as seemed likely, it is conceivable that the ships would have attempted to give a display of force by blasting away at a number of selected targets such as the ammunition factories, the Turkish War Office, the barracks on the hills and perhaps even the Sultan's palace; but to indiscriminately bombard harmless civilians, many of whom were friendly to the Entente, was unthinkable. If a revolution had not taken place within a fortnight, the fleet would have had no choice but to retire and again run the gauntlet of the Turkish batteries along the Straits.

Suppose by sheer good fortune a rebellion had swept the band of usurpers from office, the Allies would still have been confronted with at least two obstacles. First the new ministry, though

---

immense strategic and symbolic value and was the site of the only two ammunition factories in the country. More important it was the nerve centre of the Empire. Alan Moorehead has written in *Gallipoli* (London, 1956), p. 41, that 'Constantinople was the centre of all Turkish affairs, economic, political and industrial as well as military. There was no other city in the country to replace it, no network of roads and railways which would have enabled the Army and the government to have rapidly regrouped in another place. The fall of Constantinople was in effect the fall of the state, even though resistance might have been maintained indefinitely in the mountains.'

[59] Henry Morgenthau, *Ambassador Morgenthau's Story*, pp. 204–5.

perhaps desirous for peace, would not or could not have acquiesced in the partitioning of its own state. The Allies had no means to coerce the Turks, for no troops accompanied the fleet. On the other hand, if they had left Turkey intact in return for her pledge to withdraw from the war, then they could not have satisfied their appetites for Imperial gains. How the Entente expected to coax Turkey out of the conflict and at the same time wrest from her enormous territorial concessions is a question they had obviously not considered. Secondly, and it is amazing that not even the later writers have pointed this out, were the Germans simply to remain passive observers to Turkey's defection? Would they not have struck against Serbia six months before the actual invasion, poured into Turkey and restored their friends to power?

A strategic plan must be evaluated on the strength of its achievement or merit and not on speculative consequences. The naval operation was designed as a short cut to victory and on this alone it must be judged. In this sense it was an utter failure. To quote Sir Gerald Ellison, 'the underlying idea of the whole plan was Utopian in the extreme'.[60]

From this welter of confusion and illusion one thing emerges quite clearly. The Allies were trying to gain the advantage of a victory without finding the means to win that victory. Regardless from which direction the naval operation is viewed it was not likely to have succeeded on any of the terms actually available. Above all the Allies needed to agree to political ends that related not to their own Imperial ambitions but to the defeat of Germany. If there had been someone of sufficient authority and independence of mind to correlate and compare the clashing interests of the moment, a brilliant victory might have been achieved. It is well known that in 1915 no such man existed.

---

[60] Sir Gerald Ellison, *The Perils of Amateur Strategy* (London, 1926), p. 66.

Chapter 6

THE PROBLEM OF STRATEGY
AND COMMAND

'Remember, once you set foot upon the Gallipoli Peninsula, you must fight the thing through to a finish.'
Kitchener to Hamilton, March 1915

'*On ne change pas de cuisinier le jour de la fête.*'
Millerand, 1915

When de Robeck refused to send his ships for another attack on the enemy forts, it became a question either of abandoning the enterprise or of landing an army to fight on Gallipoli. It was accepted in London that there was too much at stake to think of withdrawal and that, if large military operations on the Peninsula were necessary, they must be carried through. Although the campaign was to be essentially military in character, Kitchener remained under the impression that the navy would co-operate in the next attack. De Robeck, however, had already decided that he would not rush the Straits until the army had taken the Peninsula. In the absence of specific orders from the Admiralty, de Robeck had assumed responsibilities beyond the normal limit of his command.

If the army was to help the navy get through the Straits, the exact nature of its assignment was not defined. As was so often the case, matters were allowed to drift without direction. At a conference with the French leaders at Chantilly (Joffre's headquarters) on March 29th, Kitchener was asked whether a scheme for a landing had been worked out. He replied that there was not enough information available at home to prepare a detailed plan and that the task would have to be done by the Allied Generals on the spot. Kitchener went on to indicate that the broad lines of strategy

114

amounted to the seizure of the high grounds overlooking the Narrows and later the occupation of the Bulair lines.[1]

Where, then, was the most advantageous place to disembark the troops? Hamilton had been rushed to the Dardanelles without any provision made to supply him with reliable information on the enemy, and without the General Staff memorandum of 1906, accurate maps of the area, or even a suggested plan of operation. But before the military chief could think about where the army was to be put ashore, he was faced with a serious problem, one which could have been avoided with a little foresight. British troops, supplies and war material had been loaded so swiftly on transport ships that they were hopelessly disarranged. As it was impossible to restow the ships at Mudros owing to a shortage of water on shore and inadequate harbour facilities, Hamilton decided to transfer the main base of the expedition to the Egyptian port of Alexandria.[2]

In Alexandria, besides attending to the administrative work in setting up this gigantic amphibious enterprise, Hamilton had to draw up a plan for a landing. His task was made more difficult by Kitchener's orders to avoid a serious undertaking in Asia. This left only Bulair and the Peninsula itself.

Millerand had advised d'Amade on March 16th to suggest an advance across the neck of the Peninsula near Bulair to sever the land communications of the Turkish army with Constantinople and Thrace.[3] There was much to be said in favour of this plan but Hamilton eliminated it almost from the start. He based his judgment on the following reasons. First, the area was, as he had seen for himself, commanded by elaborate networks of trenches and rows of barbed wire. The only logical landing place lay to the east of the lines, where the Allies ran the risk of attacks from Turkish forces in the south and by reinforcements in the north from Thrace. Second, the main objective was to seize the guns at the

---

[1] Noted, March 29, 1915; War Office archives; noted: March 29, 1915, Diary of Henry Wilson.

[2] Robert Rhodes James, *op. cit.*, pp. 77–8; Ian Hamilton, *The Happy Warrior: A Life of General Sir Ian Hamilton*, p. 291; *Final Report of the Dardanelles Commission*, pp. 15–17; A. J. Marder, *op. cit.*, vol. II, p. 238.

[3] Millerand to d'Amade, March 16, 1915; *Les armées françaises dans la grande guerre*, tome 8, vol. 1, annexe no. 31.

Narrows and the Army would have been forced to fight its way down through thirty miles of difficult ground, without sufficient supplies, equipment and transport facilities, to carry out its role to assist the Navy. Third, the fleet would have been attacking the Peninsula from south to north and the Army from north to south and no co-operation would have been possible. Fourth, the Turks could still have continued the struggle in the Peninsula by drawing their supplies and reinforcements from across the Dardanelles.

Insofar as d'Amade could tell, Gallipoli should be left entirely alone. He had in mind a landing in the Bay of Adramyti, opposite Mitylene, where the beach was wide and level and the water close in fairly deep. Little if any opposition was anticipated, for it was reported that the region was very lightly held and few entrenchments existed. From the place of disembarkation the plan was to cut across to Bali Kessir, march on to Panderma and Brusa, and by turning enemy defences along the rest of the route, take Constantinople by storm. D'Amade broached the idea to Hamilton who politely put him off with the excuse that he must await the arrival of all the troops before deciding on a course of action. In the interval d'Amade sought to convince the Minister of War of the merits of his scheme, while arguing against an attack at Bulair: 'Attempt on Bulair peninsula, streaked with German trenches, where we are expected by 75,000 men, and where we shall be blockaded and stopped by a force converging from Gallipoli, Adrianople, Constantinople, runs risk of bringing defeat to land forces, following that of fleet.' [4]

The Chief of the General Staff in Paris, General Graziani, issued a sharp reprimand to d'Amade for taking the initiative in pressing for a plan that did not have the endorsement of the Ministry of War. He was of the opinion that the operation was too impractical and eccentric to be considered. The objectives d'Amade sought would not assist the navy to get through the Straits. In addition the long overland march to Constantinople would call for the assembly of mass transports and the establishment of an elaborate system of communications; and give the Turks ample time to bring up reinforcements from Anatolia and Thrace to bolster their forces guarding the Asiatic shores of the

[4] D'Amade to Millerand, March 21, 1915; *ibid.*, annexe no. 41.

Straits. Recognizing that an assault at Bulair was perhaps too hazardous, Graziani instead directed d'Amade to recommend to Hamilton the idea of a landing in the vicinity of Besika Bay. Here the army in conjunction with the navy could undertake a deliberate and progressive sweep of the forts along the maritime defile.[5]

Field-Marshal Liman von Sanders, Commander-in-Chief of the Turkish army in the Peninsula, commented at a later date that a landing in the proximity of Besika Bay offered the invading forces the best opportunity for a victory. He described the area up to the Narrows as 'fertile undulating hills and large flats with meadow-land, traversed by the numerous windings of the Mendere River. . . . The most important works and batteries dominating the straits of the Dardanelles lay on the southern, Asiatic coast. . . . As the works and heavy batteries of the fortresses were arranged only for a struggle for the possession of the waterway, an advance and attack against our rear after his landing on the Asiatic shore offered excellent chances to the enemy. Road communications here were tolerably good.' [6] This view is challenged by Robert Rhodes James who maintains that the ground over which the Allied army would have had to traverse was so rugged and difficult as to prove a remarkable feat even for a large modern force. Moreover, during the march both flanks would have been vulnerable, the left to artillery fire from the Peninsula and the right to attacks by Turkish forces.[7] Whatever the pros and cons of a thrust by way of Besika Bay, Hamilton never gave it serious thought, for Kitchener had placed Asia off limits. Hence on March 30th Millerand was duly apprised of that fact.[8] Thereafter he ceased to press his view and left the entire matter in the hands of Hamilton and his staff.

A draft plan was approved in principle on March 23rd and with few minor changes was the one adopted on April 25th. Hamilton elected to strike in the southern half of the Peninsula. Under cover

[5] Graziani to d'Amade, March 23, 1915; *ibid.*, annexe no. 43.

[6] Liman von Sanders, *Five Years in Turkey* (Annapolis, 1927), pp. 58–9.

[7] Robert Rhodes James, *op. cit.*, p. 74. The author cites Major Sherman Miles, 'Notes on the Dardanelles Campaign', *U.S. Coast Artillery Journal*, vols. LXI–II, 1924–5, to support his contention.

[8] D'Amade to Millerand, March 30, 1915; *Les armées françaises dans la grande guerre*, tome 8, vol. 1, annex no. 50.

of a feint at Bulair and a demonstration at Kum Kale,[9] troops would disembark at five points on Cape Helles, while another landing force further ahead at Gaba Tepe would cut the waist of Gallipoli at Maidos and compel the defenders in the south to surrender or be taken in the rear. A division of force in battle is seldom justifiable, but in this case it was not possible to hurl all the troops at a single beachhead for a decisive push. Hamilton's strategy struck where the enemy expected it least, and in this respect was in accordance with sound military principles. The Turks would be forced to hold back their reserves not knowing where the main landing would take place until it was too late and the Allies had secured a firm foothold on the Peninsula.

As preparations were moving forward an incident occurred which threatened to embroil the Entente partners in another dispute and delay the attack. On April 12th the French Naval Attaché in London telegraphed Augagneur that quantities of oil intended for submarines were being concentrated at Budrum.[10] The Minister of Marine immediately alerted a French squadron in the Mediterranean to stand by. On April 16th, however, a message arrived in Paris that Churchill had ordered Admiral Peirse to draw a battalion of marines and two additional battleships from de Robeck's flag and to raid Budrum and destroy the oil.[11] Augagneur took exception to this directive for it violated an agreement London had made with Paris two months before. First, it was understood that the coast of Syria lay within the sphere of French command and, second, that no operations would be carried out in the region of Alexandretta without the consent of both Governments.[12]

Churchill countered these arguments by explaining that 'the operation in question being of altogether secondary importance and closely linked to that of the Dardanelles since its purpose is to

[9] Having accomplished their objectives the troops at Bulair and Kum Kale were to join the main attack at Cape Helles.

[10] French Naval Attaché to Augagneur, April 12, 1915; X a 3, Marine archives. Budrum was a small town in the south-eastern end of the Aegean.

[11] French Naval Attaché to Augagneur, April 16, 1915; X a 3, Marine archives.

[12] Augagneur to French Naval Attaché, April 17, 1915; X a 37, Marine archives.

118

protect ships operating in that area against possible submarine attacks and being furthermore under British command, it apparently could not be the subject of discussion between the two governments. At any rate it can be fruitful only if it is conducted in a speedy manner and in the utmost secrecy.' [13]

Augagneur did not feel that Churchill's reply met his case and his fears were aroused that the English were bent on making another bid for Alexandretta. Along with his other colleagues, Augagneur suspected and resented every unorthodox move attempted by the First Lord. In March the Marine Commission had fallen heavily on him for abdicating the naval command in the Dardanelles [14] and he was in no mood to be enticed away from, what seemed to him, an incontestable right. Augagneur was determined that the French navy should at all costs take the initiative in the operation. Before the dispute could develop into a major issue an Allied agent sent to Budrum indicated that the report was false. Consequently the Admiralty revoked the order to Admiral Peirse.[15]

In the meantime Hamilton began to re-embark at Alexandria and by April 20th all the troops detailed for the operation had been assembled at Lemnos. On April 25th the attack was launched. By a remarkable feat of arms the Allied force gained the shore but was denied victory when the vital Y beach, advance from which would have outflanked the defenders at Cape Helles, was suddenly evacuated on the orders of the local commander.[16]

The invasion of Gallipoli had proved far more difficult in the actual operation than in the planning. Admittedly the Allies had landed 29,000 troops but at the cost of severe losses, extreme exhaustion and infinite effort, and with the exception of the French

[13] French Naval Attaché to Augagneur, April 18, 1915; X a 3, Marine archives.

[14] A. P. L. Bienaimé, *op. cit.*, p. 172.

[15] French Naval Attaché to Augagneur, April 20, 1915; X a 3, Marine archives.

[16] On the military operations see Brig.-Gen. C. F. Aspinall-Oglander, *Military Operations: Gallipoli*, 2 vols.; Robert Rhodes James, *op. cit.*; Alan Moorehead, *op. cit.*; Ian Hamilton, *The Happy Warrior: A Life of General Sir Ian Hamilton*; J. North, *Gallipoli: The Fading Vision* (London, 1936); Sir Ian Hamilton, *Gallipoli Diary* (London, 1920), 2 vols.; Liman von Sanders, *op. cit.*; and Hans Kannengiesser, *op. cit.*

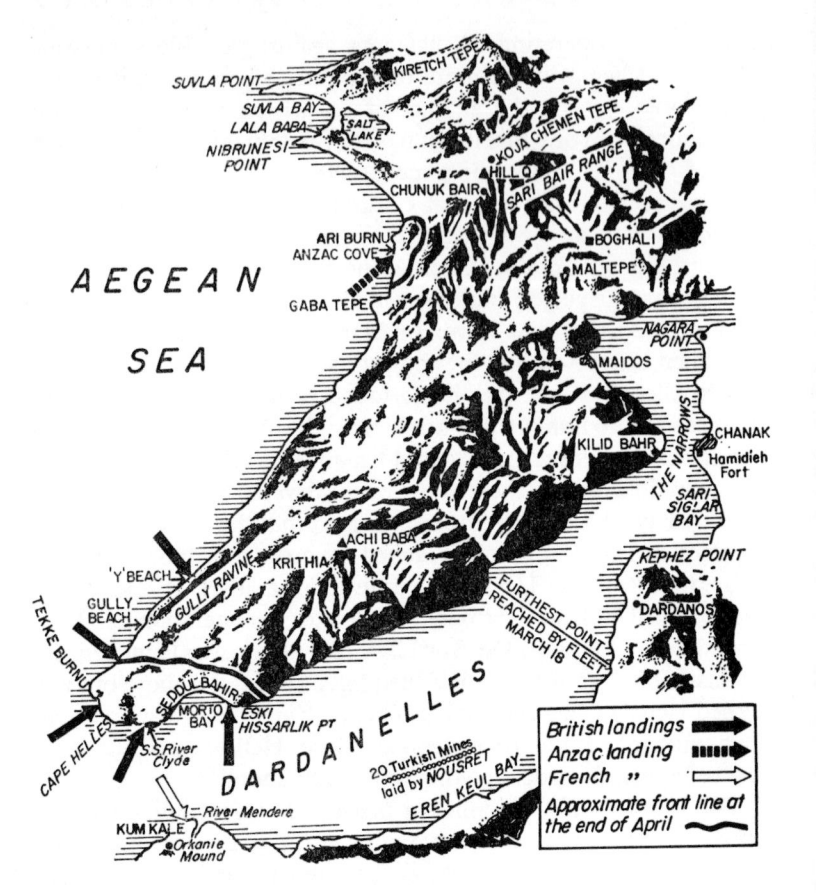

3. Gallipoli: the landings, April 25th

operation at Kum Kale, their initial objectives had not been gained. The Anglo-French force was now blocked by an enemy so firmly entrenched and secure that only planned and determined trench warfare could remove him.

It was not Hamilton but Guépratte who alerted the British Government of the army's position and serious need for reinforcements. During the night of April 26th Guépratte sent the following telegram to his naval superior at Malta, whereupon it was communicated to London the next day: 'All goes well, but in order

120

to ensure continued success it is of utmost importance to reinforce immediately the Expeditionary Force which is insufficient for such extensive operations.' [17] Hamilton confirmed the announcement on April 27th and in a subsequent cable told of a second French division being held in reserve for the Dardanelles, urging that it be despatched also.[18] Responding to the appeal, Kitchener made arrangements to provide troops from Egypt and at the same time asked Millerand if he would send the reserve division to reinforce d'Amade's corps.[19]

Millerand had hoped to retain that division until after Hamilton had seized the Gallipoli Peninsula. The campaign was beginning to take on new dimensions and he could not exclude the possibility that it was apt to cut into French military resources before it was over. With Joffre intent on assuming the offensive in the West, Millerand was not anxious to move any more troops from France than those already collected for what he still viewed as a subsidiary effort in the Eastern Mediterranean. For the moment at any rate all fears were unnecessary. There was as yet no thought of sending large reinforcements to the East.

On April 30th the Minister of War issued instructions to prepare the 156th Division commanded by General Bailloud for service in the Dardanelles. The composition of this division was similar to that of the first except that it had no Foreign Legionnaires and one of its colonial regiments had two European battalions instead of one. Under the title the 2nd Division of the *Corps Expéditionnaire d'Orient* the first units were to embark at Marseilles on May 2nd.[20]

Simultaneous with plans to augment the French force on the

[17] Brig.-Gen. C. F. Aspinall-Oglander, *Military Operations: Gallipoli*, vol. 1, p. 304.

[18] D'Amade knew of the reserve division and suggested to Hamilton on April 28th that as Commander-in-Chief he should ask for it. See Sir Ian Hamilton, *Gallipoli Diary*, vol. 1, p. 174; and Viviani's testimony before the Foreign Affairs Commission, March 11, 1915; dossier 65, C7488, National archives.

[19] French Military Attaché to Millerand, April 29, 1915; *Les armées françaises dans la grande guerre*, tome 8, vol. 1, annexe no. 101.

[20] General Staff directive, April 30, 1915; *ibid.*, annexe no. 104; Millerand to d'Amade, April 30, 1915, *ibid.*, annexe no. 105.

Peninsula was Millerand's decision to make a change in the command. Joffre wrote of the incident:

'With a view to extricating themselves from the difficulties in which they had so light-heartedly engaged, the Government for the first time turned to me and asked me to nominate a general capable of bringing this difficult undertaking to a successful conclusion. General Gouraud, who had been commanding the Colonial Corps for a short while, was at once placed at the disposal of the Minister.' [21]

The order recalling d'Amade was welcomed by Hamilton as a move to exercise greater determination in the effort against the Turks. From Hamilton's standpoint, d'Amade had not fully measured up to expectations. His precipitous evacuation of Kum Kale in the absence of serious enemy resistance and his tendency to complain and cry for help during the heat of battle at Cape Helles were clear proof of his irresolution and lack of combative spirit.[22] Shortly after being notified of the change in the leadership of the French force, Hamilton wrote to Kitchener:

'. . . d'Amade . . . is, as you know, one of the most charming gentlemen in the world. But he has lately lost a son, and the sorrow of this misfortune combined with the strain and responsibility of his present position has thrown him into an overwrought condition of mind. Directly any serious work begins I get nothing from him but pessimistic and usually quite inaccurate messages, even about the 29th Division. He appeals for help too, on the very smallest provocation.' [23]

The new commander, Henri Gouraud, at the age of forty-eight, had the distinction of being the youngest general in the French

[21] Field-Marshal Joffre, *op. cit.*, vol. II, p. 370. See also Joseph Galliéni, *Les carnets de Galliéni*, edited by Gaëtan Galliéni (Paris, 1932), p. 165; and Augagneur's testimony before the Marine Commission, May 11, 1915; C7532, dossier 1106, National archives.

[22] Robert Rhodes James, *op. cit.*, pp. 134–5, 147.

[23] Hamilton to Kitchener, May 5, 1915; PRO 30/57/61, Kitchener papers.

army. Graduating from Saint Cyr in 1888 he gained considerable attention ten years later when he executed a bold coup against the native chieftain Samory in the Sudan. Between 1912–14 he assisted Lyautey in the pacification of Morocco and at the outset of hostilities returned to France. In 1914–15 he commanded a division and then a corps of the Colonial Army in the Argonne where he won a high reputation. A solid, fearless and imperturbable soldier of the best French type, Gouraud was affectionately called the 'Lion of the Argonne' and idolized by his men.[24]

After receiving his instructions,[25] Gouraud set sail with his Chief of Staff, Colonel Girodon, and arrived at Cape Helles on May 14th. Two days later d'Amade left the Peninsula amidst the thunderous ovation of the troops who had turned out to pay him courteous homage.[26]

The relative inactivity of the fleet during the landings of April 25th had produced a painful impression among the senior naval officers. There was in the air a sense of guilt, a feeling that the navy had not lived up to its end of the bargain. The Admiralty had stated that the 'efforts of the Navy will primarily be directed to landing the Army and supporting it till its position is secure, after which the Navy will attack the forts at the Narrows, assisted by the Army'. As can be seen, the time to take the initiative was left to the discretion of de Robeck.

When the soldiers had secured a footing on the Peninsula and most of the ships were no longer required to provide covering fire, Roger Keyes tried to persuade de Robeck on April 28th to sanction another unaided naval attempt to force the Straits. But de Robeck would not hear of it until after the army had captured the guns at the Narrows.[27]

On May 3rd Guépratte had a private talk with de Robeck and

---

[24] On Gouraud, see Pierre Lyautey, *Gouraud* (Paris, 1949) and H. Colin, 'Gouraud', *Revue historique de l'armée*, juillet–septembre, 1947, pp. 7–24.
[25] His mission was practically identical with that of d'Amade. See *Les armées françaises dans la grande guerre*, tome 8, vol. 1, annexe no. 125.
[26] Brig.-Gen. C. F. Aspinall-Oglander, *Military Operations: Gallipoli*, vol. 1, p. 361.
[27] Brig.-Gen. C. F. Aspinall-Oglander, *Roger Keyes* (London, 1951), p. 163.

brought up the idea again. He advanced a plan which consisted of sending four old battleships manned by volunteers in front of the main fleet to explode the mines and create a free channel. The scheme was ambitious and daring but accurately timed and well within the bounds of possibility. The fleet's losses on March 18th had been replaced; old trawlers had been exchanged for destroyers able to operate effectively at night and their civilian crews replaced by naval personnel. It was believed, moreover, that the enemy's supply of big shells was nearly depleted and that many of the mobile guns protecting the mines had been moved inland to assist the land forces in opposing the Allied invasion. As for the mines themselves, Aspinall-Oglander [28] has written:

> 'Of the nine rows of mines, many had been in position for six months, and a large portion of these were believed either to have been carried away by the current, or to have sunk to such a depth that ships would not have touched them. For the rest, many were of old pattern, and not too trustworthy, and, owing to the shortage of numbers, they were, on an average, 90 yards apart, more than three times the beam of a ship.' [29]

According to Guépratte, de Robeck agreed in principle to the general outline of the scheme but approached him on May 7th with the news that the Admiralty had forbidden a resumption of independent naval action.[30] There does not appear to be any evidence to suggest that de Robeck informed Churchill or even his own staff of what Guépratte had in mind. If de Robeck did not make contact with London it may have been because he felt that the proposals were too unrealistic to be considered and the excuse that he offered was patently contrived to place the onus of responsi-

[28] A witness of the events in the Dardanelles, he was at this time on Hamilton's General Staff.

[29] Brig.-Gen. C. F. Aspinall-Oglander, *Military Operations: Gallipoli*, vol. 1, pp. 105–6.

[30] Guépratte gave a full explanation of the incident in a post-war study on the Dardanelles. I was unable to find it in the Marine archives though several unpublished works by young naval officers, writing on the French side of the naval operations, have made note of it. Of these works, 'L'Expédition des Dardanelles, 1914–1915' (Ministry of Marine, 1923) by Lt de vaisseau Rivoyne, is by far the best.

bility on the Admiralty, freeing him of a task which was apt to cast him in a bad light with the amiable and daring Guépratte.

When Hamilton admitted on May 8th that the attack had definitely failed, Keyes returned to the charge. The next day de Robeck held a conference with his senior British Naval Officers. Everyone present, with the exception of de Robeck, was eager to renew the naval assault and accepted the fact that perhaps only half the fleet would reach the Sea of Marmora. De Robeck was hesitant in the knowledge that a defeat at the Narrows would leave the army stranded on the Peninsula at the mercy of the enemy. Nevertheless he agreed to put the plan before the Admiralty.

After the conference broke up, Keyes called on Guépratte. In his memoirs Keyes recorded:

'Guépratte had not been summoned to the meeting, but I knew that he was of the same mind as I was, and ardently longed to renew the naval offensive, in fact, when I told him of my hopes, he said, "Ah, Commodore, that would be *immortalité*".' [31]

Elated at the chance of getting into the thick of battle again, Guépratte telegraphed the Minister of Marine: 'In order to assist army in its vigorous and violent action, we are contemplating active fleet participation in Straits with attack on fortifications. In these circumstances I need my battleships *Suffren*, *Charlemagne*, *Gaulois* as soon as possible.' A second telegram followed shortly, correcting the impression that it was to be a combined operation. [32]

The proposal met a hostile reception in Paris. Augagneur was not about to consent to a naval attack which, if unsuccessful, might prove to be the *coup de grâce* to his waning political career. The outcome of the operation now lay in the hands of the army and he was content to allow the situation to remain as it was unless, of course, it could be shown that the assault on the Straits was almost certain to succeed. He indicated to the Admiralty:

'If success is not absolutely certain, if conditions are not different from those of March 18th, I deem it foolhardy to involve the fleet in that enterprise. Apart from the risk of possible losses,

[31] Roger Keyes, *op. cit.*, vol. 1, p. 336.
[32] Guépratte to Augagneur, May 12, 1915; C a 20, Marine archives.

defeat would have a deplorable moral effect. More realistically, instead of helping the land forces in an already difficult situation, the unfortunate intervention of the fleet would dangerously aggravate their position. I would appreciate your informing me of your views and intentions on the matter.' [33]

Churchill replied: 'We have asked Vice-Admiral [de Robeck] to explain what he intends to do before taking any decisive action. I am generally in accord with your views.' [34]

Somewhat relieved by this announcement, the Minister of Marine turned his attention toward Guépratte:

'Your telegram . . . refers to an impending operation to force [the Straits] while preceding telegram mentioned combined operation, apparently due to last some time. I cannot understand a return to a plan similar to the one of March 18th which had been abandoned.' [35]

Meanwhile in London, Churchill tried to persuade the Sea Lords to agree to a limited attack on the Narrows to enable the clearance of the Kephez minefield. Fisher, however, flew into a rage and stated that under no circumstances would he be a party to such an attempt. The Admiralty had received information that a German submarine was heading in the direction of the Dardanelles and on May 12th Fisher's apprehensions were confirmed when the old battleship *Goliath* was torpedoed in Morto Bay. Churchill, in the end, was forced to give way before the fiery First Sea Lord. On May 13th, after receiving the French note, he signalled de Robeck that 'the moment for an independent naval attempt to force the Narrows has passed, and will not rise again . . .'.[36] Two days later Churchill sent a similar message to the Minister of Marine.[37]

[33] Augagneur to French Naval Attaché, May 13, 1915; X a 32, Marine archives.

[34] Naval Attaché to Augagneur, May 13, 1915; X a 4, Marine archives.

[35] Augagneur to Guépratte, May 14, 1915; E d 108, Marine archives.

[36] Churchill to de Robeck, May 13, 1915; Winston S. Churchill, *op. cit.*, vol. 2, p. 363.

[37] French Naval Attaché to Augagneur, May 15, 1915; X a 4, Marine archives.

Augagneur was under the impression, heaven knows why, that de Robeck had been the moving spirit behind the idea to renew the naval attack.[38] Already disturbed over rumours that Guépratte was showing signs of mental aberration, Augagneur reasoned that he must have someone competent on the scene to check the irrational impulses of the British Naval Commander. Therefore he decided to appoint Vice-Admiral Nicol in place of Guépratte. At Churchill's request Guépratte was allowed to remain as second in command of the French squadron.[39]

The blow stunned Guépratte who was not given any explanation for his demotion. He later wrote:

'. . . the French Government, deeming the situation incoherent and tired of my insistence and obstinacy in wanting to force the Straits, removed me from my command . . . without the courtesy of an explanation. I had to be satisfied with some vague rumours that my demotion was due to the alleged following complaints "Daredevil and dangerous visionary".' [40]

The qualities which had raised Guépratte so high in the French navy were his undoing. He was not a scientific or academic type of naval officer but essentially a man of action and of unusual gallantry. His greatest professional attributes were his ability to act on his own initiative and his intense desire to engage the enemy. A born leader, full of dash, selfless and warm-hearted, he earned the profound trust and affection of all those who served under him. In the months that he spent at the Dardanelles, thanks to his loyalty and chivalrous co-operation, there was never a single instance of friction with the British. On the other hand Guépratte was vain, full of outward show and attracted by ceremonial display. He was greedy for glory, worshipped valour for its own sake and his judgment was apt to be carried away by his enthusiasm when hazards were high. Yet whatever his failings, he was a refreshing improvement over Carden and de Robeck, both of whom reflected

---

[38] Augagneur before Marine Commission, August 4, 1915; C7533, dossier 1126, National archives.

[39] French Naval Attaché to Augagneur, May 12, 1915; X a 4, Marine archives.

[40] P. E. Guépratte, *op. cit.*, p. 238.

the creeping paralysis that had invaded the upper ranks of the Royal Navy.

It is interesting to note that until the second week in May neither Augagneur nor Vice-Admiral Boué de Lapeyrère had attempted to intervene in the conduct of naval operations or to impose orders on Guépratte contrary to those he had received from Carden and de Robeck. But this was soon destined to change. To avoid any more unhappy incidents and to gain a definite voice in the planning of future naval strategy, Augagneur sought to revise his earlier agreement with Churchill.

As part compensation for joing the Entente, Italy was promised four British battleships and four cruisers together with certain light French units, to reinforce her fleet in the Adriatic (May 10, 1915). Convinced then that de Robeck had abandoned the idea to force the Straits, Churchill proposed to remove the British cruisers from the Dardanelles division. The French, in turn, agreed to replace the British cruisers and increase the number of their battleships in the Dardanelles to six.[41]

In view of the approaching increase of size of the French squadron at the Dardanelles, Augagneur made up his mind to nominate a vice-admiral to take charge, hoping at the same time to wrest command of the entire fleet from the hands of the English. He suggested to Churchill that the present naval commander be superseded by a vice-admiral promoted to that rank before January 1, 1913.[42] Since all the French vice-admirals had received their promotion prior to this date [43] and as one of them was about to assume responsibility of the French ships in the Dardanelles, the implication here was obvious.[44] Churchill curtly declined to submit to the arrangement. He replied:

'Under no circumstances would it be possible to replace for mere reasons of seniority Vice-Admiral de Robeck in whom we have the greatest confidence. That officer was selected for the

[41] Julian S. Corbett, *op. cit.*, vol. II, pp. 395–7.

[42] Augagneur to French Naval Attaché, May 11, 1915; X a 37, Marine archives.

[43] Lt de vaisseau Rivoyne, 'L'Expédition des Dardanelles, 1914–1915', p. 519.

[44] De Robeck became a vice-admiral when he succeeded Carden.

immense task entrusted to him and his recall would compromise the success of the operations and would discourage the fleet. Moreover by giving him the privisional rank of admiral would place him above Vice-Admiral de Lapeyrère, which is in no way desirable.' [45]

Failing to place his own man at the top, Augageur sought to restrict the latitude of the British naval chief. On May 14th he gave the new French Naval Commander, Vice-Admiral Nicol,[46] his instructions and added:

'I deem it useful to inform you that in the venturesome Dardanelles expedition, Admiral de Robeck shows great daring sometimes verging on temerity. While giving him your most faithful assistance and recognizing his authority, your rank and the size of the forces at your disposal will surely influence his decisions greatly. I trust your tact, your wisdom and your experience to temper his decisions, without clashes and friction, in a way which will be compatible with the honour of our flag and our commitments towards our Allies.' [47]

Nicol arrived at Lemnos on May 21st. The army was still bogged down on the Peninsula and Hamilton could not hope to dislodge the Turks without additional reinforcements in troops and munitions. On May 17th he had telegraphed Kitchener that if the Russians could land troops on the shores of the Bosphorus and if Greece or Bulgaria could be persuaded to enter the struggle against Turkey, two army corps would suffice to accomplish the task; otherwise he would require four. But no action was taken on Hamilton's request for three weeks. England was in the midst of a political crisis and other things were occupying the minds of the politicians.

[45] French Naval Attaché to Augagneur, May 11, 1915; X a 4, Marine archives.

[46] Nicol was elevated to the rank of vice-admiral on May 14, 1915. By this time it was known in Paris that Churchill was determined to keep de Robeck in command.

[47] Augagneur to Nicol, May 14, 1915; E d 108, Marine archives.

Chapter 7

THE NEW RESOLVE

'How disgusting and disgraceful are all these intrigues and squabbles in the midst of our life and death struggle with the Huns.'
Lord Bertie, 1915

'Should the Dardanelles fall, then the world war has been decided against us.'
Grand Admiral von Tirpitz, 1915

'Things are going badly in Argonne where every day we lose a great many men and a little ground. . . . Pénélon tells me that no single General, not excepting Foch has any more faith in an offensive proving successful and the Commander-in-Chief is very unhappy about this.'
Raymond Poincaré, *Au service de la France*

In the first half of May, events appeared to conspire to frustrate British efforts everywhere. News arrived that Hamilton's army had been unable to overcome the resolute resistance of the Turks. The Austro-German offensive in Galicia had caused the Russians to retire and each day added a horrifying page to a chapter studded with disasters. In the West the use of poison gas by the Germans at Ypres, though resulting in no serious loss of ground, had left the British so ill and weary that their complementary attack a fortnight later at Aubers Ridge was easily repulsed. To make matters worse *The Times* charged, on the strength of information fed by Sir John French, that the failure of the attack had been due to a shortage of shells, and directed a heavy barrage of criticism upon the Government's management of the war. The only ray of hope was Rome's pledge to join the Entente and even this became uncertain when the Italian Premier, confronted by a Parliament hostile to his policy, was compelled to resign on May 13th. Amid the general mood of despondency, Lord Fisher announced his intention to leave his post in protest against Churchill's methods of conducting Admiralty business and the gradual draining of naval resources from the decisive theatre to augment the fleet in the Dardanelles.[1]

The shock of the resignation of Britain's most trusted and admired sailor was too great for the Tories who were still up in arms over the shells scandal. The party's leader, Bonar Law, stated bluntly that he would demand a public debate on the issue that had provoked the crisis, unless Churchill was ousted from the Admiralty. The Conservatives refused to allow a man they respected to be sacrificed for someone they disliked and distrusted. To placate the opposition, as it was undesirable for the Government to be challenged in the House in view of the imminent entry of Italy in the war, Asquith agreed to reshape the Government on a non-party basis.[2]

The coalition Government assumed office on May 26th with Balfour as First Lord and Sir Henry Jackson as First Sea Lord.[3] Churchill had been relegated to the sinecure post of the Duchy of Lancaster and given a seat in the reconstituted War Council.[4] Churchill accepted the verdict with characteristic dignity but the brutal fall removed him from playing an effective part in the war effort.

On June 7th the new War Council, now called the Dardanelles Committee, met for the first time to consider what course of action to take at Gallipoli. Serving under Asquith's chairmanship were

[1] For a balanced view of the Fisher-Churchill controversy see A. J. Marder, *op. cit.*, vol. II, pp. 266–79.

[2] On the May political crisis see Robert Blake, *The Unknown Prime Minister* (London, 1955); J. A. Spender and Cyril Asquith, *Life of Herbert Asquith, Lord Oxford and Asquith* (London, 1932), vol. II; Roy Jenkins, *Asquith* (London, 1964), as well as the accounts of those who were involved, such as Churchill, Lloyd George, Asquith, Hankey and Lord Beaverbrook, *Politicians and the War, 1914–1916* (London, 1960).

[3] Fisher sealed his own doom when he laid down a list of preposterous dictatorial terms as a condition for his return to the Admiralty.

[4] The French, while insisting that Asquith retain Grey and Kitchener, made it no secret that they wished to see him exclude Churchill from the Coalition Government. It is unlikely, however, that the feeling in Paris against Churchill was in any way connected with his removal. Noted: May 19, 1915, Esher War Journals; Esher to Kitchener, May 20, 1915; P.R.O. 30/57/59, Kitchener papers.

Grey, Lloyd George, Kitchener, Churchill, Balfour, Crewe, Bonar Law, McKenna, Lansdowne, Selborne and Curzon.[5] Before the members lay two papers, one written by Kitchener and the other by Churchill. Kitchener rejected all thoughts of evacuating the Peninsula but doubted that even with substantially increased forces Hamilton could achieve success. He favoured a compromise plan of replacing Hamilton's losses and leaving him to push on gradually and make such progress as might be possible. Churchill's memorandum made a strong plea to supply Hamilton with large reinforcements for an early decision. Despite his earlier attitude, Kitchener was apparently impressed by Churchill's arguments and he came out proposing to send Hamilton the divisions he had requested in anticipation of another major offensive during the second week of July.

By this time it was common knowledge that an ominous shadow had fallen over the operation in the Dardanelles, a predicament for which Churchill was held directly responsible. With few exceptions the press was united in condemning the gifted amateur who had interfered in technical matters and had monopolized all initiative in the Admiralty. On April 27th the *Morning Post* went one step further when it published a full account of the events dealing with the Dardanelles and in the process excoriated Churchill for overriding the First Sea Lord, for imposing an ill-conceived scheme on the Government and for the abortive naval attack. The article was so revealing that it immediately caught the attention of the high French officials in London. To the French Military Attaché it was even more surprising when reliable sources in the British Government corroborated the story. Writing to the Minister of War he cited excerpts from the article and concluded that the 'First Lord thus appears to be entirely responsible for the failure [of the naval attack] and of its consequences'.[6]

Any doubts Millerand may have had in the inherent unsoundness of the naval plan were dispelled by d'Amade upon his arrival

[5] Carson became a member in August.

[6] French Military Attaché to Millerand, April 28, 1915; Dardanelles Operation, Box 4, fol. 3, Diplomatic archives.

in Paris. D'Amade was convinced that if troops had co-operated with the navy on March 18th the Turkish forts could have been taken by a *coup de main*. He added that the Turks used the lull between the naval ·strike and the army landing to fortify their system of inner defences. The Anglo-French force was now faced with the additional task of cutting through elaborate wire entanglements, earthworks and trenches before reaching the enemy.[7] During his account of the land operations d'Amade paused to comment on the British method of conducting war. He observed that London not only laid down the broad lines of the military operations but also dictated the means to be employed.

It should be mentioned that unlike Sir John French, who enjoyed the usual prerogatives of a commander-in-chief, Hamilton's hands were often fettered by strict orders emanating from the War Office. The contrast in the structural command stemmed from the difference in the nature of the widely separated fronts. The soldiers regarded the Western front – the only place where an ultimate decision would be gained – as their private preserve and resisted the slightest interference from the civil authorities. On the other hand they dismissed the Dardanelles adventure as a useless drain on men and munitions and refused to be a party to it. Smarting over a rebuff by the army, the politicians adopted the Dardanelles expedition as their own project: they made plans, worked out the details and selected their own commander. In addition to attending to questions of higher strategy they also exerted influence over the actual operations in the field.

Ignorant that a dual system existed in the British command, Millerand was astonished by d'Amade's revelations. He felt that the English directives which denied the commander-in-chief freedom of action, were contrary to all sound military principles. It had always been the practice of the French Minister of War that while he should not surrender control of the war, he should not interfere in the line of action on the field. Thus Millerand delivered a protest note to the War Office, through which he hoped to gain a voice in determining the future course of the war in the Dardanelles:

'I think it is opportune to call to your attention . . . our joint

[7] Bertie to Crewe, June 12, 1915; F.O. 800/181, Bertie papers. Crewe had temporarily replaced the ailing Grey.

operations in the Dardanelles and to the regulations which control them.

'In France – whether it is a question of a Colonial expedition or a Continental war – the Government chooses the Commander-in-Chief in whom it reposes confidence and whom it considers to be the best fitted to exercise supreme control; it then points out to him the object to be attained – and nothing more.

'The General Officer Commanding-in-Chief enjoys full initiative in the conduct of the operations for which he becomes *ipso facto* responsible.

'Thus General Joffre has always been left free to choose the moment, the force and the method of his attacks. The Government has confined itself to pointing out to him the main object – which is to beat the Germans and to oblige them, to start with, to evacuate the French and Belgian territories which they have invaded. Apart from such indication the Government only furnishes the Commander-in-Chief with all the information which it can obtain as to the enemy army.

'It is thus also that General Gouraud, while he should receive ... from General Hamilton the directions necessary to co-operation and a clear indication of the object to be attained, has been left perfectly free to choose the means he will employ and the methods of utilizing his troops in that sector of operations allocated to him by the Commander-in-Chief.

'Now, unless I am mistaken, the conception of the British Government differs from that of the French Government and Sir Ian Hamilton in the Dardanelles does not carry out operations according to his personal views but agreeably with instructions he received from the War Office, which are not simply general in character, but which state precisely the manner of execution.

'If that is so, and if the British Government thinks that matters should so continue, do you not think it would be advantageous that the instructions which you give to Sir Ian Hamilton should be the subject of preliminary exchange of views between the British and French ministers. These instructions could thus inspire the view of the two governments; they would take exact account of the precise situation of the two

Allied expeditionary forces; and they could, in particular, take into due consideration the opinion of General Gouraud in whose experience I have complete confidence.' [8]

The firm tone of the communiqué reflects the anxiety that had begun to develop in French political circles over the Dardanelles operation. As Lord Bertie saw it:

'The French are very sore on the subject of the Dardanelles Expedition. They say that the proposal was started by Mr Churchill without proper consideration by the Military Authorities; that he obtained the concurrence of the French Ministry of Marine by flattery. . . . The French also feel that the French and British Military forces sent to the Dardanelles might, more usefully to France, have been directed to the fighting lines in Flanders. The Dardanelles Expedition is regarded by ordinary Frenchmen as undertaken in the interests of Russia materially, and of England politically, to secure her position in India and Egypt.' [9]

Paris had anticipated that the expedition against the Dardanelles, among other things, would shortly bring the Balkans and Italy into the war. So far none of these states had declared themselves for the Entente and there was an inclination to say that the 'British Child', started without sufficient thought and preparation and attempted in the first instance without adequate means, had not yielded any results. Cries of '*Cela ne marche pas bien*' and '*nous avons des embarras*' often reverberated in the chambers of the Quai d'Orsay.[10] Although d'Amade had expressed the conviction that inside a month the Allies would be in possession of the Gallipoli Peninsula,[11] the news from the embattled area did not justify this optimism.

Gouraud grasped from the outset that all individual force and bravery could achieve had been done and that the present situation

[8] Millerand to Kitchener, May 30, 1915; P.R.O. 30/57/57; Kitchener papers.

[9] Notes: July 5, 1915; F.O. 800/181, Bertie papers.

[10] Bertie to Crewe, June 12, 1915; F.O. 800/57, Grey papers.

[11] Raymond Poincaré, *op. cit.*, vol. VI, p. 228.

no longer afforded room for much hope. He found that the nature of the Turkish defences were more formidable than he had expected and though the Allies were in no danger of being pushed into the sea, the constant shelling from enemy batteries on Achi Baba rendered their position precarious. The capture of that ridge, therefore, appeared to him to be a necessity, not only from a military angle but from the point of view of the morale of the soldiers. Experience in the past had shown that the enemy would be difficult to dislodge and plans for the assault would have to be prepared with all the care of a trench attack on the main front. He cautioned against pushing beyond Achi Baba where a march to the Narrows was bound to encounter heavy opposition. Instead he recommended that with an additional two divisions the main attack on the Narrows be launched from Anzac Cove.[12] There the difficulties present were equally great but the distance was much shorter. The troops disembarking at Anzac would enlarge the beachhead occupied by the Australians as a prelude to a general attack upon the Gaba Tepe–Maidos line. In the south, meanwhile, once the Allies had seized Achi Baba, a small garrison would be left behind to hold the strong line of trenches and then the remaining troops would be transferred to Anzac to join in the operations which would cut off the defenders below the waist of the Peninsula, destroy the system of Turkish defences at Nagara and Chanak and open a passage for the fleet.

As an alternative plan, Gouraud suggested a landing in Asia near Besika Bay, and an advance on Chanak. This would also clear the Straits and permit the fleet through, but 100,000 men would be required to complete the task. The route of march would be arduous and lengthy, not to mention that the Allied force would be exposed to flank attacks.[13]

Gouraud submitted his appreciation to Hamilton who, owing to insufficient troops on hand, could do no more than take note of his colleague's proposals. Hamilton, however, arriving independently at the identical conclusion reached by Gouraud, saw the need to take Achi Baba and to begin a methodical destruction of Turkish

[12] Later named in honour of the Anzac troops (Australian-New Zealand Army Corps).

[13] Gouraud to Hamilton, May 19, 1915; *Les armées françaises dans la grande guerre*, tome 8, vol. 1, annexe no. 201.

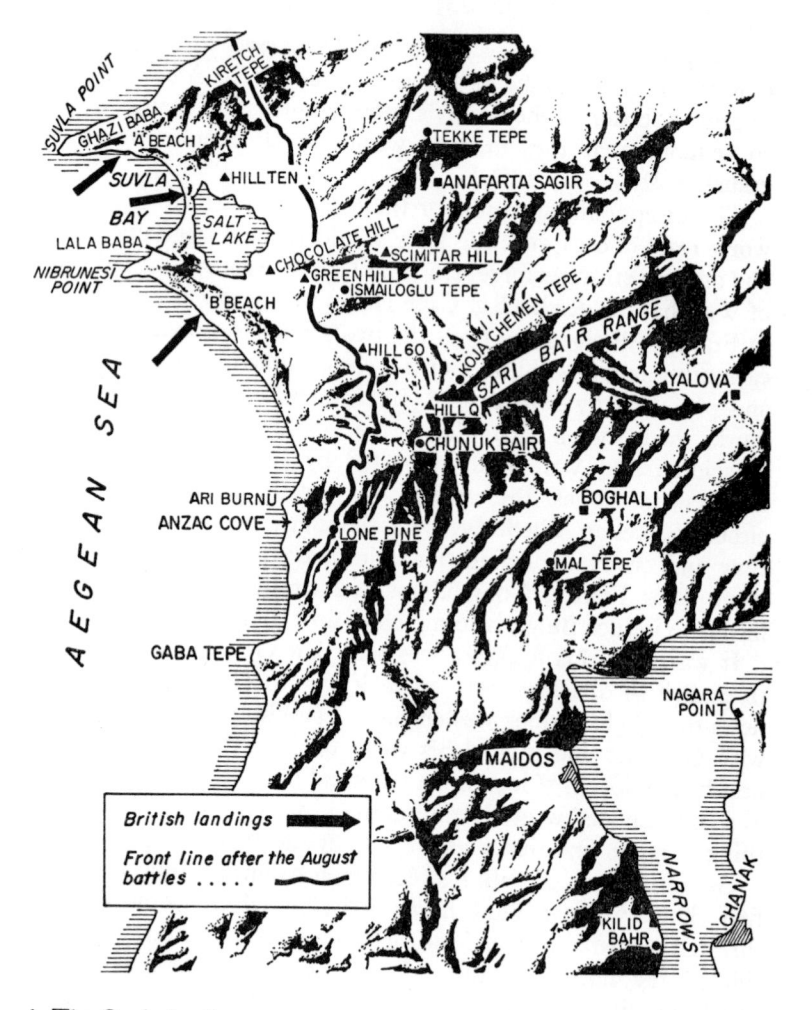

4. The Suvla landings

trenches. But for the time being he would have to limit himself to local attacks.

On June 4th the Third Battle of Krithia was launched with a view to storming the enemy's first line of trenches across the Peninsula. Plans, drawn up with painstaking care, proposed to confine the attack to about eight hundred yards, instead, as was the usual custom, of improvising as the battle progressed with no definite objective in sight. In the face of murderous fire the Allies managed to carry a section of the enemy's entrenchments but their hold was so tenuous that they had to withdraw after suffering heavy casualties.[14]

The disappointing results of the assault confirmed Gouraud's worst fears. To capture the lines would involve siege operations and an even stronger force. On June 11th he wrote to the Minister of War that the deadlock at Cape Helles was nearly as complete as in France. All along the front the two armies were fixed opposite each other in two solid lines of trenches, flanked by machine-guns and protected by barbed wire. In clinging to their positions the Turks had shown that they were good soldiers, brave and tenacious; they were well supported by artillery fire and their numbers in the last three weeks had greatly increased. In these circumstances an Allied advance in the south was bound to be both slow and costly. Knowing that reinforcements were unlikely to come from France, Gouraud made a strong plea to find some means to induce Bulgaria to march against Turkey.[15]

It was after this telegram was sent that Gouraud learned that three British divisions were on their way to Gallipoli. With this news the whole outlook was changed. Hamilton at once conferred with Gouraud and invited his views on how these troops could best be employed. 'I look upon Gouraud more as a coadjutor than as a subordinate,' wrote Hamilton in his diary, 'so it is worth anything to me to find that we see eye to eye at present.'[16]

Gouraud returned with his recommendations on June 13th. His first choice was a landing north of Bulair which would directly threaten Constantinople itself. However, if the Admirals considered the naval difficulties insuperable then the main blow should be directed at Anzac. The occupation of the Gaba Tepe-Maidos area would outflank, if it did not destroy, the enemy's closure of the Dardanelles and enable the construction of a base in Kilia Bay for British submarines lurking in the Sea of Marmora.

[14] Robert Rhodes James, *op. cit.*, pp. 211–14.

[15] Gouraud to Millerand, June 11, 1915; *Les armées françaises dans la grande guerre*, tome 8, vol. 1, annexe no. 238.

[16] Sir Ian Hamilton, *Gallipoli Diary*, vol. 1, pp. 295–6.

A third solution would be an attack in Asia to take the Yeni-Shahr heights and relieve the Allied forces on Cape Helles from shell-fire. This was a purely defensive measure and 'would not bring the campaign a single step nearer to final victory'.[17]

While in the process of searching for a plan and until the arrival of massive reinforcements, Hamilton did not feel that the army could remain quiescent. Accordingly, in the latter part of June he mounted two more limited attacks against the Turkish lines at Cape Helles. Although some progress was made it is questionable whether the tactical advantages gained were in proportion to the losses sustained.[18] Shortly after the last attack General Gouraud, on the way to visiting his men at the hospital, was struck by a shell fired from the Asiatic shore and seriously wounded (June 30th). He was later carried aboard the *Tchad* and returned to France. Gouraud had been a tower of strength to his corps. His regular tours of the trenches, sharing the same dangers and hardships with the rank and file and assuring them of the great value of their continued presence at Cape Helles to the main operation, had been instrumental in sustaining morale and affirming that the struggle was worth the sacrifice. The loss of this able soldier created a void that his successor was not likely to fill.[19] By virtue of seniority command of the French forces devolved upon General Bailloud, an old campaigner whose career had taken him to widely scattered parts of the world, including terms of service in Madagascar, China and Algeria. Recalled from retirement in 1915 he was sent to the Dardanelles in charge of a division. He was accurately described by Hankey, who visited the Peninsula at the end of July, as 'the most confirmed pessimist I have met since the war began. . . . He is a stupid old man and ought to be superseded . . .'.[20]

[17] Gouraud to Hamilton, June 13, 1915; *ibid.*, pp. 296–301. See also *Les armées françaises dans la grande guerre*, tome 8, vol. 1, annexe no. 240.

[18] Robert Rhodes James, *op. cit.*, pp. 229–30.

[19] The loss of Gouraud was of such concern to the English that it prompted the King to send the following telegram to Hamilton: 'I very much regret to hear that General Gouraud was wounded yesterday. I know what a serious loss he will be both to his own army and to you. I trust that his wounds are not serious and that he may soon recover. George. R.I.' Brig.-Gen. C. F. Aspinall-Oglander, *Military Operations: Gallipoli*, vol. 2, p. 93, fn.

[20] Lord Hankey, *op. cit.*, vol. 1, p. 381.

Hamilton was sick at heart over the unfortunate turn of events. He wrote to Asquith [21]:

> 'The . . . loss of Gouraud, who is one of the finest commanders I have ever met, and whose loss to an impressionable set of people like the French, is, to my thinking at least equivalent to the loss of a Brigade. . . . The new General is not at all a man of the same calibre as Gouraud, and he is too old for the job (67). . . . So for the moment, the French have cold feet and, as in the early days of d'Amade, we shall have to constantly act as big brother to them and try to get them to buck up.' [22]

Hamilton's lack of confidence in the French was not entirely warranted. Admittedly certain colonial units like the Senegalese and the Zouaves had proven to be unreliable, especially at night, but on the whole the French soldiers had given a good account of themselves, fighting with dash, spirit and, at times, unusual valour. Hamilton never took into consideration that the French contingent had been up 'against the most formidable part of the Turkish defences since the end of April and had lost heavily from the Asiatic shelling'.[23]

In no place was the loss of Gouraud felt as deeply as in Paris where events were rapidly moving towards a political crisis. Regarded as a talented and aggressive soldier, his absence was certain to be felt in the Dardanelles. A victory at this time was badly needed. On all fronts the Allied position was deteriorating and the parliamentarians were increasingly restive over the faulty manner in which the war was being conducted. Most of the verbal attacks were levelled at Millerand. On the one hand the Chamber took him to task for failing to control Joffre, whom he in turn defended vigorously. On the other hand the Commissions complained that he fed them inadequate and often incorrect information and that he was mishandling the production of munitions. It

[21] Each time Hamilton wrote to an official in the Government he forwarded a copy to Kitchener.
[22] Hamilton to Asquith, July 7, 1915; vol. 14, Asquith papers (Oxford, Bodleian Library).
[23] Robert Rhodes James, *op. cit.*, p. 232.

140

was evident from the growing pressure of discontent that, unless Millerand was sacrificed or the Entente Powers achieved a victory shortly on the battlefield, the Viviani Ministry would collapse under the strain.

Joffre's last offensive in Artois, begun in May, limped along painfully until mid-June producing no worthwhile gains. But Joffre was inclined to discount the immediate results, fortified by the illusion that he had inflicted enormous casualties upon the Germans and that he was one step closer to a break-through. He intended to strike again at the enemy as soon as Kitchener's New Armies arrived in France. Both Joffre and Millerand were ready to wage an all-out fight to preserve the reigning war policy – the former because he had to do something to restore a prestige tarnished by recent defeats and the latter out of his prolonged practice of unquestioned obedience.

If Joffre was bent on pursuing the slaughter in the West it was certain that he would receive no encouragement from the English. Reviewing the general military situation in mid-June, Churchill observed that since April the Anglo-French forces on the main front had cleared about eight square miles of territory which was of little strategic value and, in the process, had suffered 320,000 casualties, while enemy losses amounted to less than a third of that number. He urged that the Allies in France remain on the defensive throughout 1915 and that full provisions be made to achieve a victory at the Dardanelles.[24] At about the same time a conference between the French and British Ministers of Munitions opened at Boulogne. This meeting, presided over by Lloyd George and attended by representatives from the British and French High Commands, proposed to consider the munition requirements for the armies after taking into account the changed conditions of warfare. The conference concluded that sufficient munitions for a successful offensive in the West could not be provided before the spring of 1916 and suggested that until then an active defensive be maintained on that front.[25] Kitchener in a memorandum on

[24] 'A Further Note Upon the General Military Situation, June 18, 1915'; Winston S. Churchill, op. cit., vol. 2. See also Lord Hankey, op. cit., vol. 1, p. 342.

[25] Sir James E. Edmonds, general editor and chief compiler, *Military Operations: France and Belgium* (London, 1936), vol. 2, pp. 115–17.

June 29th expressed similar views. He wanted the Allied offensive postponed until early in 1916 when the New Armies would be fully trained and equipped, and when such a movement could be co-ordinated with a Russian attack. As the Russians were short of guns and munitions a synchronized advance at present was not possible.

Notwithstanding the recommendation of the Boulogne conference and Kitchener's strong pleas, Joffre was determined not to alter his plans. Lord Esher observed during this period:

'When by Lord Kitchener's desire the gist of this Memorandum was reported to the French Grand Quartier Général, Joffre vehemently differed. He and his officers admitted the force of Lord K.'s reasoning, but they were intractable, and explained with fire and vigour the cogent motives for the delivery of another blow before the winter set in. Considerations of morale could not be eliminated, and the fierce temper of the French armies expected another effort to be made to drive the invader out of France; and further, the French people might misunderstand if the effort were not made. . . . There were political reasons also which were not put forward, but were of common knowledge in France, that made a successful offensive indispensable to the security of the French Ministry. There had been bitter attacks in the Committee of the Senate upon the conduct of the War, upon General Joffre and M. Millerand, which were not without weight in the decision of the Grand Quartier Général to stick out for the offensive planned by the Staff. From what was said at Chantilly it was clear that the conviction of its necessity was unfaltering.' [26]

Along with G.Q.G., the British High Command persisted in claiming top priority for the Western front. Of all the British military leaders in France none was more fervent in his admiration and trust of Joffre than Sir Henry Wilson. As Director of Military Operations between 1910 and 1914, Wilson had taken a leading part in concerting plans with the French General Staff for the war with Germany which he saw was inevitable. From August 1914 he was

[26] Reginald Viscount Esher, *The Tragedy of Lord Kitchener* (London, 1921), pp. 137–9.

for five months Assistant Chief of Staff and then became principal liaison officer with the French. Although at this time he exercised no control over the course of events in the field, he busied himself with the political conduct of the war. Aware of the increasing friction on both sides of the Channel over a military policy, Wilson appeared before the British Cabinet on July 3rd to plead G.Q.G.'s case. His record of the discussion reads as follows:

'Full Cabinet discussed future plan of campaign. I represented French view of us "not being cross, but dissatisfied and a little suspicious", and pointed to Dardanelles and shortage of ammunition as chief reasons. Much discussion, and a good deal of nonsense; but in the end Kitchener said he thought that the 2nd New Army should be sent out at once. This was good.' [27]

There was as yet no definite decision to support Joffre's proposal for an autumn offensive. The 2nd New Army would merely take over part of the French line, which would then free French troops for service elsewhere. London still hoped to persuade the French to postpone their intended offensive until the spring of 1916. With this idea in mind the English requested a conference.[28]

In the evening of July 5th the English delegation consisting of Asquith, Kitchener, Crewe and Balfour, crossed over to Calais. The next morning the French Ministers – Viviani, Delcassé, Millerand and Augagneur – arrived by train. Sir Henry Wilson had arranged a private meeting between Kitchener and Joffre earlier that morning. The details of the interview were never revealed by Kitchener but it is reasonable to assume that he supported Joffre's explanation that the restive mentality of the French people made a defensive policy dangerous, despite the strong military reasons for a delay. It seems likely that Kitchener anticipated success at Gallipoli before September and that he would then be free to co-operate on the Western front. Poincaré observed in his memoirs that as a result of the various meetings at

[27] Noted: July 3, 1915, Diary of Henry Wilson.
[28] Paul Guinn, *British Strategy and Politics, 1914 to 1918* (Oxford, 1965), p. 90.

Calais, Kitchener consented to send to France during the month of July six divisions, to be followed each succeeding month by an additional six. At Joffre's insistence, Kitchener agreed to give up the idea of standing entirely on the defensive, but for the next five or six weeks there would only be local attacks 'to hold and wear out the enemy'. As for the Dardanelles, Kitchener declared that three English divisions would land there shortly, but that for the moment he had no intention of sending any more reinforcements.

The Anglo-French conference got under way at 10.00 a.m. Both Joffre and Sir John French were in attendance. No minutes of the meeting were recorded in English, an unfortunate omission as there was considerable confusion and misunderstanding. Kitchener dominated the proceedings and enjoyed a great personal triumph. He was calm, frank and consistent in his arguments and created a tremendous impression on everyone present. The French, who up to this moment had been prepared to follow Joffre's lead,[29] were apparently won over and agreed to pursue an active-defensive strategy in the West and to give priority to the Dardanelles Operation. Joffre was relatively reticent during the talks. He had obviously gained what he had sought and took no notice of the arrangements that followed.[30]

No sooner had Joffre left Calais than he resumed the development of his plans for an autumn offensive. On July 7th the first Inter-Allied Military Conference was held at Chantilly with Millerand acting as chairman. Speaking before the various military representatives, Joffre underlined the need to undertake a major drive in the West for three reasons: first, to relieve pressure on the faltering Russians; second, to bolster the morale of the troops; and finally because it was believed that the German line was weak. Sir John French concurred with Joffre's appreciation of the situation and promised that as soon as the 2nd New Army arrived from England he would be ready to occupy additional

[29] Bertie to Crewe, July 4, 1915; F.O. 800/167, Bertie papers.
[30] Philip Magnus, *Kitchener : Portrait of an Imperialist* (London, 1958), pp. 343–5; Lord Hankey, *op. cit.*, vol. 1, pp. 347–51; Reginald Viscount Esher, *op. cit.*, pp. 140–1; Paul Guinn, *op. cit.*, p. 90; Major Gerald French, *Life of Field Marshal Sir John French* (London, 1931), p. 311; Raymond Poincaré, *op. cit.*, vol. VI, pp. 314–15. Noted: July 6, 1915, Diary of Henry Wilson.

lengths of the French front. The attack was due to begin in August.[31]

Neither Joffre nor Millerand ventured to inform the French Cabinet of this decision. Both feared, with just cause, that their plans might encounter strong opposition. Buoyed up by the agreement at Calais, opinion in the Cabinet had begun to harden against further attacks in the West. For several months evidence had been accumulating in Paris that the uneasiness in the country was due more to the dissatisfaction over costly and premature attacks than to impatience at remaining idle. On July 5th Poincaré recorded: 'The war weariness which permeates many quarters has produced a fresh flow of insulting and threatening letters addressed to me.' Two days later while on an inspection tour at the front, Poincaré noted that a corps commander had taken him aside and pleaded: 'Pray Mr President, do what you can to put a stop to these local offensives; the instrument of victory is being broken in our hands.' [32] During the last offensive at least one army corps had refused to leave the trenches [33] and two battalions had gone over to the enemy singing *L'Internationale*.[34] Even Joffre's generals recognized that, unless the Anglo-French armies were heavily reinforced, there was not the slightest chance of smashing through the German lines. The effect of these warnings on the Government was to suggest that if Joffre was allowed to continue his policy of frontal assaults, the French army, which was in a complete state of exhaustion, would probably mutiny.[35]

Within the Cabinet the most questioning minds were probing to determine if there was a way out of the bloody stalemate in the West. While fully conscious of the importance of massing troops where decisive blows were to be struck they were no longer unanimous that France should be regarded as the only primary

[31] Noted: July 7, 1915, Diary of Henry Wilson. There is a somewhat different version in *Military Operations: France and Belgium*, vol. 2, pp. 87–8.

[32] Raymond Poincaré, *op. cit.*, vol. VI, pp. 307, 313. See also Brig.-Gen. John Charteris, *At G.Q.G.* (London, 1931), p. 98.

[33] Noted: June 22, 1915, Diary of Henry Wilson.

[34] Raymond Poincaré, *op. cit.*, vol. VI, p. 234.

[35] Basil Collier, *Brasshat: a Biography of Field-Marshal Sir Henry Wilson* (London, 1961), p. 228.

theatre. Even those who felt that the final decision must be sought on the Western front had come to recognize that troops should be sent to some other theatre where operations might lead to more productive results. As the Government began to search for an alternative strategy it fastened on the current campaign in the Dardanelles.

On July 22nd the Cabinet had a long and lively session which lasted nearly all day. Viviani conducted a reappraisal of the Allied position on the Peninsula and pointed to the staggering casualties the French forces had sustained since the first landing. The Ministers had now to decide what they would do. They could abandon the enterprise or send large reinforcements and seek a rapid conclusion. Poincaré was instrumental in trying to justify the second course.[36] This would restore communications with Russia, probably force Turkey to capitulate, open the door for Balkan intervention and assure for France those portions of the Ottoman Empire deemed vital to her interests. The President argued that the Germans did not have the power, nor could they obtain it in the foreseeable future, to break the Allied line in the West. On the other hand he was convinced that no strategic benefits could be gained in France and that further offensives would produce nothing but a continuation of the very heavy losses of the previous attempts. A condition of stalemate had in fact gripped the home front and was likely to last for some time. In these circumstances Poincaré urged that the French Commander be supplied with all the troops he needed to storm the Turkish trenches. Millerand was clearly uneasy over this suggestion. He stated that the war on the Eastern front was going very badly and it was possible that, with the sudden collapse of the Russians, numerous German divisions would be free to return to France and unleash a gigantic assault on the Allied line. He therefore laid down the general principle that the safety of France must not be jeopardized by a secondary operation, no matter how important it seemed. Millerand tended to understate the inadequacy of the existing military policy but the bare facts could not be concealed. Everyone was dejected over Joffre's recent failures, especially as there was nothing to show for the heavy losses incurred. Seeing there was no

[36] Abel Ferry, *Les carnets secrets, 1914–1918* (Paris, 1957), p. 103.

possibility of a breakthrough in the mud, barbed wire and trenches in France, they were anxious to find another place which might afford greater opportunities. For them, as Poincaré had maintained, the key to victory appeared to lie in the Dardanelles. If the British proved unequal to the task of defeating the Turks, it would be up to the French to seize the initiative. To this end the Cabinet agreed to send large-scale reinforcements to the East.[37]

There was no thought of discussing a strategic line of action until the result of Hamilton's projected offensive were known. The civil authorities tended to favour a landing in Asia and hoped that Hamilton could yet be induced to move in that direction. Their preference for operations in Asia clearly reflected the views of their successive military commanders in the Dardanelles.

Shortly before he was wounded General Gouraud, discarding an appreciation of a fortnight earlier, suggested that a subsidiary campaign be undertaken to silence the Turkish batteries on the southern side of the Straits. The pounding from the Turkish guns had become unbearable and it was seriously undermining the morale of the men on Cape Helles.[38] Bailloud went beyond his predecessor's proposal and implored that the landing take the shape of a major operation. He asked the Government to insist that Hamilton divert two of his three divisions for an offensive in Asia. 'If a solution for this state of affairs is not promptly found,' Bailloud added, 'it will mean the material and moral ruin of the French Expeditionary Corps.'[39]

Hamilton never tried to understand the marked effect the constant shelling had produced on the French troops even though he was the first to admit: 'From the point of view of moral[e] one man killed by a shell from Asia is equivalent to ten men killed in action.'[40] Given a copy of Bailloud's plan, Hamilton immediately shrugged it off. He calculated that a landing in Asia would be difficult and dangerous unless the Allies could weaken the Turkish garrison there by heavy attacks in the Peninsula. At the moment

[37] Raymond Poincaré, *op. cit.*, vol. VI, p. 335.

[38] Gouraud to Millerand, June 19, 1915; *Les armées françaises dans la grande guerre*, tome 8, vol. 1, annexe no. 253.

[39] Bailloud to Millerand, July 4, 6, 8; *ibid.*, annexes nos. 269, 270, 271.

[40] Sir George Arthur, *Life of Lord Kitchener* (London, 1920), vol. III, p. 158, fn.

147

he had no intention of abandoning his own scheme for what he believed to be a mere defensive measure. Once his objective had been attained, the Turkish guns would cease to be a problem. In the meantime Hamilton proposed to use battleships to keep the activity of enemy batteries in Asia at a minimum.[41]

But in Paris nothing short of decisive action would quell the unrest, and pressure was being exerted on Millerand to persuade the English to agree to operations in Asia. On July 19th General Gouraud, who was convalescing in the hospital, wrote to the Ministry of War and stated pointedly that as long as the Turkish guns remain in place 'the very existence of the French corps is at stake'.[42] Gouraud was no alarmist and if his letter reflected a sense of urgency he had to have good reasons for doing so. The next day Millerand appealed to Kitchener to consider a landing on the shore of Asia.[43]

Kitchener in turn asked Hamilton for his views on the matter:

'The French state that the fire from the Asiatic side allows them no rest. . . . They propose secondary operations on the Asiatic side to deal with enemy artillery, and suggest employment of 20,000 British assisted by French 75 monitors. Would the main scheme of our operation be jeopardized by thus detaching a considerable force, which may find itself employed with hostile forces of unknown strength?'[44]

Hamilton replied: 'I am sure you will agree, that a diversion if and when necessary, must be made at my own time, not at Bailloud's, to whom I have not yet confided my plans.'[45]

Kitchener concurred with this decision. He had always sought to avoid involvement in Asia and as he felt confident that

[41] Brig.-Gen. C. F. Aspinall-Oglander, *Military Operations: Gallipoli*, vol. 2, p. 146.

[42] Gouraud to Millerand, July 19, 1915; *Les armées françaises dans la grande guerre*, tome 8, vol. 1, annexe no. 284.

[43] Millerand to Kitchener, July 20, 1915; *ibid.*, annexe no. 285.

[44] Kitchener to Hamilton, July 21, 1915; tel. no. 1612, War Office archives.

[45] Hamilton to Kitchener, July 23, 1915; tel. no. 1630, War Office archives.

Hamilton's attack would succeed, he was unwilling to interfere with his plans. On July 28th Kitchener wrote to Millerand: 'You will understand, how difficult it is to impose upon a commander-in-chief an operation which does not fit in with his own most carefully prepared plan.' [46] To allow a military chief freedom of action in the field was a principle from which Millerand himself never deviated and he could hardly fault Kitchener for pursuing the same line. Still the Minister of War did not rule out the possibility of an Asiatic landing at a future date. Everything would hinge on Hamilton's next attack.

On the Peninsula meanwhile, Hamilton was busy making last-minute adjustments before the great battle. The plan that he selected was similar to the one that he had adopted on April 25th, the main difference being that the focal point of attack would take place at Anzac instead of Cape Helles. The idea was to break out from the Anzac beachhead and, after making a feint at Lone Pine to the south, converge on the Sari Bair ridge. At the same time a complementary attack would be mounted at Suvla Bay to the north to protect the Anzac flank. Once the enemy had been swept from the hills at Suvla, the two forces would join hands and push forward to the Narrows. There would also be a feint landing at Bulair to delay the enemy and a diversionary attack at Cape Helles to hold the Turks there and attract reinforcements from the Anzac front. The plan was sound enough although insufficient consideration was given to the difficult ground over which the Anzac troops had to traverse.

On August 6th Hamilton signalled for the attack to begin. At Suvla the landing force was virtually unopposed. The local commander, General Stopford, was a muddled and mediocre officer. He wasted invaluable time and forfeited the opportunity to occupy the high ground. By the time Hamilton arrived on the scene to take personal charge, the enemy was present in strength and an advance was no longer possible. Without any support from Suvla, the few Anzac units that scaled the heights of Sari Bair could not hold their position and were obliged to fall back. The fighting dragged on until August 29th though the issue had been

[46] Kitchener to Millerand, July 28, 1915; *Les armées françaises dans la grande guerre*, tome 8, vol. 1, annexe no. 294.

decided by the 10th. The second attempt to bring the Gallipoli campaign to a close had failed.*

Weary and disillusioned, Hamilton admitted in a telegram to Kitchener that his attack had not fared well and that he would require 95,000 more troops to give him 'the necessary superiority'. Kitchener was hard pressed to find surplus troops at this time because he had promised to support Joffre's plan for an autumn offensive. He told Hamilton that the utmost that could be done was to supply him with drafts to replace his casualties. Hamilton replied that he would utilize the troops at his disposal to the best of his ability but that, unless reinforcements arrived shortly, he would have to consider reducing his front.

As the British began to give up hope for a solution, the French Government suddenly came forward on August 31st with an offer to add four divisions to the two they already had in the Dardanelles. The English were puzzled. It was well known that the French had always been opposed to the idea of diverting troops from the principal scene of action. What then had precipitated this proposal? To this story we must now direct our attention.

* See map on p. 137.

Chapter 8

L'AFFAIRE SARRAIL

'One can say without offending anyone that . . . Sarrail is one of the greatest generals the war has produced.'
Gustave Hervé, in *La Guerre Sociale*, August 7, 1915

'It is the task of the government to determine the theatre where a general should operate and the goal which he must achieve.'
General Sarrail, *Mon commandement en Orient*

'From his headquarters . . . Joffre kept one eye on the front and the other – as well as both ears – on Paris, for in a man as devoid of political interests his interest in politicians was as remarkable as his skill in dealing with them, ever alive to incipient intrigues and quick to counter-act them through his faithful entourage and press supporters.'
B. H. Liddell-Hart, *Reputations: Ten Years After*

As the immediate threat of a further German breakthrough receded and as the abortive attacks against the German lines continued to mount, opposition to Joffre in the Chamber of Deputies rose steadily in the summer of 1915. Criticism of the French Commander ranged from dissatisfaction over his military policy to a belief that he was trying to set up a dictatorship at Chantilly. Even the Government had begun to lose faith in his judgment, but it was unthinkable to replace a soldier who was still popular with the press, idolized by the rank and file of the French army and respected in Allied countries. Joffre's strength was derived from the enormous prestige that he had gained as the 'Saviour of the Marne', a prestige which he sustained by denying subordinates public credit for performances which were apt to dim his own glory. In the first part of 1915 a popular rival appeared in the person of General Maurice Sarrail. Responding to the challenge, Joffre provoked an incident which not only endangered his own

151

position, but 'introduced a new phase of conflict into the relations between the command, the government, and Parliament'.[1] This chapter in French history is known traditionally as *l'affaire Sarrail*.

Maurice Sarrail was born near the Pyrenean border, at Carcassonne, in 1856. He graduated third in his class at Saint-Cyr in 1887 and passed to a commission in the infantry. During his military ascent he pursued a course which set him apart from his colleagues. While orthodox French officers were apt to be devout Catholics and even harbour Royalist sympathies, Sarrail was a freethinker, an anti-clerical Republican and was suspected of having associations with freemasonry. In the 1890s he had been the only officer in the higher ranks who had spoken in defence of Dreyfus and after the vindication of the martyred Jew had found the door open for rapid advancement. He became an orderly officer for General André, the Minister of War, and later served as commandant of the guard at the Palais Bourbon.[2] Here he used every opportunity to make political contacts and in 1911 this paid off when Joseph Caillaux became Prime Minister and he (Sarrail) was promoted general of division. As soon as the war broke out Sarrail took the field at the head of the 6th Corps of the 3rd Army.

If Sarrail made good use of his political connections to accelerate his rise, it was on the strength of his ability in the field that Joffre appointed him to command the entire Third Army on August 30th. It was a happy event for the country that Sarrail should be given so important an assignment one week before the start of the battle of the Marne. Attacked by a superior German force, Sarrail ignored Joffre's orders to fall back and clung to the Verdun pivot without losing touch with the Fourth Army on his left. This had the effect of disrupting Germany's modified plan which aimed for a pincer-like squeeze on either side of Verdun. 'So also by maintaining a solid front while the issue was being decided farther west by the Allied left wing, Sarrail's Third Army contributed to the victory of the Marne, and the German decision to withdraw.' Almost overnight Sarrail became a national hero. Pictured as a knight in shining armour, a champion of the people, he was especially popular among Republicans, the working classes

[1] J. C. King, *op. cit.*, p. 67.
[2] Home of the Chamber of Deputies.

and political groups on the left, the most powerful of which was the Radical Socialist party.[3]

So fervent were some of his admirers that they sought his elevation to commander-in-chief. In the spring of 1915 they passed around two anonymous memoranda to certain Parliamentary members whereby they condemned G.Q.G.'s military policy and acknowledged Sarrail to be superior to Joffre. The authors went on to say that 'if General Joffre were unavailable for a period of two weeks and if supreme command were entrusted to General Sarrail, the Germans would surely be expelled from the national territory, for there would be an entirely different military conception and a brutality of execution that would cost us less dearly than the war of attrition which we have endured for five months and which we shall go on enduring, leaving our richest regions of the north completely ruined'.[4]

Whether Sarrail was informed of these circulars in advance is open to debate, but it is certain that he had knowledge of, and was implicated in, the movement on his behalf. That Sarrail should take a jaundiced view of Joffre's self-attrition strategy was natural enough. But Joffre's obtuseness cannot condone the underhanded methods of intrigue which Sarrail permitted himself to employ against his chief. Such a state of affairs could hardly have escaped the vigilant eyes of Joffre. He noted that 'as soon as the front was stabilized, matters of a political and personal nature took the place of purely military affairs which, up to then, had sufficed to engage his attention. He received all the Members of Parliament who passed near him, in particular M. Doumer,[5] to whose machinations against myself I have already referred.' [6]

[3] B. H. Liddell-Hart, *Through the Fog of War* (New York, 1938), pp. 126–127; Alan Palmer, *op. cit.*, pp. 29–30; J. C. King, *op. cit.*, pp. 67–8; Paul Coblentz, *The Silence of Sarrail* (London, 1930), pp. 23 *et seq.*; Jean-José Frappa, *Makédonia : souvenirs d'un officier de liaison en Orient* (Paris, 1921), pp. 24 *et seq.*; Gabriel Terrail, *Sarrail et les armées d'Orient* (Paris, 1920), pp. 17–19.

[4] Gabriel Terrail, *op. cit.*, p. 178.

[5] He was a senator and Galliéni's former secretary of civil affairs.

[6] Field-Marshal Joffre, *op. cit.*, vol. II, p. 372. Doumer made a habit of visiting army commanders and of telling them that it was inevitable that Galliéni, the real hero of the Marne, should replace Joffre. See Joseph Galliéni, *Les carnets de Galliéni*, edited by Gaëtan Galliéni, p. 131.

The two Generals were temperamentally incompatible as well as having important differences in strategic outlook. Joffre was simple in manner and tastes, yet he was authoritative and a strict disciplinarian. He considered himself supreme in military matters and was accustomed to unflinching obedience. He expected daily and complete reports from his commanders in the field and insisted that they remain aloof from politics. Sarrail was not in the least awed by Joffre's reputation or concerned about military precedent. He had no regard for Joffre's ability, did not hesitate to rake him over the coals in public and had an insatiable appetite for political intrigue. Impatient of delays and higher control, Sarrail showed a reluctance to co-operate with Chantilly.[7] It was alleged that he often falsified his reports to conceal his tactical blunders and ignored the directives from his superior. What Sarrail desired was to be left alone, to use his strength and energy to develop his own plans [8] and to await the call to unseat Joffre. 'He became a bogy,' wrote Sir Compton Mackenzie, 'sitting there at Ste Menehould, the headquarters of the Third Army, ready it might be, in the event of disaster to make a bid for supreme power . . .'.[9] There were obviously faults on both sides and neither was an apostle of compromise. By mid-1915 Joffre's personal relationship with Sarrail had finally collapsed and he could no longer remain a passive witness in this struggle, upon the outcome of which his command depended. A mishap at the front afforded Joffre a pretext to eliminate his rival.

A two-month period of relative inactivity along the Argonne front was shattered on June 30th when the Germans struck in force against the Third Army. Accompanied by heavy artillery fire and poison gas the well co-ordinated drive, carried out on a wider front than the former attacks, endangered Sarrail's position and

[7] Emile Herbillon, *Souvenirs d'un officier de liaison pendant la guerre mondiale* (Paris, 1930), vol. 1, pp. 167–8; Yarde-Buller (Head of British Mission at French Army Headquarters) to Kitchener July 26th and August 8th, 1915; War Office archives; Raymond Poincaré, *op. cit.*, vol. VI, pp. 136–7.

[8] Poincaré comments on Sarrail's preference for an offensive either in Belgium or in Alsace in *op. cit.*, vol. VI, p. 137. On the same subject see also A. Percin, *Sarrail et Galliéni* (Paris, 1919), pp. 5–6.

[9] Sir Compton Mackenzie, *First Athenian Memoirs* (London, 1931), vol. II, p. 374.

154

inflicted heavy casualties on his forces. Joffre immediately dispatched two divisions of reinforcements to allow Sarrail to regain the upper hand. On the day before the counter-attack was due, the Germans captured Hill 285 on the Haute-Chevauchée. Sarrail's counter-offensive was started too late and in spite of two violent assaults the 3rd Army was thrown back to its own line.[10]

Joffre then decided that it was time to intervene. He appointed General Dubail, a staunch republican and favourite of the far left, to investigate the operations in the Argonne as well as Sarrail's personal conduct. Joffre calculated that in case Dubail made an unfavourable report against Sarrail, the radical and socialist elements in Parliament could not claim that his removal was due to political pressure. In military matters Joffre was not known for great astuteness, flexibility or imagination, yet in his dealings with politicians he suddenly revealed himself to possess an almost 'Oriental' guile.

On July 20th Dubail submitted the results of his inquiry in the form of two long papers. The first report charged Sarrail with gross incompetence: that he failed to support XXXII Corps in the front line; that in refusing to intermingle his units he had divided the front into watertight compartments with the result that insufficient reserves were kept on hand; and that delays in beginning the counter-attack had turned what might have been a spectacular victory into a decisive defeat. In the second note Dubail found that Sarrail's hostility toward certain generals whom he held in low esteem, and partiality with regard to officers he favoured, had created a spirit of unrest throughout the Third Army. Dubail recommended a change in the leadership of the Third Army and suggested that Sarrail be assigned to take command of the less important Army of Lorraine.[11] Joffre was

[10] Joffre's version of the events, *op. cit.*, vol. II, pp. 373–4, differs sharply from Paul Coblentz's account, *op. cit.*, pp. 89–95. A more balanced view is given in the unpublished 'Notes de guerre' (July 28, 1915), by William Martin, a correspondent in Paris. The author was acquainted with many of the leading political figures and he has drawn from them valuable information. The manuscript is housed at Stanford University Library.

[11] Field-Marshal Joffre, *op. cit.*, vol. II. The memoranda are reproduced in the appendix, pp. 607–15. See also Raymond Poincaré, *op. cit.*, vol. VI, pp. 336–7. There is a reference to the incident in Abel Ferry, *op. cit.*, pp. 100–1.

now justified on military grounds to relieve Sarrail of his command.

On July 22nd Sarrail was informed of his removal and instructed to report to the Ministry of War the following day. Upon arrival at the French capital Sarrail, in response to a telephone call, stopped by the office of the Minister of the Interior, Louis Malvy, a Radical Socialist whose faith in the old soldier remained undimmed. Malvy revealed to the General that he was due to succeed Gouraud at the head of the Dardanelles Expeditionary Force.[12]

As shown in the previous chapter, the Cabinet had consented on July 22nd to send additional reinforcements to the Dardanelles. Later during the meeting the Sarrail case was brought up. Several ministers believed that Joffre's treatment of Sarrail was unduly severe. Alexandre Ribot, Minister of Finance, felt it was unfair to punish Sarrail for his setback in the Argonne, whereas no one had been disciplined for the recent failure at Arras. It was decided to ask Joffre if he would accept General Dubail's advice and entrust Sarrail with the command of the Army of Lorraine. Of course no pressure could be exerted, for Joffre had always been given a free hand in selecting local commanders and he would probably resign rather than brook any interference from the Government. Briand opposed the suggestion on the basis that a discontented Sarrail, if left in France, would provide an excuse for continued controversy in the restless Chamber. Colonel Buat, Millerand's chief of cabinet, had confided that Joffre would prefer to send Sarrail to the Dardanelles. This seemed like an ideal solution and the ministers agreed to sound out Joffre on the matter.[13]

After leaving Malvy's office, Sarrail went directly to the Ministry of War, where he was received by Millerand and Viviani. Grimly aware of what was to happen, he listened politely to the two men until they had finished and then flatly rejected the offer of a command in the Dardanelles. Sarrail would not accept a post inferior to the one he had been deprived of. And the two French divisions in the Eastern Mediterranean could hardly be said to have constituted a real army. Moreover, Sarrail correctly discerned

[12] Maurice Sarrail, *Mon commandement en Orient* (Paris, 1920), p. vii.
[13] Raymond Poincaré, *op. cit.*, vol. VI, pp. 336–7.

that Joffre and Millerand were anxious to throw him out of the country and he had no intention of playing into their hands. He announced that he would return to his home at Montauban and await his retirement from the Army.[14]

News of Sarrail's dismissal rocked the Chamber of Deputies. The sacking of generals was not an uncommon occurrence and it usually evoked little outside interest. In the first six weeks of the war Joffre had retired three army commanders, ten corps commanders and thirty-eight division commanders, on the grounds that they were incompetent or had collapsed under pressure.[15] The royalist and clericist generals may have been dominant in the upper echelon of the army but their support in Parliament was negligible – 'three dozen rattlepates', according to Clemenceau.[16] The same was not true of republican generals who commanded a large following in the Chamber.[17] And Sarrail was especially popular for he was viewed as a republican Maid of Orleans. As one parliamentarian put it: 'Sarrail is a flag. . . . Removing him from his command would be a slap at Parliament.'[18] Although Caillaux was no longer in office to take up the cudgels for Sarrail's reinstatement, his numerous friends in Parliament could be counted on to prevent his being relegated to a minor assignment. Viviani had to steer a careful course, for he could not afford a breach with the Radical Socialists if he wanted to continue in his present capacity. The socialists in the Chamber were becoming unruly despite all efforts to show that Sarrail's removal was founded on a report by General Dubail. 'They refused to look upon it in any other light than a manifestation of spite.'[19] The Prime Minister remarked to Poincaré on July 23rd: 'The Chamber is in an

---

[14] Maurice Sarrail, *op. cit.*, pp. vii–viii; Paul Coblentz, *op. cit.*, pp. 101–3.

[15] Abel Ferry, *op. cit.*, annexe no. 7, p. 248. The journalist Léopold Marcellin in *op. cit.*, p. 98, claims that up to the Sarrail incident Joffre had broken 138 generals. He neglects to mention, however, how many of these actually commanded armies. For more details on this subject see Paul Allard, *L'oreille fendue: les généraux limogés pendant la guerre* (Paris, 1933).

[16] Jean Martet, *Georges Clemenceau* (New York, 1930), p. 281.

[17] J. C. King, *op. cit.*, pp. 70–1.

[18] Emile Herbillon, *op. cit.*, vol. 1, p. 171.

[19] Field-Marshal Joffre, *op. cit.*, vol. II, p. 376.

157

incredible state of agitation. Violette [20] on the one hand and the socialists on the other have been trying to see me all day. I managed to keep out of sight. But the situation is becoming impossible, since Parliament must be reckoned with.' [21]

To avoid a rupture of the 'Sacred Union' the ministry had to find Sarrail an important army command. Accordingly, Doumergue [22] and Millerand were delegated to try to get Joffre to withdraw his objection to place Sarrail in charge of the forces at Lorraine. When the two men arrived at Chantilly they were dismayed to find out that Joffre had already chosen General Gérard, a strong republican, for that post. It was a move worthy of a consummate politician and confirmed Galliéni's observation that Joffre was the most 'cunning of men'.[23] No one could reproach him for naming a good republican to head the Army of Lorraine. Nor did Joffre give the impression that he was trying to exclude Sarrail altogether from an assignment. He explained that he could see no reason why Sarrail could not be appointed to lead an army corps or the French troops in the Dardanelles.[24] Secretly Joffre harboured the hope that Sarrail would be packed off to the obscurity of a colonial garrison.

It was felt in Government circles that since Sarrail would unquestionably reject an army corps, he must be made to accept the command of the Dardanelles Expeditionary Force. On April 24th the Cabinet arranged to send Albert Sarraut, Radical Socialist minister of Public Instruction, to hold talks with Sarrail. The Radical Socialist Minister pleaded with Sarrail to reconsider his decision, underlining the importance of the mission and the need to capture the Ottoman capital post haste.[25] He hinted that the Expeditionary Force would be enlarged and that in all probability supreme command would be entrusted to the French General.[26]

---

[20] A radical republican.

[21] Raymond Poincaré, *op. cit.*, vol. VI, p. 340.

[22] Minister of Colonies.

[23] Joseph Galliéni, *Les carnets de Galliéni*, edited by Gaëtan Galliéni, p. 208.

[24] Raymond Poincaré, *op. cit.*, vol. VI, p. 341.

[25] *Ibid.*, p. 342.

[26] Bertie to Grey, August 6, 1915; F.O. 800/58, Grey papers.

Sarrail had reservations about the entire operation,[27] but he could hardly overlook the fact that the French general who entered Constantinople in triumph 'would have a unique page in history'.[28] He began to waver but refused to make a formal commitment. As soon as Sarraut left, Briand called on Sarrail. The Minister of Justice had a personal stake in putting everything in order. He had his mind set on replacing Viviani, if there was a change of ministries, and by conciliating Sarrail he would be strengthening his hand with the Radical Socialists in the Chamber.[29] Using his famed powers of persuasion, Briand succeeded in converting the General, subject to certain conditions. 'I would accept the command offered if it were augmented but I would assume possession only after the increase had been carried out,'[30] declared Sarrail.

It was, of course, another matter to meet this condition, but as a first step Millerand signalled Bailloud to furnish him with information on several strategic plans that were under consideration, and an estimate of the number of divisions that would be required in each case: '(1) What effectives do you judge necessary and sufficient for an operation designed to occupy the battery emplacements on the shore [of Asia]? (2) Same question for an operation of greater scope, comprising the preceding but continuing along the coast of Asia to open the Dardanelles. (3) Do you believe that the first operation can be accomplished without entailing the second?'[31]

On July 26th Bailloud forwarded his memorandum to the Ministry of War. In reply to the first question he considered that two divisions would suffice to silence the guns in Asia. As for the second query he felt that five or seven divisions would be needed, depending on which of the two following schemes the Government preferred – an advance along the shore in conjunction with the fleet or a march outside the main line of Turkish

---

[27] Paul Coblentz, *op. cit.*, p. 102.

[28] Speech by Georges Leygues, July 26, 1915; C7488 Foreign Affairs Commission, National archives.

[29] Yarde-Buller to Kitchener, August 6, 1915; War Office archives.

[30] General Sarrail, *op. cit.*, p. viii.

[31] Millerand to Bailloud, July 24, 1915; *Les armées françaises dans la grande guerre*, tome 8, vol. 1, annexe no. 287.

defences which would mean forsaking the assistance of the ships. The last suggestion was not only possible but advisable since it would not entail lengthy preparations. Bailloud saw that after the occupation of Kum Kale an additional operation would be required with the view to seizing Chanak, otherwise the Turks could build another fortress there and resume their shelling.[32]

In submitting to pressure from numerous quarters to act expeditiously, the Cabinet reaffirmed its intention to send three or four divisions to the Dardanelles and left it up to Viviani and Millerand to make the necessary arrangements with Joffre (July 27th).[23] On July 29th Joffre arrived at the Ministry of War for an appointment with Millerand. As soon as he sat down he was bluntly told that the Cabinet planned to send reinforcements to the Dardanelles. Since the Minister of War no longer had at his disposal an organized force it would become necessary to call on the armies of the North-East to make up this expedition. But Joffre was not partial to any suggestion that would decrease his striking power in France. He stiffened his back and outlined his position, which he confirmed later in the day in a letter to Millerand:

'The action now going on in the Gallipoli Peninsula should not be abandoned but should be carried on with the means required to bring it to a successful conclusion. At the same time care must be taken that the situation in France should not be compromised by untimely withdrawals from that theatre. At this period, the end of July 1915, it seems to me impossible to withdraw any troops. It would be a different matter in September when the battle which I propose to engage in Champagne and Artois has come to an end. Moreover, an interval of this duration appears necessary to enable a definite plan of operations against Constantinople to be drawn up, and for preparations to be made. It is clear that our setbacks in the East were due to defects in the general plan of operations, and to insufficiency of means. I, therefore, propose that a rational plan of operations be drawn up and that, with this end in view, an officer of my staff be sent

---

[32] Bailloud to Millerand, July 26, 1915; *ibid.*, annexe no. 290.
[33] Raymond Poincaré, *op. cit.*, vol. VI, p. 347.

to the Dardanelles to establish contact with the troops and obtain all necessary information.' [34]

Millerand was in the midst of a Cabinet meeting when the note was brought to him and he felt compelled to read part of it [35] to his colleagues. There was nothing of consequence in what was revealed except an inference that further preparations for the proposed operation should be placed under the supervision of the High Command. In order to set the record straight, the Ministers invited Joffre to confer with them the next day. At the meeting Joffre made no reference to his paper and simply stated that it would be difficult for him to spare four divisions, especially on account of a shortage of artillery and ammunition. When the Cabinet refused to accept this explanation, Joffre began to give way and conceded that the idea of a secondary operation should be studied but that it should not be attempted unless Hamilton's attack miscarried. In the afternoon the civil authorities convened without Joffre and decided to nominate Sarrail commander of the Expeditionary Force. He was to start immediately to make arrangements and would leave in a fortnight to take charge of the two divisions already on the Peninsula.[36] This was the first time since August 1914 that Joffre's views on military matters had not prevailed. The Government had begun the process of liberation from the role of Joffre's obedient servant.

On August 3rd Sarrail was summoned to the Ministry of War to state his conditions for accepting command of the French forces in the East. He listed them clearly: (1) an army was to be constituted and known as the Army of the Orient; (2) unlike his predecessors he did not wish to be under the orders of the British Commander; (3) he would not leave without the promised units.[37]

If Joffre ever had any plans to enlarge the expeditionary army, he cancelled them once he learned that Sarrail would be sent to the Dardanelles. He had hoped that the Government would take his hint and appoint Franchet d'Espèrey, a personal friend, to head the

[34] Field-Marshal Joffre, *op. cit.*, vol. II, p. 371. See also *Les armées françaises dans la grande guerre*, tome 8, vol. 1, annexe no. 296.
[35] No allusion was made to Joffre's autumn offensive.
[36] Raymond Poincaré, op. cit., vol. VI, pp. 350–1.
[37] Maurice Sarrail, *op. cit.*, p. viii.

French forces in that theatre.[38] He had hated the side-show from the start and his attitude hardened every time he was confronted with an item of business that related to the expedition. His patience was wearing thin. On August 3rd Joffre addressed a lengthy letter to the Minister of War, strongly objecting to the proposals advanced by Gouraud and Bailloud, and added:

'Despite a considerable numerical superiority the Russians, owing to lack of arms and ammunition, are obliged to withdraw before the Austro-German forces. As regards the future we must on no account allow ourselves to be deluded by false hopes. The reconstruction of powerful modern armies cannot be improvised nor cadres created or shells and rifles turned out in large numbers from one day to another; several months may therefore pass before the Russians can again assume the offensive. . . . Do not forget that we have reached the maximum of our military strength; if the English in the course of next winter bring new forces to help us, we still cannot ourselves do otherwise than decrease from the point of view of effective strength. Now everyone knows that the French Army alone can stand up to the German Army and defeat it.[39] Not only is the occasion favourable to take action but our strict duty towards the Russians is to do so, a duty in which, under analogous conditions, they for their part have not failed. Finally we are formally bound by the protocol of the conference of last July 7, which was approved by the military representatives of all the Allied Powers, and I consider that your signature and mine pledge France. In short, circumstances are too uncertain at the moment for us to be able to take away troops from the Armies of the North-East in order to send them to the Dardanelles.'[40]

It is remarkable that the revision in Joffre's military thinking was dictated largely by his political prejudice. He was apparently

[38] Raymond Poincaré, *op. cit.*, vol. VI, p. 348.

[39] It would require enormous self control not to ask: 'If this is the case what have you been doing all this time?'

[40] Raymond Poincaré, *op. cit.*, vol. VII, p. 12; Field-Marshal Joffre, *op. cit.*, vol. II, p. 377.

willing to acquiesce in the plan to send an expedition to the Dardanelles until he learned that Sarrail would be in command of the French troops. Joffre realized that if he had no influence with the officer leading the venture, he would be unable to exert any control over the conduct of operations, or flow of reinforcements to the East. Furthermore, Joffre was not averse to embarrassing Sarrail and possibly inducing him to resign from the army by blighting his chance of obtaining a new appointment. The exercise of power and the ruin of a rival appear to have become more important to Joffre than the immediate task of finding a way to defeat the enemy.

When the Cabinet met on August 5th, attention was directed to Millerand's recent interview with Sarrail. Some of the members were uneasy about the whole situation and were prepared to go to any lengths rather than humiliate a popular Republican General. Failure to come to terms with Sarrail would endanger the Viviani Ministry. Poincaré reminded his colleagues that any decision affecting the Dardanelles expedition should not be guided by personal consideration.[41]

Actually the President was not anxious for Sarrail to go to the Dardanelles.[42] It is true that he wanted Sarrail pacified, but he preferred to see him given an honorific position that carried no authority, or banished to a remote outpost. He suspected that Sarrail would not fit easily into this narrowed groove in the Eastern Mediterranean, and that nothing could stifle all the bitterness he would feel at being transferred to a secondary assignment. On the basis of this Poincaré did not feel that Sarrail could be counted on to collaborate with the English, work in harmony with his subordinates or provide inspirational leadership to the rank and file. Similar views had been expressed by Gouraud and Bailloud, who even indicated a desire to return to France rather than serve under Sarrail.[43]

Still, all suggestions or hints that Sarrail was temperamentally unsuited to command in the Dardanelles did not seem to register

[41] Raymond Poincaré, *op. cit.*, vol. VII, p. 11.

[42] Bertie to Grey, August 3, 1915; F.O. 800/58, Grey papers.

[43] Bertie to Grey, August 3, 1915; F.O. 800/58, Grey papers; Yarde-Buller to Kitchener, August 8, 1915, War Office archives.

with most of the Ministers. Anxious to see Sarrail removed from Paris, the Cabinet readily accepted his terms.

A new issue was unfolded when Millerand produced the full text of Joffre's memorandum (of August 3rd). The Ministers were angry and surprised that Joffre had made arrangements for an autumn offensive without their knowledge and, save for Millerand, were unanimous in deprecating such action. It was evident also that the decision to mount another attack in the West could interfere with plans to send divisional reinforcements to the Dardanelles. After the meeting broke up, Poincaré returned to his office and wrote a sharp note to Millerand:

'What is this? What are these contemplated operations? Is it to be a repetition of Champagne, Woevre, Eparges or Souchez? Joffre told us himself, in his long letter relative to the Dardanelles, that the wear and tear of his fighting strength was far beyond what he calculated. I must formally ask you that no new offensive be set afoot without my being fully informed as to its conditions and objective, or without my being able to consider whether, in a war which anyhow will go on till next year, anything like premature action may not constitute a dangerous squandering of strength. When I know all about it we will consider, you and I consider, the situation, and if there is good reason, lay the matter before the Government. Tell them no definite or irreparable step must be taken; the question is not one for purely military consideration but affects our diplomatic and national concerns.' [44]

It had always been Millerand's contention that his duty as Minister of War was to be the Intendant General of the Commander-in-Chief. During the early months of the war he set out uncritically and untiringly to support Joffre and to supply him with everything he required. His policy was seldom challenged as long as the welfare of the country lay entirely in the hands of the army. When in 1915 the civil authorities sought to reoccupy a place so patriotically vacated at the outset of the war, they grew to resent Millerand for his continued self-effacement before Joffre.

[44] Raymond Poincaré, op. cit., vol. VII, p. 14.

In the ensuing and expanding conflict the soldiers looked to Millerand to help them obviate Government interference and defend the authority of the High Command. Millerand was under obligation to carry out the wishes of his Government, yet he could not bring himself to renounce his loyalty to the army. He stood between the two institutions and became the convenient scapegoat of both.

In the late afternoon of August 5th, Millerand apprised Sarrail that he had been formally selected to command the Army of the Orient. The Minister of War made no reference as to whether Sarrail would be independent or subordinated to Hamilton, but did promise that he would not be sent to the Dardanelles without new forces unless the acting commandant there, General Bailloud, were to pass away suddenly. In the meantime Sarrail was invited to express his views on what 'a French army ought to do in the Orient'. This was a highly irregular request since it was normally the responsibility of the Government to set the aim of the expedition. It was nonetheless politically expedient to assign work to Sarrail so as to keep him from intriguing with politicians. As Sarrail was about to leave the Ministry of War, Millerand warned him: 'Do not associate with Parliamentarians.' [45]

Fed by *l'affaire Sarrail*, the dissident leftists showed no sign of letting up on the Government. A number of these politicians began a disguised campaign to marshal British opinion in France in support of the appointment of Sarrail as chief of the Allied army in the Dardanelles. They circulated reports, largely fictitious, of the circumstances under which Sarrail was removed from his post and of the petty persecutions he suffered at the hands of the High Command in their attempt to weave around him the halo of martyrdom. Chief among the lobbyists was Franklin-Bouillon, Radical Socialist deputy from Seine-et-Oise and heir-apparent to Caillaux.[46] In conversations with Lord Murray of Elibank, he hinted that the French were starting to think that perhaps the English did not have the ability to end the conflict in the Eastern Mediterranean. He claimed that a crisis was building up in Paris

[45] Maurice Sarrail, *op. cit.*, p. ix; J. C. King, *op. cit.*, pp. 76–7; Emile Mayer, *op. cit.*, p. 279.

[46] He was also Vice-President of the Chamber Commission on Foreign Affairs.

and that unless the Dardanelles expedition succeeded there would be a serious revulsion of opinion in the country which could then lead to a movement for a separate peace. Not too surprisingly Franklin-Bouillon argued that the much-needed victory in the Dardanelles could be accomplished by a competent commander like General Sarrail.[47]

A play upon fear, especially when there is good cause for alarm, can be a valuable crutch and the Radical Socialist deputy made full use of it when he addressed himself to Lord Bertie. Brimming with messianic zeal, he asserted that Russia was beaten and would undoubtedly conclude a settlement with Germany. France was near exhaustion, one-eighth of her territory was occupied by the enemy and it was evident that she could not continue for more than a year. The anxiety in the country could be dispelled if the Allies, by executing a bold coup in the Dardanelles, succeeded in carrying the Turks before the end of the summer. According to Franklin-Bouillon, General Sarrail, who had been unjustly derpived of his command in France, was the logical choice to lead the combined force in the Dardanelles. He reasoned that 'such command ought not be governed by the number of troops furnished by each of the two Allies, nor by questions of national pride. National safety should be the sole deciding factor.'[48]

Bertie was not the least bit interested in considering the claims of Sarrail, but he was worried over Franklin-Bouillon's allegation that France was approaching the limit of endurance. He called on Briand and related his encounter with the Radical Socialist leader. Briand dismissed Franklin-Bouillon as a 'busy-body' with an inflated sense of his own importance and currently in search of a portfolio. He added that this politician carried no weight outside the rue de Valois [49] party and that he had no authority to speak on behalf of the Viviani Ministry. The Minister of Justice assured Bertie that there was no substance to the charges and that the French Government intended to fight to the very end. As for Sarrail, he would be assigned to take over the French troops in the

[47] Murray of Elibank to Drummond (of the Foreign Office) August 4, 1915; F.O. 800/60, Grey papers.
[48] Bertie to Grey, August 4, 1915; F.O. 800/181, Bertie papers.
[49] Radical Socialist headquarters.

Dardanelles but there was no question of proposing to London that he be placed in supreme command.[50]

To set his mind at ease, the British Ambassador sought corroboration of this statement from the Quai d'Orsay. The results of his interview with Delcassé do not appear to have been to his satisfaction:

> 'I inquired of M. Delcassé as to the truth of the report which I had heard from Socialist quarters that General Sarrail is to succeed General Gouraud at the Dardanelles. Delcassé said: "not that I know of". On coming out of his room I read in *Le Temps*: "*Le conseil des ministres a désigné le Général Sarrail comme commandant en chef de l'armée d'Orient.*" I suppose that Delcassé must be deaf or an awful liar.' [51]

The battle of wits was sharpened by a rumour, designed to underline British bungling and spread freely by radicals and leftists, to the effect that the French had consented to join the expedition on the strength of assurances from London that the Turkish Commanders in the forts had been bribed and would allow the ships to pass through the Straits. The story went on to say that Enver Pasha discovered the plot shortly before the naval attack and brought in German officers to replace his own commanders.[52] Lord Bertie took up the matter with the French political authorities and could turn up no evidence of any kind. He came to the conclusion that the recent scraps of gossip had been put about town 'partly to shield Augagneur [53] from responsibility for a failure'.[54] Unknown to Bertie, however, there was some basis for these rumours.

In February 1915 the Director of British Intelligence, Admiral Sir Reginald Hall, entrusted two agents to meet a Turkish delegation at the Thracian port of Dedeagatch to negotiate a treaty

[50] Bertie to Grey, August 6, 1915; F.O. 800/58, Grey papers.

[51] *Ibid.*

[52] Bertie to Grey, August 4, 1915; F.O. 800/58, Grey papers. There is a brief reference to this incident in the biography of General Gouraud by Pierre Lyautey, p. 124.

[53] He was a socialist-republican.

[54] Bertie to Grey, August 4, 1915; F.O. 800/58, Grey papers.

whereby the Turks would withdraw from the war in exchange for £4,000,000. The representatives from both sides met on March 15th–16th but failed to reach an agreement because the British Government would not guarantee that Constantinople would remain in Turkish hands.[55] One of the British agents wrote after the war: 'The whole country desired peace, and their leaders [56] would have accepted any terms had we been able to assure them of their retention of Constantinople. They knew full well that signing away that city would also mean signing their own death warrants.' [57]

Even after more than half a century the details of this bizarre episode remains unclear. Captain G. R. G. Allen, son-in-law of one of the British delegates, in his article 'A Ghost from Gallipoli' maintains that Admiral Hall kept both Fisher and Churchill in day-to-day contact with events by sending them copies of all important telegrams. But these telegrams, if they do exist, cannot be found in the official archives. Admiral Sir William James, the biographer of Hall, relates a different version. He is convinced that Hall had acted on his own initiative, without the consent or knowledge of the British Government. James admits that Lord Fisher was told of the negotiations, but only after hope of a settlement with Turkey had practically disappeared.[58] He gives no indication that any minister was ever consulted, although this seems hardly credible. A possible explanation is that the Admiralty leaders were too absorbed with the impending naval attack to devote much thought to the clandestine talks which they felt were not likely to produce fruitful results. There does not appear to be the slightest hint in the available sources to suggest how the French became aware, or at least suspected, that something was going on. Perhaps they picked up rumours of the discussions from their own intelligence system in the Near East. Many questions

---

[55] London had already acknowledged Russia's right to annex Constantinople and the Straits.

[56] The Turkish Minister of War, Enver Pasha, a Germanophile, was excluded from the secret discussions.

[57] Captain G. R. G. Allen, 'A Ghost from Gallipoli', *Journal of the Royal United Service Institution*, May 1963, p. 138.

[58] Admiral Sir William James, *The Eyes of the Navy: A Biographical Study of Admiral Sir Reginald Hall* (London, 1955), pp. 62–3.

are still unanswered and it may be that what actually happened will never be known.[59]

The backstage activity of the Turkish war was relatively calm in comparison with the complex and multiple intrigues that bedevilled *l'affaire Sarrail*. In cashiering the republican general, Joffre touched off a chain of events that he could not foresee. One consequence was that Parliament set an ominous precedent by intervening in military appointments. Another result was that it placed a strain on the 'Sacred Union' as the political groupings resumed their struggles of the pre-war era. Then, also, Millerand came under fresh fire from political critics for showing devotion to Joffre which far transcended his sense of obligation to Parliament.

Fully aware of his own powers and confident of broad political support, Sarrail refused to be rushed into accepting a definite commitment. On August 11th he turned in his appreciation of what a French Army might do in the Orient. Sarrail observed that the two French divisions on Gallipoli were crowded into vulnerable positions and reduced to fighting under conditions of trench warfare and that progress would be difficult, slow and costly. He suggested leaving the English to pursue operations in the Peninsula, while his own forces, including the two divisions presently under Hamilton, were used in another theatre. A number of schemes were put forward. These included a march on Chanak to capture the Asiatic forts, a more ambitious operation to begin farther to the south in the Bay of Adramyti; a landing at Smyrna, at Alexandretta or, as he preferred, an advance into Serbia by way of Salonika.[60]

The first two projects were in keeping with the original idea of taking Constantinople. The remaining three, which envisaged different objectives, signified an abrupt and all-embracing change

---

[59] This was not the first time that the British had ventured to buy Turkish officials. Enver Pasha complained to the American Ambassador, Henry Morgenthau, that the English had tried unsuccessfully to plot his overthrow in the capital as well as bribe certain key officials, such as the Governor of Smyrna. Enver Pasha to Morgenthau, March 14, 1915, Box 1, Diary of Henry Morgenthau (Library of Congress, Washington).

[60] 'Note on the subject of the military situation in the Orient', August 11, 1915; *Les armées françaises dans la grande guerre*, tome 8, vol. 1, annexe no. 315.

of strategical conception. Having seized Smyrna the plan was to dig in and defend the city-port against Turkish attacks until the end of the war. The only advantage to what otherwise appears to be a useless manœuvre would be to relieve some pressure on the British troops in Gallipoli. A similar action at Alexandretta would place the French in a position to capture the Baghdad–Bahn railroad at some future date, incite the Arabs to revolt, and further the progress of the English in Mesopotamia and the Russians in the vicinity of Van Lake. At Salonika the presence of French troops would very likely induce the wavering Balkan states to join the Entente. The French and Balkan forces could then link with the Serbian army preparatory to launching a great offensive against Austria-Hungary.[61]

The report was referred to Joffre, who was quick to point out its defects. He considered the plan too sketchy, with no thought for the size of the force that would be required, the chances of success or the many other problems that usually attend operations of this nature.[62] Sarrail admitted that the criticism was probably valid but, as he remarked, 'the duty of deciding where an army should be sent and what it should do is the task not of a soldier but of the Government'.[63] In all fairness to Sarrail it should also be noted that he had not been provided with expert advice nor given any information about the enemy.

French policy in the Near East was in a state of uncertainty and flux. When the Chamber Commissions of the Army, Marine and Foreign Affairs could not draw from the Government precise facts on what was occurring in the Dardanelles, they turned directly to the President. They complained that the Government had evaded their questions and it was from the press they had discovered that the naval attack and the first landing had failed. Such was the situation when they learned that an Army of the Orient would be constituted. The three Commissions were unanimous in their decision to urge that French reinforcements be dispatched immediately to the Dardanelles.[64] Poincaré remained non-

[61] *Ibid.*
[62] Joffre to Millerand, August 18, 1915; *ibid.*, annexe no. 318.
[63] Maurice Sarrail, *op. cit.*, p. x.
[64] J. M. G. Pédoya, *La commission de l'armée pendant la grande guerre* (Paris, 1921), p. 353. Select documents.

committal, saying only that he could not offer any views independently of the Ministers nor engage in debate with Parliamentarians.[65]

Here again, the President thought, was further evidence that the country desired to shift the main action to a theatre which offered greater prospects of victory. On August 14th Poincaré, Viviani and Millerand motored to Chantilly to confer with Joffre. The military chief had prepared for the occasion a paper in which he underlined the need for complete freedom of action in the conduct of future operations. 'A single man must conceive, decide and command.' [66] Once Joffre reaffirmed his position he announced his intention to mount an offensive in Champagne in September. The President challenged Joffre's pretension to ignore control from Paris and there followed a sharp exchange of words between the two men. Joffre held the opinion that an Allied offensive in the West was not only urgent but expedient in the sense that it would honour French commitment to Russia. Poincaré objected to the General's ambition to take on responsibilities that were not within his purview: 'No, the questions of alliance are for the Government, and not for the soldier, to consider; you must only look at the situation from the strategic point of view, the rest is our concern.' Joffre repeated his absurd claim that from purely military considerations it was necessary to keep the men active, otherwise they would deteriorate physically and morally.[67]

As for the Dardanelles, Joffre maintained that he could not spare the four required divisions until the results of his projected offensive were known. He commented tartly: 'What is to be done at the Dardanelles? Prepare an expedition for a factious general.' Joffre then tore into Sarrail with unmatched savagery, only to be reminded by Poincaré that it was not Sarrail but Gouraud, and Bailloud, as well as the Government and Parliamentary Commissions, who had recommended that the Expeditionary Force should be augmented. Poincaré, finally, was able to extract a promise from Joffre that he would release two army corps in

[65] Raymond Poincaré, *op. cit.*, vol. VII, p. 30.
[66] Charles Bugnet, *Rue St Dominique et G.Q.G.* (Paris, 1949), p. 76; J. M. Bourget, *Gouvernement et commandement: les leçons de la guerre mondiale* (Paris, 1930), p. 139.
[67] Raymond Poincaré, *op. cit.*, vol. VII, p. 37.

September. It was clear that if the civil authorities tried to impose their will on Joffre, he would resign. And the Government's fear of the effect of his resignation enabled Joffre, as usual, to follow his own plans.[68]

While Joffre had been able to coerce the political leaders in Paris into accepting his proposals, he found that Sir John French was not so easily led. The British Commander refused to co-operate with Joffre for he was convinced that the fall offensive could not possibly succeed. Joffre arranged to invite Kitchener to Chantilly, hoping that his pleas would fall on a more receptive ear. If Joffre was eager to drag in Kitchener's trained reserves his attitude was very different so far as his own reserves for the principal theatre were concerned.

On August 15th Kitchener crossed the Channel and held talks with Joffre and Millerand. By then signs were not wanting that the German drive in the East was meeting with great success. Warsaw had fallen on August 4th and the Russians were in full retreat. The French leaders concluded that if vigorous action were not taken immediately in the West, the Russians might be defeated and forced to make a separate peace. The French even went so far as to hint to Kitchener that they themselves might seek a release from the war rather than remain inactive. This threat was confirmed by Sir Henry Wilson who asserted that Joffre's failure to attack would bring in a new government, one which would be bent on making peace with the enemy.[69] The belief had begun to spread among the parties of the left, especially in the ranks of the Radical Socialists, that a negotiated peace was the only alternative to endless meaningless slaughter.

The theory of attack had become so rooted in Joffre's mind that he seems to have lost all sense of proportion. It was well known in military circles that a superiority of at least two to one was required in an offensive and the Allies clearly did not enjoy that advantage. The French had proclaimed the coming attack so loudly that the Germans had ample time to prepare for it. With the help of reconnaisance planes, which spotted troop activity behind the Allied line, and the indiscreet announcement by the mayor of St

[68] *Ibid.*, pp. 37–8.
[69] Paul Guinn, *op. cit.*, p. 95; Sir Llewellyn Woodward, *op. cit.*, pp. 135–6. Noted: August 16, 1915, Diary of Henry Wilson.

Omer of the impending drive,[70] the Germans were able to pin down the approximate area and time of the assault. Joffre was aware that he could not achieve a tactical surprise [71] and that the chances of success were minimal, yet he paid no heed to the thought of sacrificing 200,000–300,000 men in his obsession to avenge his series of defeats.

Kitchener had long since realized the futility of such attacks but he had to face a disastrous commitment only because he saw no other way of avoiding a fatal rupture with the French. As he told Churchill on August 20th: 'Unfortunately we had to make war as we must, and not as we should like to.' [72] Having deferred to Joffre's formula, Kitchener instructed the British High Command to 'act with all our energy, and do our utmost to help the French, even though, by doing so, we suffered very heavy losses indeed'.[73] In all probability Kitchener would have adopted a different line had he known that Joffre's views were contrary to the declared policy of the Government. Actually Joffre used Kitchener's assent to his advantage in dealing with the civil leaders. It was no secret in Paris that the Secretary of State for War had hitherto advocated a postponement of further offensives in the West, and so his change of heart was all the more meaningful.[74]

As Joffre was concluding his bargain with Kitchener, the Cabinet met and decided that Viviani should ask Sarrail to examine closely how the Dardanelles could be forced, dismissing the extraneous operations he had mentioned in his first memorandum.[75] When Sarrail reported to the Prime Minister's office he was told to devote full consideration to the possibility of a landing

---

[70] The mayor had unwittingly revealed at a public meeting that the French offensive would take place around September 15th. Recorded in the minutes of the Dardanelles Committee meeting of August 20, 1915; CAB 22/3.

[71] G. R. Alexandre, *Avec Joffre d'Agadir à Verdun* (Paris, 1932), p. 206.

[72] Minutes of the Dardanelles Committee, August 20, 1915; CAB 22/3.

[73] Field-Marshal Sir Douglas Haig, *The Private Papers of Douglas Haig, 1914–1919*, edited by Robert Blake (London, 1952), p. 102.

[74] Philip Magnus, *op. cit.*, pp. 347–8; Brig.-Gen. C. F. Aspinall-Oglander, *Military Operations: Gallipoli*, vol. II, p. 372; Sir Llewellyn Woodward, *op. cit.*, pp. 135–6.

[75] Raymond Poincaré, *op. cit.*, vol. VII, p. 42.

at Bulair, Gaba Tepe or in Asia. Sarrail complied with the request and returned on August 24th to submit an appreciation of his findings. He concluded that an attack at Bulair was fraught with danger but if successful would bring substantial results; an advance at Gaba Tepe would be extremely difficult and would only prolong the struggle on the Peninsula; an operation in Asia was not likely to encounter serious resistance but it offered less important gains.[76]

As might be expected Joffre instinctively disliked the plan. He complained that it was not particularly clear nor sufficiently detailed, in short that 'no decision had been arrived at as to the number of divisions which would be necessary for the completion of the mission assigned to the future Army of the East, and that the conditions under which the expedition was to be organized had not been defined'.[77] Joffre then asked the Section d'études de la défense nationale [78] to produce a 'very concise Note' on the Dardanelles. Rejecting the idea altogether of a new assault in Gallipoli, this committee would do no more than cast a net in Asia.

[76] 'Operations in the region of the Dardanelles', a memorandum, August 24, 1915; Les armées françaises dans la grande guerre, tome 8, vol. 1, annexe no. 323.

[77] Field-Marshal Joffre, op. cit., vol. II, pp. 377–8.

[78] Toward the end of August 1915, at the suggestion of Joffre, the Conseil Supérieur de la défense nationale was reconstituted from the defunct Conseil Supérieur de la guerre, which had not assembled since the outbreak of the war. Presided over by Poincaré, this committee was originally composed of Joffre, Millerand, Delcassé and Augagneur. After the early meetings the membership tended to increase in size. To guard against possible leakage of secret information no official records of the sessions were kept. The Conseil Supérieur was, in theory, a purely advisory body but in practice, as its members constituted a powerful voice in the Cabinet, its conclusions were usually acted on at once. It could best be described as a supplement to the Cabinet, charged with exploring major questions of policy, rather than a device for meeting the day-to-day emergencies of the war. Until late in the war it was the Government's main instrument for the correlation of political and military leadership.

The Conseil Supérieur had a permanent secretariat, known at first as the Section d'études de la défense nationale, which functioned at the Ministry of War under the direction of General Graziani, Chief of the General Staff. Summoned only when Joffre or Millerand deemed it desirable, its role was to examine questions relating to the war as a whole, forward its

It was seen that Sarrail's estimate of four divisions would be inadequate and that an additional nine would be required as the Turks could assemble 165,000 men by the tenth day after the landing.[79] Since the French obviously could not spare all the necessary divisions, the Italians should be requested to make up the difference and the entire Allied force in the Dardanelles, the army as well as the navy, should be turned over to a French commander-in-chief. The report concluded by suggesting that no further offensives take place in the Dardanelles unless it was certain that progress could not be achieved on the main front. This meant that for the time being the Allies on the Peninsula would have to adopt a strategic defensive policy and cling to their existing positions.[80]

The note could hardly have been more to Joffre's liking if he had drawn it up himself. But it was to no avail. The tide of opinion in the country, already flowing strongly in favour of a renewed effort in the Near East, was further fortified by events in the last week of August.

On August 25th the three Parliamentary Commissions (Army, Marine and Foreign Affairs), in an unusual gesture, made written representations to the President, to the Prime Minister and to all the Ministers. While acknowledging they had no right to discuss war policy, they were emphatic in their request for regular sessions with Viviani at which he could keep them posted on important issues. They expressed concern at the indecision over the Dardanelles Operation and urged haste on account of the approach of bad weather conditions after September 15th, which

---

reports to the *Conseil Supérieur*, draft the final decisions and supervise their execution.

Much of the information about the French War Councils was kindly provided for me by Dean Pierre Renouvin. There are passing remarks on one or both of these Councils in the following works: Pierre Renouvin, *The Forms of War Government in France*, p. 83; G. R. Alexandre, *op. cit.*, pp. 191–2; and *Les armées françaises dans la grande guerre*, tome 8, vol. 1, p. 521, fn.

[79] As a basis for this exaggerated calculation it was alleged that Gouraud himself had asserted that ten divisions would be required.

[80] 'Note on the subject of the Dardanelles', August 31, 1915; *Les armées françaises dans la grande guerre*, tome 8, vol. 1, annexe no. 332.

would make a landing either in Europe or Asia uncertain, and also because of the threat of a German attack on Serbia, which would open a direct route between Berlin and Constantinople. The Commissions were astonished by the irresolute attitude of the Government and especially at the delays in concerting a Dardanelles policy with England and the Balkans. They added:

'At first you spoke to us of more than 100,000 men, then of four divisions, then of two divisions. Finally you have told us that military reasons will not allow you to decide before September 15 if reinforcements will be available for the Orient. Yet, a general, who formerly was at the head of an army, has been named commander-in-chief of the Army of the Orient. Despite this, the Minister of Marine has admitted that all transport preparations have been suspended. What can this general do then as long as he does not know whether he will be given a man; what preparations can be made if the transport facilities are not known?' [81]

Failing to receive an answer, the Commissions passed a resolution on August 27th which they 'set out in an allocutional address' to the Prime Minister. They reiterated their desire for periodic meetings with Government leaders, as well as their conviction of the need to press on at the Dardanelles, alluding to the great benefits that would accrue from the capture of Constantinople. The letter concluded by inviting the Government to organize without delay, in agreement with its allies, an expedition of sufficient scope to force the Dardanelles and occupy the Ottoman capital.[82]

This time Viviani replied to the motion. He recognized the right of the Commissions to be kept informed and asserted that henceforth all important matters would be discussed with them in advance.[83]

On August 27th Cambon forwarded a copy of Hamilton's latest telegram. The British General admitted his attack had failed and

[81] J. M. G. Pédoya, *op. cit.*, pp. 354–8.

[82] *Ibid.*, pp. 358–9.

[83] *Ibid.*, p. 359.

claimed that unless substantially reinforced he would have to remain entirely on the defensive and might even be forced to withdraw from Anzac or Suvla. The next day the Cabinet convened to decide what should be done about the British telegram. Poincaré wrote in his memoirs:

> 'The Council resumes the examination of the Dardanelles question, revived again. . . . All the Ministers are clear that the British set-back renders a dispatch of fresh French troops nothing else but indispensable. They have learned that Sarrail has sent in a second memorandum, unfortunately again rather superficial and vague. But Millerand reads out to us a report drawn up by the General Staff,[84] which concludes quite definitely that some intervention on the Asiatic coast is absolutely necessary.' [85]

In the afternoon Joffre made his way to the Elysée to keep an appointment with Poincaré, Viviani, Millerand and Augagneur. He was told upon his arrival that events dictated the immediate dispatch of reinforcements to the Dardanelles. Appearing somewhat deceived, Joffre claimed that he would need the four divisions in question, either for an offensive or possibly to hold back a German attack. When reminded of an earlier promise he had made, Joffre clasped his head with his hands and would only say that he could not abdicate his responsibilities as Commander-in-Chief. To this argument Poincaré replied that the Government also had obligations. He added: 'If the offensives which you are preparing in France are inspired by purely military considerations, all is well; that is your business and we shall bow to your authority as Commander-in-Chief. But if your plans are in any way based on our relations with the Allies, please let me say that the opening of the Narrows is of far greater importance, affecting as it does Russian opinion and the supplies to the Russian Army, than the gain of a few kilometres on our front.' [86] The upshot of the

---

[84] The note was occasioned by Sarrail's unsatisfactory appreciation and based on the recommendations of Gouraud and Bailloud. See *Les armées françaises dans la grande guerre*, tome 8, vol. 1, annexe no. 320.

[85] Raymond Poincaré, *op. cit.*, vol. VII, p. 64.

[86] *Ibid.*, p. 68.

discussion was that Joffre half-heartedly consented to release the required troops by September 20th, or the 22nd at the latest, if he failed to achieve a breakthrough on the main front.[87] The military direction of strategy had received its first check. Never again would it recover its earlier freedom of action.

On July 31st the Cabinet concluded that the four divisions should be ready to start for the Dardanelles on September 20th, and, if necessary, these would be followed by an additional four. After the meeting Delcassé telegraphed the Foreign Office that the French Government was prepared to send reinforcements to the Dardanelles, subject to four conditions: that the Expeditionary Force led by a French general be allowed to operate in a new theatre, independent of, but in close liaison with, the English on Gallipoli; that the Royal Navy co-operate in transporting the new divisions; that the Allied fleet cover their disembarkation; and that the French be permitted to establish a separate naval base at Mudros or Mitylene.[88] A subsequent message from the Quai d'Orsay requested that the English use their own units to replace the two divisions under Bailloud at Cape Helles.[89]

Up until this time the Dardanelles operation had been treated like an illegitimate child in Paris, fed only by the troops and ammunition that could be spared from the country without offending G.Q.G. or prejudicing offensive operations on the main front. It cannot be argued that the politicians themselves had shown much of a disposition in the first half of 1915 to go beyond local affairs. Attracted to the 'side show' in the Dardanelles largely out of a desire to protect French interests, they did not see the venture with the same eyes as did London. The majority were 'Westerners' who hesitated at the difficulties of waging a distant campaign and who were apprehensive lest the Allies be left with insufficient reserves to hold the line in France. It was natural that so long as French soil was under the heel of the Germans every

---

[87] *Ibid.*, pp. 68–9.

[88] Delcassé to Cambon, August 31, 1915; England, Box 70, Military archives.

[89] Millerand to Delcassé, August 31, 1915; *Les armées françaises dans la grande guerre*, tome 8, vol. 1, annexe no. 331; Delcassé to Cambon, September 1, 1915; Dardanelles Operation, Box 6, fol. 1, Diplomatic archives.

effort should be made to break the enemy's hold. The Government was assured that continued attacks in the West would gradually eat into, and in a few months effectively pierce, the German front. But all the Allied offensives began and ended in the same way. Even if the enemy's first line was carried, there was behind it a second line and sometimes a third. By the end of June the heavy lists of casualties were out of all proportion to the meagre gains of a few square miles and no breach in the defences was achieved. The vision of an early victory disappeared; gloom and frustration settled upon the country. The civil authorities came around to the view that any further offensives in France would be a waste of blood unless a very great preponderance of strength had been gathered, and for this they could see nothing but to develop the unlimited manpower potential of Russia. To open the Dardanelles, therefore, and resuscitate the Russians appeared to be the only hope of salvation. Once Russia was fully armed then a great concerted attack by all the allies might succeed in overcoming the Central Powers.

The French Government found itself committed by force of circumstances, rather than by choice, to the possibility of extensive military operations in the Dardanelles. The idea of half-measures and limited risks had disappeared. In their place now stood a definite determination to see the matter pressed to a conclusion.

In all probability Joffre would have succeeded in deterring the Government's projected plan until the end of 1915 had it not been for the intrusion of Sarrail into the political scene. Spurred on by the Parliamentarians and to some extent by the Commissions and the successive army commanders in the Dardanelles, the Government found the courage to confront and surmount Joffre's opposition. It would be unfair to suggest that the decision to send an Expeditionary Force to the Dardanelles had been motivated solely by the desire to mollify Sarrail and his partisans. Sooner or later an alternative to the war of attrition, which was exacting an inhuman toll, had to be found, for France could not sustain a policy of bankruptcy indefinitely. The Sarrail incident was the catalyst that drove the politicians to shift from a Western to an Eastern strategy.

The attempt to divert troops from the West extended the scope of the conflict between Chantilly and Paris. As a result of his recent military setbacks, Joffre's arguments no longer carried the

179

same conviction. Aware that his popularity and prestige were waning, the military chief was forced to recognize, at least for the moment, the Government's claim to a greater share in determining the future course of the war.

The arrival of large-scale reinforcements in the Dardanelles was certain to reinvigorate the flagging operation. But would the troops be allowed to leave France? Would Joffre acknowledge defeat and submit to civilian rule or would he make an effort to regain his former position of strength? The fate of the Expeditionary Force hinged on the outcome of the struggle between Joffre and the Government over the conduct of the war.

Chapter 9

THE RACK OF CHOICE

'If news of our preparations had not leaked out, if the fine weather had continued, if fleeting opportunities had been seized by local commanders, heaven knows how far we might have been able to drive the enemy.'
General Joffre, *Personal Memoirs*

'The English really have had luck in meeting failure in the Dardanelles. . . . England has simply gone mad from fear of Germany. This absurd "German madness" . . . has caused the best of English statesmen . . . to lose sight of England's best interests, so causing the English to do that which, if successful, would be the worst possible thing for England's future. Russia is England's great future enemy. . . . So England's endeavour to conquer the Dardanelles, to take Constantinople and deliver her to England's greatest rival of the future, is nothing short of political madness. . . .'
New York World, September 6, 1915

'Salonika is a chimera which is driving us to make useless sacrifices.'
Lord Kitchener, 1915

In London the French announcement 'caused a great sensation in the Dardanelles Committee'.[1] Spirits were lightened. Lord Kitchener stated that he would gladly make arrangements to relieve the two French divisions on the Peninsula, while Balfour began to assemble the necessary transport ships. Even Bonar Law, who had constantly opposed diverting troops to the Near East,[2] joined Churchill in urging the dispatch of additional British units to 'make a good job of it'.[3] Seldom since the start of the war had the

[1] Lord Hankey, *op. cit.*, vol. 1, p. 410.
[2] An avowed 'Westerner', Bonar Law had assured Henry Wilson on July 3rd that he would resist the dispatch of more drafts to the Dardanelles. Although the obstructionism of the Conservative leader did not prevent reinforcements from reaching Hamilton, he did succeed in holding them long enough to delay the second Allied offensive.
[3] Winston S. Churchill, *op. cit.*, vol. 2, p. 492.

English acted with such singleness of purpose and alacrity. But delays were still destined to occur.

As all thoughts in English ministerial circles focused on the Dardanelles, Joffre was trying to keep the attention of the French Government fixed on the Western front. On September 1st he informed the Cabinet that his great offensive, originally scheduled for September 7th, was postponed until the 26th of the same month. He also drew up another report on the Dardanelles to urge that no troops be sent to the Eastern Mediterranean until a precise plan had been worked out. Sarrail's proposals, he pointed out, had merely considered possible landing places in Europe and Asia without arriving at any definite conclusion. He seriously questioned the wisdom of sending four divisions, arguing that if the landing force was held up he would be compelled to support it with further reinforcements, thereby weakening the home front and exposing the Allies to a crushing defeat. Joffre made it clear that in any event he could not release the requested divisions before the first week in October and suggested that in the meantime Sarrail leave to make a detailed study of the situation on the spot. Appealing to French ego Joffre declared: 'It was the English who led us to the Dardanelles. Today the abandonment of the attack would be an English defeat. Tomorrow, if we were to send reinforcements, and to claim the chief command, we should be faced, in case of failure, by a French disaster.' [4]

Joffre followed up this note by appearing before the Cabinet to give added weight to his case. He knew there were certain Ministers open to pressure and he hoped to use any split to bend the Cabinet to his will. Like many taciturn men, Joffre was capable of impressive eloquence when his deepest interests and convictions were at stake.

In his opening remarks Joffre outlined the progress of his plans for the coming offensive, contending with paralysing regularity that hope would soon dawn for the Allies. He claimed that if by misfortune his drive did not succeed he would change to a defensive strategy, but threatened to resign if pressed to detach any divisions from his front before October. The army chief promised that four divisions would be available after that time but felt that,

[4] Joffre to Millerand, September 1, 1915; *Les armées françaises dans la grand guerre*, tome 8, vol. 1, annexe no. 336.

in the light of the memorandum by the *Section d'études*, these would be insufficient to clear the passage at the Narrows. He repeated that it was indispensable that Sarrail assess the Allied position at the scene of action and return to report what could be done in the Near East. On the last point there was total agreement among the Ministers in the Cabinet.[5]

Sarrail, however, did not welcome the suggestion. Millerand in vain tried to coax him to leave for the Dardanelles. Sarrail was adamant: he would leave with the divisional reinforcements or not at all. He later wrote: 'It was the continuation of the same idea: my removal at any price; I absolutely declined the offer, desiring to remain to arrive at something; the Minister of War wanted me to leave so as to avoid a settlement. The war of attrition persisted.'[6]

On September 2nd a meeting was held at the Ministry of War between Millerand, Augagneur and Sarrail in order to determine the size and work out the basic plans of the future Army of the Orient. The following decisions were taken: (a) that the Expeditionary army sent from France be composed of four divisions; (b) that the two divisions under Bailloud join the Expeditionary army which would be concentrating at Lemnos and Mitylene; (c) that the whole French force be landed at a single place; (d) and that the navy assure the supply of stores.[7]

Any such understanding was an exercise in futility unless troops were available and ready to leave. And it was evident at the moment that Joffre was determined not to send a single man out of the country. The Government was caught between the irresistible force, Sarrail's demand for immediate satisfaction, and the immovable object, Joffre's refusal to yield. The Government's task was rendered many times more difficult by the absence of a trusted body of experts which could offer reasoned and impartial professional advice on the general conduct of the war. For want of this advice, France's wavering war policy in the summer of 1915 violated every principle of sound strategy.

From the outset Sarrail had made his position clear and he

[5] Raymond Poincaré, *op. cit.*, vol. VII, p. 79.

[6] Maurice Sarrail, *op. cit.*, p. xi.

[7] General Staff Report of the meeting of September 2, 1915; Ed 108, Marine archives.

showed no signs of wavering. It now became a simple matter as to who would give in first, the Cabinet or Joffre. The military chief could not openly flout the Government, but he could stall and play a waiting game, ready to exploit any opportunities and use them to his advantage.

In the spring of 1915 Italy aligned herself with the Entente after bargaining skilfully with both groups of belligerents. The Italians had proclaimed their neutrality in August 1914 on the ground that the terms of the Triple Alliance were specifically defensive and no longer applied after Austria attacked Serbia. The search for allies, busily pursued by the two warring coalitions as the deadlock settled in the West, placed Rome in a position of vantage. She could afford to sit back and await the highest bid. Much of the regions coveted by the Italians, namely the *terre irredente*, belonged to Austria. This might be obtained as a reward from Austria in exchange for their neutrality, or from the Entente for their active support. Under German pressure Austria agreed to some of Italy's demands. The Allies quite naturally were free to offer more. Russia was slow to give her consent for she was loath to promise Italy territory which the Southern Slavs hoped to acquire. Eventually the Italian Government, under Premier Salandra, came down on the side of the Entente. By the secret Treaty of London, signed on April 26th, it was agreed that if the Allies won the war, Italy should receive the Trentino and Tyrol up to the Brenner Pass, Trieste, Istria, part of Dalmatia, the Dodecanese and certain islands in the Adriatic. She was also promised Libya and Somaliland if France and England increased their territorial holdings in Africa; and the port of Adalia and its hinterland in Asia Minor in case Turkey was divided. Having received these generous promises the Italians declared war against Austria-Hungary on May 23rd.

A strong factor in bringing the Italians into the conflict was the fear that Turkey would collapse under the strain of the Dardanelles campaign before they could stake a claim for a portion of the Sultan's realm.[8] It was understood in Rome that, short of intervention, she would be omitted from the share-out after the

[8] W. W. Gottlieb, *op. cit.*, p. 314; Barrère (French Ambassador at Rome) to Delcassé; Italy, Box 3, fol. 11, Diplomatic archives.

liquidation of the Ottoman Empire. Well might Churchill observe in *The World Crisis* that while this was not the main objective of the Salandra Government 'the Dardanelles and Turkey were the real "motor muscle" of Italian resolve'.[9]

Both Grey and Delcassé were eager to introduce a fourth Power into the Eastern question to balance the claims of Russia and to serve as an example for Rumania and the other neutral states to follow. Sazanov, quite naturally, was loath to accept any such arrangement. He recognized that the presence of Italian troops on Turkish territory could draw several Balkan states into the war but thought that this did not justify the exorbitant price he would have to pay. He had already been forced to sacrifice South Slavic interests to Italy and saw no reason to acquiesce in the creation of an anti-Russian league. Italy's clearly stated opposition to Russian rights to annex Constantinople and the Straits was bound to complicate the relations between Petrograd and the Western Entente capitals. Since Rome had not been informed of the Straits Agreement she might later, by eliciting the support of London and Paris, demand its revision.

From the moment Italy declared war on Turkey (August 21st) [10] the French looked to the Salandra Government to substitute a contingent for the forces which they themselves could not yet provide for the Dardanelles. At the same time Delcassé defended the idea of Italian collaboration in the presence of Isvolsky, pointing out how much it would help the Dardanelles campaign and assuring that it would not threaten the existing agreements among the Allies.

By granting the Russians their principal aspirations the French, as well as the English, acquired the whip-hand over them elsewhere. Any impediment Petrograd placed in the way of Italian co-operation in the Near East was apt to jeopardize her prospects of possessing Byzantium. The firm tone of the French message had the effect of softening Sazanov's intransigence. He came forward with a compromise whereby, if the Allies undertook operations in Macedonia, the Italian Government could be invited to replace those troops leaving the Peninsula for the new theatre.[11]

[9] Winston S. Churchill, *op. cit.*, vol. 2, p. 105.

[10] Italy waited until August 28, 1916 to declare war on Germany.

[11] Paléologue to Delcassé, August 24, 1915; Italy, Box 4, fol. 11, Diplomatic archives.

The Salandra Ministry, though not excluding involvement in the Dardanelles, was inclined to favour sending an expedition to Asia Minor.[12] Occupation of the desired territory was the only solid guarantee to its incorporation within the Italian Empire. The response to this in diplomatic circles on both sides of the Channel was cool. Delcassé and Grey were highly annoyed and thought it senseless since the Treaty of London recognized Italy's right to Adalia in case of the breakup of the Ottoman Empire. They cautioned Rome against plunging into Asia Minor without previous consultation with them and strongly advised that an Italian expedition could best serve the Allied effort in the Dardanelles.[13]

As the controversy raged, the Italian Cabinet asked General Cadorna, Commander-in-Chief, to comment on the advisability of embarking on a venture in the Near East.[14] A high priest of the offensive spirit, Cadorna's strategic plan provided for the maximum number of divisions concentrated as battering rams along Austria's defensive line. He made it clear that he could not accept the withdrawal of men from the decisive theatre of war for some months to come.[15] No one felt justified in challenging the General's conviction. Italy had begun the war ill-prepared, short of heavy artillery and lacking the means to manufacture military material on a large scale, and with her treasury and stores still depleted as a result of the Libyan campaign of 1911–12. The General Staff was given about three weeks to prepare for a conflict after having based its plans on an alliance with Austria. The main advance at the opening of hostilities was along the Isonzo River, where the mountainous terrain and lack of munitions made Cadorna's task particularly difficult. By the end of the Second Battle of Isonzo (August 3rd) the Italian forces had barely eaten into the enemy

[12] French Military Attaché (at Rome) to Millerand, August 25, 1915; Italy, Box 4, fol. 11, Diplomatic archives.

[13] Bertie to Delcassé, August 28, 1915; Delcassé to Barrère, August 26, 1915; Cambon to Delcassé, August 27, 1915; Italy, Box 4, fol. 11, Diplomatic archives.

[14] French Military Attaché to Millerand, August 25, 1915; Italy, Box 4, fol. 11, Diplomatic archives.

[15] Barrère to Delcassé, August 30, 1915; Italy, Box 4, fol. 11, Diplomatic archives.

position.[16] Although the Italians were superior by more than three to one they were up against organized defences and it was apparent that to break through they must resort to siege warfare with limited objectives. For that reason Cadorna would not consider sending troops abroad while the course of events at home remained in doubt.

At this juncture Joffre entered into the picture. While on a goodwill visit to Italy in the first week of September [17] the French Commander had a long interview with Cadorna. From Cadorna he obtained a solemn pledge that no Italian troops would be sent to the Dardanelles.[18] This came as a relief to Joffre. He had been nagged by fears that if the Italians offered to bolster the Allied effort in the Dardanelles, the French Government might feel compelled to match their contribution with at least an equal number of units.

The more pressure Joffre applied to wreck the intended operation, the harder Poincaré laboured to hold it together. On September 7th the President wrote to Millerand, reporting a recent conversation he had engaged in with Gouraud. It seemed that Gouraud had no recollection of mentioning anything like ten divisions to Colonel Alexandre,[19] and, although he would not commit himself, implied that four divisions would suffice to clear the forts on the Asiatic side of the Narrows. The General persisted in the belief that it was sheer folly to leave the French troops at Cape Helles exposed to the constant shelling from Kum Kale. He estimated that for this limited enterprise, one infantry and one cavalry division would be required and stressed that these should be sent out no later than the first week of October.[20]

Millerand was prompted then to telegraph the War Office to obtain Hamilton's views on the prospects of a landing in Asia. Kitchener had indicated several days before that he supported the French plan, though in truth he could scarcely do otherwise. In a

[16] Cyril Falls, *The Great War* (New York, 1959), pp. 143-4.

[17] Barrère to Delcassé, September 6, 1915; Italy, Box 4, fol. 12, Diplomatic archives.

[18] Joffre to Wilson, September 8, 1915, Diary of Henry Wilson.

[19] He was a member of the *Section d'études*.

[20] Raymond Poincaré, *op. cit.*, vol. VII, pp. 88-9.

rare mood of optimism, especially astonishing in the light of his previous outlook concerning military activity in Asia, Kitchener maintained that an expedition made up of four divisions had a good chance of breaking the resistance of the Turks. He urged haste and absolute secrecy in order to deny the Turks time to concentrate their forces in Asia and to forestall the impending Austro-German movement against Serbia. Kitchener explained that the two English divisions, which would relieve the French corps on the Peninsula, would be withdrawn from the Western front but that these would be replaced by two fresh divisions from England.[21]

In accordance with Millerand's wishes, Kitchener signalled the Dardanelles to sound out Hamilton: 'Sarrail backed by General Bailloud is greatly in favour of the French expedition being employed independently on the Asiatic shore – Joffre greatly doubts the wisdom of this course, and Millerand requested me to ask you to state fully and confidentially for his personal information, your opinion on this matter.'[22] Hamilton, like Kitchener, had originally disapproved of the project, but he was not going to bite the hand that was about to feed him. He replied at once that under altered conditions he was not unfavourable to it.[23]

On the same day (September 7th) Millerand directed Joffre to have four divisions ready to embark at Marseilles in the first week of October.[24] Joffre maintained that, owing to his present plans, he could not spare the units in question by that date and urged that the Government reconsider carefully the findings of his appreciation of September 1st before ruling on a course of action.[25] Henry Wilson wrote in his diary on September 9th: 'Joffre has temporarily stopped the business until some proper plan of operation is drawn up. Here is the whole thing. Joffre would crush it

[21] French Military Attaché to Millerand, September 1, 2, 1915; *Les armées françaises dans la grande guerre*, tome 8, vol. 1, annexe nos. 337, 345.

[22] Kitchener to Hamilton, September 7, 1915; tel. no. 2045, War Office archives.

[23] Hamilton to Kitchener, September 7, 1915; tel. no. 2047, War Office archives.

[24] Millerand to Joffre, September 7, 1915; *Les armées françaises dans la grande guerre*, tome 8, vol. 1, annexe no. 348.

[25] *Ibid.*, annexe no. 351.

altogether if he could but he can't do more than he has done.'[26] Evidently Joffre was laying the barriers for a last-ditch stand.

In the midst of this tug-of-war the English learned through Sir John French that Joffre intended to go ahead with his offensive in the fall. French added that on no account would Joffre allow the levy of any troops from his command until the results of the attack were known. Once this was revealed, the British Government, which had assumed that the French would postpone their grand offensive on the main front in order to concentrate their resources in the Near East for a decisive push,[27] decided it was time to find out precisely the designs of Paris.[28]

On September 11th an Anglo-French conference was held at Calais. The French were represented by Millerand, Joffre and Sarrail; the English by Kitchener, Hankey, French and Wilson. The meeting got under way at 9.00 a.m. with Kitchener invited to take the chair. The first topic of business concerned the dispatch of reinforcements to the Dardanelles. Joffre rose from his seat and made an impassioned protest against denuding his front. He declared that he did not mind parting with four divisions as much as he feared that if the offensive in Asia was not immediately successful, it would necessitate more troops and munitions which he could not spare without due regard for the safety of France. Kitchener, whose exasperation had never ceased to grow, replied that he did not envisage a far-reaching commitment in Asia. The Secretary of State for War asserted that the army's role was only to help the fleet get through the Narrows, after which its task would be completed.[29]

Instead of opening up a new dialogue, these remarks passed

[26] Noted: September 9, 1915, Diary of Henry Wilson.

[27] French Military Attaché to Millerand, September 2, 1915; England, Box 70, Military archives.

[28] J. A. Spender and Cyril Asquith, *op. cit.*, vol. II, pp. 183–4; Paul Guinn, *op. cit.*, p. 96; Lord Hankey, *op. cit.*, vol. 1, p. 410.

[29] 'Lord Kitchener said he did not anticipate this. The scope of the operation was to open the Dardanelles for the fleet and he had no intention of committing himself to further operations.' Anglo-French and Allied Conferences between September 11, 1915 – November 16, 1916; CAB. 28/1.

unchallenged. It is quite obvious that the French did not comprehend the full implications of Kitchener's statement. Exactly what Kitchener was contemplating is not known but it would seem that he had given up the idea of an assault on Constantinople. Sir Henry Wilson has left an account of his private talks with Kitchener while at Calais: 'Kitchener's one idea is to get out of the mess he is in, and he said so specifically, and that there was now no intention of going to Constantinople.' [30] The British war lord was opposed to an immediate withdrawal partly because of the effect which such an admission of failure would exercise in the East and partly because he believed that it could not be carried out without appalling losses. He confided to Wilson that he would be thankful if a line could be drawn between Gaba Tepe and Maidos. From the higher ground of the Peninsula where lay the principal defences of the Narrows, it was possible to dominate the Asiatic guns and gain possession of the waterway. This appeared to be an effective means of restoring the shattered power of Russia and facilitating Allied re-embarkation when the time came.[31] Hence Kitchener was willing to leave Constantinople alone if he could link up with the Russians.[32] The sudden change of heart was occasioned by a belief that Joffre could not be counted on to supply the divisional reinforcements. Lacking the troops in England, Kitchener realized that without Joffre's co-operation a major undertaking in the Eastern Mediterranean was out of the question.

The change in policy had been decided on the spur of the moment without the strain of taking thought. Even more astonishing, it was in disharmony with the declared purpose of the Dardanelles Committee. It meant modifying the concept of the campaign, scaling-down the objective to re-opening communications with Russia. Originally the need to help Russia had been a subterfuge used by some to persuade the British Government to engage in this experiment in 'grand strategy', now by a strange twist of fate this subterfuge was to become the real aim of the campaign. Kitchener must have known that with ammunition already in short

[30] Kitchener to Wilson, September 11, 1915, Diary of Henry Wilson.
[31] Kitchener to Wilson, September 10, 11, 1915, Diary of Henry Wilson.
[32] This strange turn has not been mentioned in the other works on the campaign.

supply on the Western front, even if a sea route could be opened to the Black Sea very little could be done in the way of resuscitating the Russians. But in his mind, the idea of avoiding defeat in the East and its possible consequences overshadowed all other considerations.

Throughout the meeting Joffre made no secret of his dislike of the whole affair and refused to fix a date when it would be possible to remove the divisions from his line. It was hoped that the troops would be ready to leave on October 10th and that operations could begin around the middle of November. But nothing was definite. If the grand attack in the West succeeded the expedition to the Dardanelles would be cancelled to permit Joffre to use those troops to follow up initial gains.

Millerand wanted to reserve the supreme command of the Allied forces in the Dardanelles for Sarrail, but Kitchener objected on the grounds that Hamilton had more troops under him, greater experience and was senior in rank. Nonetheless Kitchener agreed that Sarrail could work independently in Asia but in close liaison with the English on the Peninsula.[33]

After the conference Joffre told Kitchener that the Asiatic scheme was ill-advised and that in any event it would require more than six divisions. He lashed out against Sarrail with all sorts of accusations and placed grave doubts on his fitness to command. Later Kitchener had occasion to chat with Sarrail and was not favourably impressed with him. At Hankey's suggestion, Kitchener invited Sarrail to visit the Dardanelles for several weeks but the French General politely declined, claiming that he could not absent himself from the country.[34]

It can be surmised that the results of the conference gave Joffre a good deal of satisfaction. As Sir Henry Wilson put it, even if the troops sailed from France around October 10th 'the whole thing will fall down of itself, because it will be impossible for Sarrail to land with six divisions before the end of November; beginning of December and the weather will decide the question then'.[35] Joffre had no policy for the Dardanelles since he could not make up his

[33] Anglo-French and Allied Conferences between September 11, 1915–November 16, 1916; CAB. 28/1.

[34] Lord Hankey, *op. cit.*, vol. 1, p. 411.

[35] Noted: September 11, 1915, Diary of Henry Wilson.

mind. He was torn between a desire to retain all Anglo-French troops in the West and a realization that retirement would involve the horrors of loss of life and prestige. A glimpse of his views is provided by Henry Wilson: 'I had a long talk with General Joffre about the Dardanelles. It is quite clear he is opposed to the landing in Asia Minor. He is equally opposed to a landing in Gallipoli and he thinks K's idea of sending out six divisions in order to bring the whole lot away . . . is ridiculous. . . . He agrees we are in a morass but his plan is to dig in and stick it out.' [36]

No sooner had the French Ministers been briefed on the proceedings at Calais than they were presented with a second memorandum by the *Section d'études* which urged that, owing to the importance of the approaching attack in the West, Joffre be permitted to employ all available troops until the outcome had been decided. It was conceded that the first projection calling for thirteen divisions was perhaps excessive and that six divisions might be adequate if the landing was carried out rapidly and energetically and if the plans remained unknown to the enemy. The committee did not minimize the dangers involved and assumed that the English would make another effort on the Peninsula while the French swept down on the Asiatic forts from the rear. The ultimate objective was still to occupy Constantinople, though no attention was given as to how this would be accomplished should the fleet break into the Sea of Marmora.[37]

The note did not reveal much that was not already known, but it was significant in that it was the first time that a group of experts under the aegis of G.Q.G. admitted that an operation of moderate scope in the Dardanelles had a reasonable chance to succeed. Any doubts that lingered among some members of the Cabinet as to the feasibility of an enterprise in Asia were quickly dispelled. On September 14th Millerand reminded Joffre that, in accordance with the decision reached at Calais, he was to assemble four divisions at Marseilles by October 10th.[38] Sarrail meanwhile was straining with impatience at the endless cat and mouse game

---

[36] Joffre to Wilson, September 14, 1915, Diary of Henry Wilson.

[37] 'Note on the subject of the Dardanelles', September 10, 1915; *Les armées françaises dans la grande guerre*, tome 8, vol. 1, annexe no. 354.

[38] Millerand to Joffre, September 14, 1915; *ibid.*, annexe no. 358.

between St Dominique and Chantilly. He passed the time travelling from Montauban to Paris, frequently visiting his socialist political cohorts and allegedly plotting against Joffre and the Government. There was talk in the Cabinet of creating for Sarrail a new position, *Président du Conseil supérieur de la guerre*, prestigious, but under current circumstances little more than a sinecure. It is improbable that Sarrail would have shown any enthusiasm over the doubtful compensation which this post entailed. If anything his terms had hardened during the past weeks. He now demanded as a condition for departing to the Dardanelles, 100,000 men, supreme command of the Allied force and guarantee of Italian participation. When Millerand told him that he had set his sights too high, Sarrail exclaimed angrily: 'You have merely to put me in the place of that old goat Joffre.' [39] Several days later a more subdued Sarrail consented, upon the request of the Minister of War, [40] to furnish a plan for an operation in Asia.

Before the Cabinet could sit back and await developments on the scene Jean Cruppi, a deputy, who had just returned to Paris after a visit to Russia and the Near East, made an alarming statement as to conditions on Gallipoli. Cruppi had long discussions with General Baumann [41] and several French officers and they were full of fear that, unless reinforcements arrived there shortly, the Allied force would be driven into the sea. [42]

Poincaré did not hesitate to wave the report in front of the Ministers in the hope that it would break down the barriers of listlessness and inertia. He was fast losing heart at the Cabinet's inability to make a decision and enforce it. He recognized that so long as the Government allowed itself to be checkmated by Joffre, Allied strength would continue to be siphoned away on the Western front in fruitless and costly attacks.

Although the military reasons for going to the Dardanelles still remained sound, the political inducements no longer held the same attraction since the Russians had run off with the main prize. Stamped with the old traditions of French foreign policy, Poincaré

[39] William Martin, 'Notes de guerre', September 13, 1915.
[40] Millerand to Sarrail, September 15, 1915; *Les armées françaises dans la grande guerre*, tome 8, vol. 1, annexe no. 360.
[41] French Commandant at Mudros.
[42] Raymond Poincaré, *op. cit.*, vol. VII, p. 103.

could not bring himself to accept the Straits Agreement. To hand over to Russia the most cherished possession of the Sultan's territory, after the French and English had done the hard work, did not make any sense. The President was convinced that the assurances given to Petrograd had been premature and went beyond what the Russians themselves had anticipated. He reckoned, however, that the presence of Anglo-French troops in Constantinople would compensate for the signing of the treaty. The Entente partners would be in a position to exercise a limitation of the Russian demands and could remain in possession of the Ottoman capital until satisfactory terms had been arranged with the Tsarist Government in consultation with all the interested Powers. As far as Poincaré was concerned the entry of Italy on the side of the Allies and especially the failure of the Russian forces to assist in the land operations in the Dardanelles [43] had freed the English and French from their promises to Petrograd. The President put forward his case to Lord Bertie in the expectation of winning British support. He added that, for the time being, the subject should not be brought to the attention of Petrograd as it would have a bad effect on the Russian people.[44]

Poincaré's attitude was indicative of the growing feeling not only in the Government but in many quarters of France as well as in Catholic circles.[45] On September 15th the former Minister of Foreign Affairs, Gabriel Hanotaux, a staunch Catholic, told the British Ambassador that he hoped Constantinople and the Straits would be internationalized.[46] The *Journal des débats* came out with the proposal that unless Russia co-operated more fully against

[43] The Russian troops gathered at Batum for an attack on Turkey were ultimately drawn away by more urgent needs on the Polish front.

[44] Bertie to Grey, August 27, 1915; F.O. 800/58, Grey papers; Bertie to Grey, August 26, 1915; F.O. 800/172, Bertie papers; Bertie to Grey, September 18, 1915; F.O. 800/181, Bertie papers.

[45] Vatican interest in this affair is summed up in a note to the Quai d'Orsay: 'If Constantinople were taken and the historic temple of St Sophia wrested from the Mussulmen, the Holy Father would greatly wish it to be assigned to France and thus restored to Catholic worship. . . .' G. Tabouis, *The Life of Jules Cambon* (London, 1938), pp. 293–4. See also Raymond Poincaré, *op. cit.*, vol. VI, pp. 111–12.

[46] Lord Bertie, *The Diary of Lord Bertie of Thame*, edited by Lady A. G. Lennox, vol. 1, p. 236.

Turkey, Britain and France would have to revise their position with regard to the Straits question. A number of Paris papers went so far as to suggest that Petrograd bring about Rumanian intervention by ceding a strip of Bessarabia.[47] In the latter part of October the Vatican-inspired *Corriere d'Italia* advised 'that for the diplomacy of the Triple Alliance to succeed in the Balkans, it was essential for Russia to renounce her Byzantine dreams'.[48]

In Paris, meanwhile, Millerand kept badgering Joffre to have the four divisions ready to sail early in October. Joffre, however, considered it his 'duty to protest once more'. On September 20th he produced his third document on the Dardanelles, explaining that, in view of the operations under way on the Western front, he could not promise that the divisions earmarked for the Near East would be in Marseilles on the appointed date. Joffre felt that the expedition, which was badly organized, would risk the danger of being held up and lead to a call for additional troops. He alleged that Lord Kitchener had confided to him after the Calais Conference that an Asiatic operation was full of danger and that it had been rejected by Hamilton in favour of an attack on the Peninsula. Joffre added that a fresh attempt in the Dardanelles would get the English off the hook but, in case of defeat, the responsibility and consequences would have to be borne entirely by the French.[49]

The note caused considerable dismay in the ranks of the Cabinet Ministers, for it was interpreted as a ploy on the part of Joffre to wriggle out of a promise he had twice made to them. 'You see,' cried Viviani, 'it is as I had told you. The Dardanelles Operation will not materialize. G.Q.G. will not allow it because Sarrail is to command.'[50]

On September 23rd, Sarrail submitted his report to Millerand. He proposed to establish separate bases at Lemnos, Mitylene and perhaps later at Kum Kale. The general landing of the French

[47] Isvolsky to Sazanov, October 12, 1915; *Constantinople et les détroits*, vol. 1, p. 234.

[48] W. W. Gottlieb, *op. cit.*, p. 130.

[49] Joffre to Millerand, September 20, 1915; *Les armeés françaises dans la grande guerre*, tome 8, vol. 1, annexe no. 365.

[50] Raymond Poincaré, *op. cit.*, vol. VII, p. 111.

troops would take place in the Bay of Yuk Yesi where the beach offered ample room for manœuvre. While the French forces pushed beyong Kum Kale to occupy Chanak and Cherdak, Sarrail deemed it indispensable that the English mount an attack on the Peninsula, claiming that without control of both shores the fleet could not get through.[51]

But the hour for Constantinople had passed. In the late summer of 1915 General Falkenhayn, Chief of the German General Staff, decided that in order to keep Turkey in the war he must dispose of Serbia and open a direct route to the Ottoman capital. To collect a force for the task without seriously weakening the German line in the West, Bulgarian assistance was vital.

The imminence of a German-Bulgarian pact spurred the Allies on to desperate efforts to coax Bulgaria over to their side, or at least to induce her to remain neutral. Bulgaria's attitude had not changed since the opening days of the conflict. She wavered back and forth in tantalizing fashion, biding the time when her services would command a higher price. The Allies hesitated to promise territory belonging to a neutral state (Greece) and to an ally (Serbia) and Sofia was unwilling to accept a promise of Turkish regions contingent on their victory. The Germans, however, were in a position to make good their commitments.

The lure of instant territorial gains together with the belief that the Russian disasters and the English failure at Suvla Bay presaged the ultimate triumph of the Central Powers prompted Bulgaria to sign a military convention with Germany and Austria on September 6th.[52] In return for her pledge to declare war on Serbia, Bulgaria was guaranteed Serbian Macedonia, a loan of 200,000,000 francs and restoration of the land lost to Greece and Rumania in 1913 – should these countries align themselves against the Central Powers. On September 23rd Sofia decreed general mobilization. The imminent threat of being overrun led the Serbian Government to make a frantic appeal to London and Paris for aid. Almost at the same hour Premier Venizelos, who was back in office again,

[51] Sarrail to Millerand, September 21, 1915; *Les armées françaises dans la grande guerre*, tome 8, vol. 1, annexe no. 366.

[52] An agreement with Turkey on September 3rd had given Bulgaria a strip of Thrace up to the Enos–Midia line.

asked for Allied assistance to enable Greece to honour her treaty obligations with Serbia.[53]

As the Ministers gathered in Paris, in the light of this sudden development, they were faced with a difficult decision. A large-scale offensive was pending on the Western front and until the result of that attack was known it would be impossible to divert from France any substantial detachments for Serbia. France's quota of 75,000 men could be met but this would mean abandoning the Dardanelles venture.

Briand led the fight in pressing for a Balkan landing, insisting that the new military situation created a need to undertake new objectives. Events in the Dardanelles had shown that it was hardly possible to repair errors committed in the original conception. A fresh attack on positions which had proved to be impregnable would end in heavy losses with nothing achieved. On the other hand there was much to be said for an expedition to link up with the Serbs. Here was the surest means to frustrate Germany's dream of establishing a *Mitteleuropa* by barring the road to Constantinople, while the French Army could be counted on at a future date to assist French colonial ambitions in the Eastern Mediterranean. Here again lay the key in uniting the Balkan states in a common front against Turkey and Austria.

The Cabinet grasped the plan as a solution to all its problems. The lone dissenter was Delcassé, who questioned the wisdom of embarking upon so uncertain an adventure which was apt to lead to a futile dissipation of manpower and material resources. But by this time there was growing mistrust of Delcassé's judgment and his arguments had lost all power to convince.[54] Poincaré was apparently converted to the merits of a Balkan scheme, despite his earlier attitude in support of a renewed offensive in the Darda-

---

[53] This military convention applied in case either state was attacked by Bulgaria. Under the terms of the agreement Serbia had to provide 150,000 men to defend her eastern frontier. She could not do so since she had to protect her northern front and Venizelos refused to take the field against Bulgaria unless supported by an outside force of equivalent strength. Lord Hankey, *op. cit.*, vol. 1, p. 417; Alan Palmer, *op. cit.*, pp. 31–2; Paul Guinn, *op. cit.*, pp. 97–100.

[54] Delcassé's failure to gain Bulgaria was the final disaster in a series of diplomatic checks. See next chapter in this text.

nelles. The prospect of disengagement from an inconvenient commitment to Russia, coupled with a report from General Bailloud alleging that Hamilton had admitted to him that nothing more could be done in the Dardanelles, had obviously tempered Poincaré's enthusiasm. On September 23rd the Cabinet agreed to send an expedition to the Balkans and asked Millerand to study the possibility of a landing either at Salonika or Dedeagatch.[55]

More than Briand's forceful oratory is needed to account for the precipitate decision to leap into the Balkan theatre. Weighing heavily upon the Cabinet was the feeling that abandonment of Serbia would be fatal to Allied prestige throughout the world. The helplessness of four great Powers to save from destruction a small state that relied on their protection would deter any neutral from joining the Entente. Then also Serbia's stubborn and gallant resistance had inspired overwhelming sympathy in France and public opinion was already demanding that some form of assistance be rendered to their ally. Lastly there was anxiety in ministerial circles of a possible Parliamentary revolt over their inaction in dealing with a potentially dangerous situation. It cannot be said that the Government had been short of time for a decision on the Serbian question. Since mid-1915 the Parliamentary Commissions had repeatedly warned the civil leaders to take measures against an impending Austro-German attack on Serbia: in every instance they were put off by assurances that any such threat was premature.[56] If the Parliamentarians found out that the Cabinet had been taken by surprise and not the slightest preparation had been made to block the German offensive, their confidence in its capacity to conduct the war would vanish. It was obviously the hope of the Government that the hurried revival of the project of a Balkan base might yet set everything right.[57]

[55] Raymond Poincaré, *op. cit.*, vol. VII, p. 117. Since Serbia had no sea-coast, Salonika and Dedeagatch were the only practical routes by which Allied assistance could reach her.

[56] See especially the scathing attack levelled by Georges Leygues (President of the Chamber Commission on Foreign Affairs) at the Government for misleading Parliament and for taking no timely action; October 19, 1915, C 7488 dossier 104, Foreign Affairs Commission, National archives.

[57] The fact that Alan Palmer's work on Salonika makes no attempt to examine the underlying causes for the expedition, much less assess its practicability, is beyond comprehension.

The sudden shift of attitude was striking evidence of how completely the French had withdrawn their confidence in the need or efficacy of the Dardanelles adventure. Yet to drift into a new campaign without definite objectives, adequate preparations and a precise plan of action, after having dismissed the operation in the Dardanelles as a lamentable succession of improvisations, revealed a shocking lapse of judgment. The proposed drive in the Balkans was another example of politicians determining the benefits to be derived from successful action before considering the means to achieve that victory.

It needs no rhetoric to describe the difficulties that lay ahead and no special military training to understand them. Sir William Robertson, who made a tour of the Balkans in 1906, observed 'that of all the countries in Europe none was less defensively stronger, and therefore none less favourable to the offensive, than the Balkan Peninsula'.[58] The terrain was mountainous, the few roads that existed were in poor condition and there was no room for wide manoeuvring. The only railway connecting Salonika (the best available route) with the interior had a single line of rail and in case of war it could easily be demolished. It would be almost impossible to supply an army any distance from Salonika.

The second difficulty was that the element of surprise was unattainable. By using the utmost caution and by sheer good fortune, secrecy might be maintained to a point, but once the troops landed there could be no further concealment. Greece was neutral and dozens of German agents milled about the city port, complete with notebooks in which to record details of units, their equipment and their probable destination. It would take several months before the Allies were ready to march inland and by then the enemy would know what to expect.

This introduced a third problem. Informed as to the intention

---

[58] Field-Marshal Sir William Robertson, *Soldiers and Statesmen, 1914–1918* (London, 1926), vol. II, p. 88. This view was shared by General von Falkenhayn, then Chief of the German General Staff, who maintained that with the Germans holding the high ground in the Balkans, a thrust from the direction of Salonika would be extremely disadvantageous. General Erich von Falkenhayn, *General Headquarters 1914–1916 and its Critical Decisions* (London, 1919), pp. 190–2.

and imminence of Allied movements, the Germans would have ample time to counteract this strategy. Unlike the circumstances at the Dardanelles where the Turks had to cling to their trenches or open the way to Constantinople, the Germans did not need to hold any ground south of the Danube. They could attack immediately or withdraw north and await a more favourable opportunity. As the Allies marched deeper into the interior they would have to extend their lines of communications, inviting the risk of being cut off from their base. From a military point of view, the Germans were clearly in a superior position.[59]

It is quite evident that Briand and his colleagues had rushed into this imbroglio without being aware of the great military risks involved. After all, what did they know about logistics or the obstacles imposed by geography to the movement of armies? These were questions that concerned the military specialists in the *Section d'études* or the Ministry of War. The experts may have harboured serious misgivings about the projected venture in the Balkans but they did not dare challenge the official army view. Personal initiative and independent thought were anathema to the High Command. With few exceptions the reports the military authorities framed were remarkably consistent with the attitude of the Commander-in-Chief.

Traditionally disdainful of side-shows, Joffre shuddered at the prospect of creating a new front in the East.[60] This would have been the proper moment for him to counter the proposals of the Government with the same resistance he had shown in preventing the Asiatic landing from materializing. But Joffre, in desperate need of enhancing his dwindling popularity, laid aside his personal feelings and accepted the Government's decision. Still the army chief found the Balkan diversion less objectionable than the Dardanelles campaign, for at least it would serve to draw German reserves from the main front. He suggested that the new expedition be composed of units from Gallipoli since he could spare none from France and also to give the impression that this was a 'manœuvre and not a withdrawal'. Joffre observed that the main

[59] Gen. C. R. Ballard, *Kitchener* (New York, 1930), pp. 333–5.

[60] Esher to Kitchener, October 7, 1915; vol. V, Esher papers; Esher to Kitchener, October 3, 1915; P.R.O. 30/57/59, Kitchener papers.

purpose of the Dardanelles operation was to open the sea route to Russia, but having failed in this attempt, it was necessary to maintain communications with Salonika and the Danube.[61]

The acquiescence of Joffre was the point of final decision. The French had left the region of discussion, of balancing the pros and cons and were ready to set their plans in motion. Their reckoning, however, was based on the assumption that London would move in the same direction.

Across the Channel the English, already straining every nerve to meet the needs of their various fronts, were far less in a hurry to overreach themselves. Kitchener had no surplus troops on hand and none could be drawn from France until the end of the month. As a last resort drafts could be obtained from Hamilton's camp but only at the expense of evacuating Suvla. Kitchener saw no immediate threat to Egypt even if Serbia fell [62] and, as he was still fuming over the collapse of the intended Asiatic landing, his first instinct was to wait upon events. But nothing short of swift action would satisfy Paris. Rather than risk a quarrel with the French, Kitchener relented and agreed to supply England's portion (75,000) of troops.[63]

Kitchener had no option but to turn to Hamilton for the necessary troops. However, Hamilton, seconded by de Robeck, pleaded against retirement from Suvla, claiming that such a course would lead to disastrous consequences. Hamilton's fear of a possible withdrawal from the entire Peninsula was increased upon the receipt of a message from General Bailloud on September 25th that Paris had instructed him to prepare one of the French divisions at Cape Helles for service elsewhere.[64] There was no indication of the destination of the troops nor reason for their diversion. During the night Hamilton received a cable from the War Office, explaining the ramifications of Bulgarian mobilization

[61] Joffre to Millerand, September 24, 1915; *Les armées françaises dans la grande guerre*, tome 8, vol. 2, annexe no. 43 (official military documents relating to the Salonika expedition).

[62] Brig.-Gen. John Charteris, *op. cit.*, p. 120.

[63] Lord Hankey, *op. cit.*, vol. 1, pp. 417–18; Paul Guinn, *op. cit.*, pp. 97–101.

[64] Hamilton to Kitchener, September 25, 1915; tel. no. 2204, War Office archives.

and commanding him to arrange the dispatch to Salonika of two English divisions and one French division or brigade. The British General replied that he could spare the 10th and 53rd divisions and no more than a French brigade, otherwise he could not possibly hold the line at Suvla. No sooner had the telegram left than Bailloud forwarded another notice, saying he had been directed to concentrate a French division at Mudros. Hamilton answered that as he had received no such order and as his own instructions were specific he could not permit the departure of any troops from the Peninsula.[65] A directive from London soon put an end to the controversy. Hamilton was to assemble the 10th division at Mudros and to alert the 53rd division until it was known whether the French planned to send a brigade or a division.

Relations between Hamilton and Bailloud, seldom on a cordial basis, were strained by the events of the last week of September. From the very beginning Hamilton had taken a poor view of Bailloud, thinking that he was incompetent and that he had no stomach for war. He resented the French General acting independently of him so that he was never fully aware of what was happening. For his part Bailloud could not understand why he should be faulted for using caution and for clearing his plans in advance with the Ministry of War as he was supposed to do. He considered Hamilton to be reckless and stubborn and questioned his competence. By this time Bailloud had become weary of the petty bickering with Hamilton, doubly irritating because of his conviction of the futility of persisting in the face of an immovable enemy, and looked forward to the prospect of leaving with the French division, in the mistaken belief that he was to assume charge of the land operations in the new theatre.

On September 30th Kitchener asked Hamilton to corroborate Bailloud's claim that the remaining French division at Cape Helles could resist any attack on its line.[66] Hamilton could no

[65] Hamilton to Kitchener, September 27, 1915; tel. no. 2216, War Office archives.

[66] Kitchener to Hamilton, September 30, 1915; tel. no. 2270, War Office archives. The suggestion does not appear to have come from Bailloud but from Millerand himself. See *Les armées françaises dans la grande guerre*, tome 8, vol. 1, annexe no. 367.

longer suppress his rage. He concluded that Bailloud had fed false information to Paris in order to suit his own ends: 'He is perfidious and determined to play entirely for his own hand the moment a cloud shows above the horizon.' Hamilton complained to Kitchener that Balloud had 'leaped at the prospect of getting away from a position which I have had the greatest difficulty in persuading him to hold with two divisions, and which he now thinks can be held with one division, comprised largely of unreliable black troops; this is startling enough to need no comment. If you want to get at his real opinion, suggest that he stays here with one division while Brulard [67] goes to Salonika.' [68]

Back in Paris, meanwhile, Millerand informed Sarrail of the new destination of the Army of the Orient and asked him to draw up a note on the subject of French intervention in the Balkans. The likelihood of more useful employment dictated the results of Sarrail's memorandum of October 3rd. He warned that retirement from Gallipoli would not only cause irreparable damage to French prestige throughout the Moslem world, but would also liberate a large part of the Turkish Army which could be used in another theatre against the Allies. He indicated, however, that as the operation was the 'Brain Child' of the English, the responsibility for sustaining it should rest with them. Sarrail then touched on the advisability of mounting an offensive in the direction of Sofia and fixed the number of French divisions at three or four, if any important objectives were to be attained. He added that in order to avoid complications the English force should be subordinated to the French General. [69] The paper left little doubt as to who should inherit the post of Supreme Commander. Within hours the Government responded by appointing Sarrail Commander-in-Chief of the French Army detailed for Salonika. The purpose of the expedition was to maintain communications between Salonika and Serbia and to co-operate with the Serbians

[67] Second in command.

[68] Hamilton to Kitchener, October 1, 1915; tel. no. 2274, War Office archives.

[69] 'Note on the subject of French intervention in the Balkans', Sarrail to Millerand, October 3 (erroneously listed as the 2nd in the French official account), 1915; Les armées françaises dans la grande guerre, tome 8, vol. 2, annexe no. 96.

in fighting their enemies.[70] To say that Sarrail's orders were vague would be an understatement.

On October 5th an Anglo-French Conference was held at Calais to determine the number of troops to be provided by both sides for the operations in the Balkans. The French and the English each agreed to furnish 64,000 men, thus falling short by some 20,000 of the number promised. The difference was to be made up at a later date but it was understood that the troops would not be drawn from Gallipoli. In addition arrangements were made by the two fleets for the transport of troops but no decision could be reached with regard to the nature of the operations. The French had directed General Bailloud, who at the time was in the process of disembarking, to advance to the Serbian town of Nish. The English, however, were unwilling to travel through difficult mountainous country unless the Greeks agreed to join in the march.[71] This is how matters stood when the meeting came to a close.[72]

During the course of the day Sarrail called on Delcassé with the view to learning the exact aim of his mission. Unable to get clarification from the Quai d'Orsay, the General visited Poincaré, but here too received no help.[73] Sarrail's political admirers rallied around him and advised him not to leave the country. Léon Blum, chief of the cabinet of the Ministry of Public Works, recommended an exchange of posts between Sarrail and General Franchet d'Espèrey.[74] Paul Benazet, a deputy, warned Sarrail not to hurl himself into the 'Oriental wasp nest'. Even Georges Clemenceau got into the act and made it clear to Sarrail that he

[70] Millerand to Sarrail, October 3, 1915; *ibid.*, annexe no. 100. In the official account the date is given as the 2nd but it is a misprint.

[71] The Greek King had overruled Venizelos, holding that the treaty with Serbia applied only to a purely Balkan conflict. As a result Venizelos resigned on October 5th.

[72] Anglo-French and Allied Conference between September 11, 1915 – November 16, 1916; CAB 28/1; Raymond Poincaré, *op. cit.*, vol. VII, p. 158–9; *Les armées françaises dans la grande guerre*, tome 8, vol. 2, annexe no. 108.

[73] Maurice Sarrail, *op. cit.*, p. xv.

[74] As already shown he had been one of the few French generals to advocate that the war be carried to the Danube once the deadlock settled over the Western front. He alone among the French generals knew the terrain in the Balkans.

could still change his mind. 'The Tiger' was convinced that the Allied front in the East would never come off because the French had no available troops and the English were unlikely to support such a mad scheme.[75]

But Sarrail had wearied of inactivity and wanted to leave. Under the present conditions he could do nothing more by remaining in the country. Sooner or later the ineffectiveness of Joffre's methods would become apparent and when his friends gained control of Government he would almost certainly be recalled to save the homeland. In the interval he had to keep his name before the public by an occasional spirited victory. Of course, the General was very sensitive about keeping his prestige intact and did not need to be reminded to avoid taking unnecessary chances. Moreover, he was careful to prepare the ground in advance. In public conversations he often created a scene, protesting: 'They are sending me to be slaughtered.' If he experienced unforeseen hardships his high hopes would not necessarily be dashed as long as he could say, 'I told you so'. On the other hand if he was able to overcome all obstacles and return triumphant he would add immeasurable glory to his name.[76] Sarrail's version of the events does not correspond with the above account. He claimed that he accepted the assignment so that 'it might not be said that I had evaded a most disgraceful task' in spite of the unpromising outlook: 'I did not have the requested reinforcements; I did not have a supply chief, having been denied the one that I had demanded; graver yet, I still had no directive.'[77] Such selflessness was hardly in keeping with Sarrail's past behaviour.

Sarrail's departure on October 7th served to rule out any possibility of meeting Hamilton's demands for reinforcements. Dragged into a new undertaking the English also were confronted with the prospect of fighting alone in the Dardanelles. They had barely managed to support two theatres of operations; they certainly could not sustain three. The end of the Dardanelles adventure was clearly in sight.

[75] Paul Coblentz, *op. cit.*, p. 108; Maurice Sarrail, *Mon commandement en Orient*, p. xiv; J. C. King, *op. cit.*, pp. 80–1.

[76] Léopold Marcellin, *op cit.*, vol. 1, p. 100; Gabriel Terrail, *op. cit.*, pp. 9–13.

[77] Maurice Sarrail, *op. cit.*, p. xv.

Chapter 10

THE END OF THE ADVENTURE

'In politics you must never retreat, never retrace your steps, never admit a mistake – otherwise you are discredited. If you make a mistake, you must persevere – that will put you in the right.'
Napoleon.

'I asked my colleagues to picture the situation . . . a moment must come when a *sauve-qui-peut* takes place and when a disorganized crowd will press in despairing tumult on to the shore and into the boats. Shells will be falling and bullets ploughing their way into this mass of humanity. . . . Conceive the crowding into the boats of thousands of half crazy men, the swamping of craft, the nocturnal panic, the agony of the wounded, the hecatombs of the slain. . . . It requires no imagination to create a scene that, when it is told, will be burned into the hearts and consciences of the British people for generations to come. What will they say of those who have brought about this supreme and hideous disaster?'
Lord Curzon, 1915

'Honourable retreats, are . . . no ways inferior to brave charges, as having less of a fortune, more of discipline, and as much valour.'
Lord Bacon

In the first week of October, in the heat of the Balkan controversy, the English had to decide whether they should concentrate in France or extend their commitment in the Near East. The grand offensive was an admitted failure and in view of the French promise to send troops to Serbia a renewed effort on the Western front was not likely for at least three months. This narrowed the choice down to Gallipoli or Salonika. While Lloyd George, Carson and the Unionist leaders urged that a Salonika expedition be formed, Asquith, Balfour, Curzon and notably Churchill were hopeful that reinforcements could be sent to the Peninsula for one final determined push. With such forceful characters pulling in

206

opposite directions the very life of the Government seemed threatened.

The conflict-torn Dardanelles Committee dropped the entire question in the lap of the War Office and Admiralty Staffs on October 6th. Reporting three days later the combined Staffs deprecated sending more troops to Salonika since it was too late to save Serbia. Instead they urged that a decision be sought in France with all possible forces but, if this was unacceptable, advised a fresh assault in Gallipoli. The advocates of the Salonika campaign, however, were not disposed to follow this suggestion. To fend off a rupture Asquith proposed sending 150,000 troops to Egypt as soon as these could be spared from France and decide at a subsequent date in which theatre they would be used. A General would be specially appointed to select the most advantageous place for the troops to operate in.[1] On October 12th Kitchener asked Hamilton for an estimate of the probable losses in case of an evacuation of the Peninsula. When Hamilton replied that he might lose half his force the Dardanelles Committee ordered his recall at once. His last defeat in August coupled with military and civilian criticism of his competence had led to a growing mistrust of his judgment. General Monro was set from France to replace Hamilton and was instructed to report back to the Government 'fully and frankly' on the military situation in Gallipoli.[2]

The change of command in the Dardanelles coincided with the break in the Balkan dam. On October 11th Bulgarian troops clashed with Serbian units and two days later each side declared war on the other. On October 13th the Bulgarians also clashed with French forces and by the 17th both Paris and London had declared war on Bulgaria. Greece and Rumania, however, steadfastly refused to exchange their position of neutrality for the dangers involved in active participation.

On October 22nd the Bulgarians advanced across the railway south of Uskub, severing the communications of the Serbian

---

[1] Sir Edward Carson resigned in protest, convinced that the delay would mean the ruin of Serbia.

[2] Lord Hankey, *op. cit.*, vol. 1, pp. 428–31; Robert Blake, *op. cit.*, pp. 266–7; Paul Guinn, *op. cit.*, pp. 103–4; *Final Report of the Dardanelles Commission*, p. 53; Brig.-Gen. C. F. Aspinall-Oglander, *Military Operations: Gallipoli*, vol. II, pp. 381–6.

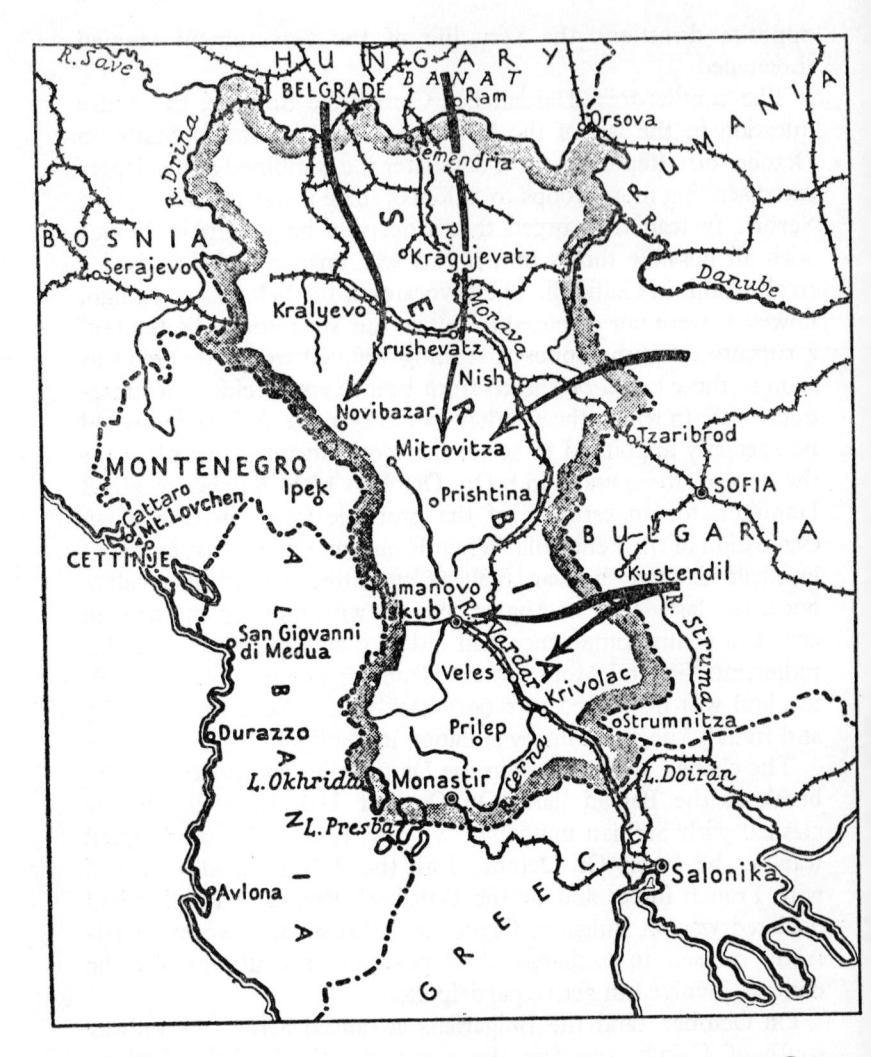

5. Serbia overwhelmed. The direction of the arrows refers to the Austro-German attack in conjunction with Bulgaria in October 1915.

Army with Salonika. Consequently Paris directed Sarrail [3] to march inland to join hands with the Serbs, but the English were unwilling to follow as long as the Greeks hesitated to take the field.[4] An Anglo-French military conference held at Chantilly on October 27th failed to resolve the impasse. Joffre was so upset over the results that he crossed the Channel to London to deliver a personal plea. He intimated that a British refusal to join the French in sending reinforcements to Salonika would place his position as well as that of the Alliance in grave jeopardy. Confronted by what Churchill termed 'this outrageous threat' the British Government agreed to co-operate on the understanding that if it proved impossible to reopen and maintain contact with the Serbian army, the Anglo-French force would be withdrawn.[5]

Joffre returned to Paris to find that a new administration was in office. The fall of Viviani's ministry had not been unexpected. Trouble had been brewing ever since Delcassé had fallen out with the Government's Balkan policy.

In the very beginning the Foreign Minister had stood against the opening of a new front in the Balkans but had been brought around to the idea when it was pointed out that, with the Greeks, Russians and possibly Italians providing troops, only a token force would be taken from the West. But the expected aid never came through. Greece clung to its neutral status and neither Russia nor Italy would agree to provide any troops. Alarmed at the prospect

---

[3] Sarrail arrived at Salonika on October 12 and took charge of the single French division (the only one to have landed in Greece thus far). The English division, acting independently, was under the command of General Mahon.

[4] The situation with regard to Greece was indeed unusual. The French and British had been invited to land at Salonika by Premier Venizelos who was subsequently forced to resign. This seemed to cancel the invitation but the Allies went ahead as if nothing had changed. They were unwelcome guests in Greece, but King Constantine did not dare protest too loudly.

[5] Cyril Falls, *Military Operations: Macedonia*, vol. 1, pp. 44–5; Sir Llewellyn Woodward, *op. cit.*, pp. 90–1; Philip Magnus, *op. cit.*, p. 358; Brig.-Gen. C. F. Aspinall-Oglander, *Military Operations: Gallipoli*, vol. II, pp. 397–8; Winston S. Churchill, *op. cit.*, vol. 2, pp. 504–6; Lord Hankey, *op. cit.*, vol. 1, pp. 433–4; Minutes of the Dardanelles Committee meetings of October 29–30, 1915; CAB 42/4.

of having to weaken the French line on the Western front, Delcassé began to oppose the sending of any more troops to Greece. His pleas were to no avail. One mistake after another had lowered his prestige and weakened his influence and there were some in the Cabinet who felt that his usefulness had been exhausted.

Except for Italy's entry into the war, Delcassé did not have much reason to boast of his achievement in 1915. In spite of everything his office had done there was still a divergence over military strategy in the Allied camp. To avoid a breach with the Russians, Delcassé had consented to their annexation of Constantinople and the Straits, an act made more unpopular in France by the conviction that it had driven Greece, Bulgaria and Rumania away from the Entente and by Petrograd's refusal to co-operate either in the Balkans or in the Dardanelles. His dealings with the Balkan states had come to a disastrous end. It was claimed that by not offering the right inducements at the proper time Rumanian assistance had been lost. Having earmarked Bulgaria as the main target of his diplomacy, Delcassé had gone to extraordinary lengths to win her over, ignoring the advice of his colleagues not to place too much reliance on King Ferdinand's promises. His desire to gratify Bulgaria, he was reproached, had led to the sacrifice of the interests of Serbia and Greece, thus discouraging the latter's intervention.

Towards the second half of 1915 Delcassé's health began to fail. Moreover, he was sick at heart over the possible fate that awaited his aviator son, shot down and captured by the Germans.[6] Constantly at loggerheads with his colleagues over the Salonika expedition, shaken by his diplomatic setbacks, ill and worried, the daily duties of his office became unbearable. Finally on October 12th Delcassé tendered his resignation, overriding the protest of Poincaré who wanted him to remain at the Quai d'Orsay in order to uphold French prestige among the Allies.[7]

---

[6] The name Delcassé was anathema in Germany.

[7] Charles W. Porter, *op. cit.*, pp. 330–4; A. Neton, *Delcassé* (Paris, 1952), p. 423; Raymond Poincaré, *op. cit.*, vol. VII, pp. 175–6; Gordon Wright, *Raymond Poincaré and the French Presidency* (Stanford University Press, 1942), pp. 157–8; C. J. Smith, *op. cit.*, pp. 341–3; Henri Leyret, 'Delcassé parle', *Revue des deux mondes*, tome 41, 15 septembre 1937, pp. 346–81; William Martin, 'Notes de guerre', October 13, 1915.

The first rumblings in the Cabinet 'let loose all the complaints and ambitions which had been accumulating for a year'. Viviani met the emergency by assuming the portfolio of Foreign Affairs and by attempting to reshuffle his Ministry, but the announcement that Joffre's gigantic drive in the West had faltered brought matters to a head. The endless and calamitous loss of life, for no apparent gain, produced a spirit of disillusionment which reacted on the French High Command. Defeatism was in the air. Beneath this military bungling the fabric of the French nation was slowly being torn apart. France was already straining to make good her losses and could not continue at the present pace very much longer. There had to be a change in war policy. But how could this be effected? Since the start of the conflict Joffre had been at liberty to manage the war as he pleased. Cloistered in the small town of Chantilly he struck back at those who sought to diminish his authority and dismissed with disdain and outrage any advice which the government might have to proffer. Such methods would have been tolerated, much as they infuriated the politicians, had they brought victory. But the 'nibbling' action throughout 1915 had been devoid of any tangible results, except that it had consumed enormous manpower resources, and the laurels that Joffre had won at the Marne were rapidly receding into the pages of history.

The despair of the nation found expression in unrelenting attacks on the Government. The parliamentarians freely castigated the lack of grip in the direction of the war, pointed to the high casualty lists and ridiculed the optimistic predictions of the Government. It was felt that the Viviani Ministry was handicapped in the vigorous prosecution of the war by allowing G.Q.G. too much independence. If the country was to fight on to victory leaders with new ideas were needed, who would maintain close supervision over the army.

Responding to demands for a full account of the Government's Balkan policy, Viviani summoned up enough courage to confront the Chamber in mid-October. A vote of confidence was passed by 372 to 9 with 150 abstentions. But this was not so much a manifestation of faith in his leadership as it was a desire to present a façade of political harmony to the watching world. In fact, feeling against Viviani in the Chamber ran high. Off the record, even some of his partisans had joined the chorus of cries of 'Away with you'. As the violent scenes in Parliament persisted Viviani reluctantly concluded that his days were numbered. On October 25th he called on the President to tell him that he could no longer continue in office.

After accepting Viviani's resignation, Poincaré decided to entrust the formation of a new ministry to the outgoing Minister of Justice, Aristide Briand, a durable and experienced politician who had the ability to reconcile persons of widely different beliefs and to retain their friendship and respect. Briand went to work assigning the various portfolios, retaining some of the former incumbents and keeping for himself the Ministry of Foreign Affairs. The difficult task of finding a suitable replacement for Alexandre Millerand was exacerbated by the suggestion of King George that his presence in the Government was desirable in the interests of Anglo-French harmony.[8] The much-maligned Millerand was considered 'dead-weight' and an obvious liability to any ministry. To assume the duties at St Dominique, Briand's choice fell on General Galliéni. The old soldier did not want the post but an appeal to his sense of patriotism overcame his reluctance. Stubborn, authoritative, inarticulate and tactless, he was nonetheless a man of action with strength of character. His arrival at the Ministry of War was likely to create a new phase in the relationship between G.Q.G. and the Government.[9] In another important change Augagneur was dropped in favour of the highly-regarded Admiral Lacaze at the Ministry of Marine. The new

[8] Acting on the advice of Lord Esher the King asked Poincaré to intercede on behalf of Millerand. The President, who was known to interfere in the selection of ministers (see Gordon Wright, *op. cit.*, p. 144) had already made up his mind that as Millerand was the main cause of friction 'both between cabinet and legislature and between cabinet and president' his elimination was in order. He replied to the British Monarch that regretfully Millerand could not be included in the new cabinet. Esher to King George, October 23, 1915; King George to Esher, October 25, 1915; vol. 5, Letters and Memoranda, Esher papers.

[9] The activity behind the scenes with regard to Galliéni's appointment to the Ministry of War is explained in P. B. Gheusi, *Guerre et théâtre, 1914–1918* (Paris, 1919), p. 229; Marius-Ary Leblond, *op. cit.*, vol. 1, pp. 87–9; and Pierre Lyautey, *Galliéni* (Paris, 1959), p. 274.

Government[10] was slightly more to the right than the previous one, but it was not expected to produce any radical changes in the conduct of state affairs.[11] Briand himself was a stronger personality than Viviani; his high statesmanship, composure, judgment and resourcefulness would bring new lustre to the office of the national leader. His independence of behaviour was shown in his unceasing condemnation, before it became fashionable to advocate eccentric strategies, of the policy of concentration on the Western front. More than any other politician in the country, Briand was identified with the adventure in the Balkans. His political survival now depended on that policy being carried through.

Shortly after Monro replaced Hamilton, a new element was introduced into the Dardanelles campaign by an aggressive coterie of naval officers who pressed for a resumption of maritime activity in the Straits. The moving spirit in this group was Roger Keyes. Admiral de Robeck, remaining unconvinced that ships could produce decisive results, nevertheless allowed his chief of staff to plead his case personally to the Admiralty. Keyes arrived in

[10] Consistent with the principle of the 'Sacred Union' the Cabinet was shaped on a broad base and included: Aristide Briand (Prime Minister and Minister of Foreign Affairs), René Viviani (Minister of Justice), General Galliéni (Minister of War), Admiral Lacaze (Minister of Marine), Alexandre Ribot (Minister of Finance), Louis Malvy (Minister of Interior), Paul Painlevé (Minister of Public Instruction), Etienne Clémentel (Minister of Commerce and Industry), Jules Méline (Minister of Agriculture), Marcel Sembat (Minister of Public Works), Albert Métin (Minister of Labour), Gaston Doumergue (Minister of Colonies) and five ministers without portfolio, Charles de Freycinet, Léon Bourgeois, Emile Combes, Jules Guesde and Denys Cochin. The newly created position of Under-Secretary of State for Munitions remained in the hands of Albert Thomas.

[11] Lacking the personal testimony of the main participants, French historians have found it difficult to reconstruct a detailed picture of the political crisis. Bits and pieces of information may be gleaned from the following sources: Georges Suarez, *op. cit.*, vol. III, pp. 164–72; Georges Bonnefous, *Histoire politique de la troisième république: la grande guerre 1914–1918* (Paris, 1957), vol. II, pp. 93–5; Marcel Laurent, *Nos gouvernements de guerre* (Paris, 1920), pp. 44–5; Raymond Poincaré, *op. cit.*, vol. VII, pp. 197–211, Gordon Wright, *op. cit.*, pp. 159–62; Michel Corday, *The Paris Front* (New York, 1934), p. 115; Charles Benoist, *Souvenirs* (Paris, 1934), vol. III, p. 281; Emile Herbillon, *op. cit.*, vol. 1, pp. 195–6; William Martin, 'Notes de guerre', October 25, 1915.

London on October 28th and wasted no time in laying his scheme before the proper authorities. Balfour and Sir Henry Jackson, the First Sea Lord, were rather well disposed to a naval strike if the army could be counted on to lend a hand. This condition all but killed the naval project. Kitchener had already promised the French to co-operate at Salonika and presumably it meant sending all available troops to the Balkans. At any rate nothing final could be decided until General Monro made his report.

Monro landed at Mudros on October 28th and took charge of the Expeditionary Force. Since the beginning of the war he had been fighting in France and, like all the other 'Westerners', did not believe in 'side shows'. It cannot be said that he came with an open mind. He spent about six hours inspecting the three fronts and conferring with the local commanders and then wrote a supposedly conclusive appreciation: 'It is my opinion that another attempt to carry the Turkish lines would not offer any hope of success. . . . On purely military grounds . . . I recommend the evacuation of the Peninsula.' [12]

Kitchener was so dismayed by the report that he refused to accept it. He had just been informed of Keyes's plan and was hopeful that this option might be grasped. On November 3rd the new War Committee [13] convened to consider the future of the Dardanelles expedition. It was decided in the end to postpone the evil day of reckoning. Lord Kitchener was to proceed to the Near East to survey the scene and to report upon the best policy. The next day Balfour told Kitchener that the naval attack would be sanctioned only if the army advanced simultaneously to seize the

[12] *Final Report of the Dardanelles Commission*, p. 54; Roger Keyes, *op cit.*, vol. 1, pp. 437–55; Brig.-Gen. C. F. Aspinall-Oglander, *Roger Keyes*, pp. 176–85; Julian S. Corbett, *op. cit.*, vol. III, pp. 202–4; A. J. Marder, *op. cit.*, vol. II, pp. 314–19; Brig.-Gen. C. F. Aspinall-Oglander, *Military Operations: Gallipoli*, vol. II, pp. 398–404; Lord Hankey, *op. cit.*, vol. II, pp. 456–7; Robert Rhodes James, *op. cit.*, pp. 321–6.

[13] This body replaced the Dardanelles Committee and its original membership consisted of Asquith, Balfour, Kitchener, Grey and Lloyd George. Within ten days Bonar Law and McKenna were included. Churchill, who had been left out, resigned his office and assumed command of a battalion in France.

forts at the Narrows. On leaving London that evening Kitchener's spirits could not have been much lower.[14]

In passing through Paris, Kitchener unexpectedly found that the new French Government was strongly opposed to the evacuation of Gallipoli. During the past two weeks the question of determining the next step in the Dardanelles had been debated off and on in the French war councils. The *Section d'études* adopted the line that if the front in the Balkans was to be reinforced, withdrawal from the Eastern Mediterranean was inevitable.[15] The *Conseil Supérieur*, however, rejected this pronouncement and resolved to cling to the Peninsula, at least for the present.[16] Two recent developments helped to promote this attitude. First, General Lyautey had warned his civilian chief that an acknowledged defeat in the Dardanelles would be the signal for the Turks to release their hordes against the Anglo-French possessions in North Africa and that, unless he was substantially reinforced for such a contingency, he could probably hold Morocco but not Algiers.[17] Second, the French were eager to support the Arab nationalist movements in the Near East but they had no available troops to foster it. They thought that all these movements would have little chance of succeeding if Gallipoli was evacuated.[18]

On the afternoon of November 5th Kitchener met Galliéni for the first time [19] and learned that he, too, considered it a folly to retire from the Peninsula. The two men were inclined to think in

[14] Brig.-Gen. C. F. Aspinall-Oglander, *Military Operations: Gallipoli*, vol. II, pp. 406–8; Ian Hamilton, *The Happy Warrior: A Life of General Sir Ian Hamilton*, pp. 406–7; Robert Rhodes James, *op. cit.*, pp. 327–8; Winston S. Churchill, *op. cit.*, vol. 2, pp. 522–3.

[15] Notes submitted to the Ministry of War, October 24 and November 3, 1915; 3837 G.Q.G., fol. 1 and 2, Military archives.

[16] Raymond Poincaré, *op. cit.*, vol. VII, pp. 200–1; G. R. Alexandre, *op cit.*, p. 218.

[17] Kitchener to Balfour, November 6, 1915; 49726 vol. XLIV, Balfour papers (British Museum).

[18] Kitchener to Asquith, November 5, 1915; P.R.O. 30/57/66, Kitchener papers.

[19] P. B. Gheusi wrote in *La vie prodigieuse du maréchal Galliéni* (Paris 1939), p. 108, that Galliéni and Kitchener were old friends, having fought together in the Franco-Prussian War. I have found no evidence to support this assertion.

the same way except for slight differences over the merits of the Salonika expedition. In the early days of the deadlock in the West, Galliéni had been among the first in the country to advocate a diversion in the Balkans, and brought up the idea at every possible opportunity thereafter. On each occasion the Government had rejected the proposal, explaining that it had not the means to take on the responsibility for supplying another theatre. The right moment had slipped by and now Galliéni saw, as he pointed out to Kitchener, that the relief force would arrive too late to save Serbia. Nonetheless, like his colleagues in the Cabinet, he was reluctant to face the consequences of disengagement from Balkan affairs. This provoked Kitchener into the brusque remark: 'Your Government seems to have no plans, only aspirations'. No statement better fitted the circumstances and Galliéni could only shrug his shoulders.[20]

This interview set the tone for Kitchener's subsequent talks with the other French leaders. Briand, while fearful of the effect of evacuation from the Dardanelles on Moslem feeling in North Africa, insisted on sending massive reinforcements to Salonika to rescue the remnant of the Serbian army and possibly tempt Greece and Rumania to forsake their neutral course. Kitchener replied that for the moment he could not remove any more troops from the Peninsula and tried in vain to dissuade Briand from pursuing his Balkan policy. Writing to Asquith in the evening, he reflected his frustration: 'They simply sweep all military dangers and difficulties aside and go on political lines. . . . I could get no idea when the troops could come out: they only said they must watch events.'[21]

Kitchener was not alone in his disenchantment with the French Government's tendency to base its plans on imaginary results, and on its inability to forge a direction. Colonel Girodon,[22] who had been invalided home after a serious lung wound and was currently

---

[20] Reginald Viscount Esher, *op. cit.*, p. 170; Pierre Lyautey, *Galliéni*, p. 272; Marius-Ary Leblond, *op. cit.*, vol. 2, p. 109.

[21] Kitchener to Asquith, November 5, 1915; P.R.O. 30/57, 66, Kitchener papers; Kitchener to Balfour, November 6, 1915; 49726 vol. XLIV, Balfour papers; Bertie to Grey, November 6, F.O. 800/172, Bertie papers.

[22] Gouraud's Chief of Staff at the Dardanelles.

attached to Galliéni's staff, was making the political rounds, asking that the Near East problem be resolved in accordance with the views of the British war lord.[23] At the British embassy, Kitchener was introduced to the French Colonel and was drawn to him at once. Girodon was no ordinary officer. He had won his laurels by displaying exceptional skill and courage on the field of battle. He was reserved, charming, handsome, alert and held in high regard by every officer and soldier who served with him. An accomplished professional, full of fire, he never shrank from a difficult assignment and his anxiety to get at the enemy never waned for a second. But he was aggressive and fearless to a point where he had no regard for his own personal safety. The day was not far away when, as a newly-commissioned General, he would be killed during reckless reconnoitring at the Somme.

Kitchener was eager to secure the services of Girodon in order to have someone along who could supply him with first-hand information. On November 10th Kitchener lunched with Galliéni and not without difficulty prevailed upon him to allow Colonel Girodon to accompany him to the Dardanelles as a member of his staff.[24] Galliéni was in a bargaining frame of mind. He was disposed, if Girodon deemed it necessary once he arrived on the spot, to divert two French brigades destined for Salonika to Gallipoli.[25] More important, he was willing to send fresh troops from France to the Mediterranean provided an equal number of battle-weary soldiers from Cape Helles or Suvla were put ashore at Salonika.[26] This arrangement revived Kitchener's hope of staving off evacuation. With fresh forces on hand it would be possible not only to

[23] Girodon to Galliéni, November 4, 1915; *Les armées françaises dans la grande guerre*, tome 8, vol. 1, annexe no. 376; Raymond Poincaré, *op. cit.*, vol. VII, pp. 220–1, 226.

[24] 'Lord Kitchener's report to the Cabinet on his East Mediterranean Mission in November, 1915', December 2, 1915; P.R.O. 30/57/66, Kitchener papers. Bertie to Grey, November 6, 1915; F.O. 800/172, Bertie papers; Reginald Viscount Esher, *op. cit.*, p. 172.

[25] Kitchener to Balfour, November 6, 1915; 49726, vol. XLIV, Balfour papers.

[26] 'Lord Kitchener's report to the Cabinet on his East Mediterranean Mission in November, 1915', December 2, 1915; P.R.O. 30/57/66, Kitchener papers.

dig in for the winter but even to take the initiative if the navy agreed to co-operate in an attempt to rush the Straits. The Minister of Marine, Admiral Lacaze, a former commander in the Eastern Mediterranean, had already expressed confidence that another naval assault upon the Straits would succeed.[27] Now it remained for the Admiralty to show the same enthusiasm.

On the last leg of his visit, Kitchener stopped at Chantilly, where he was received with all ceremony by the French military chief. The two men engaged in private conversation for several hours. Surprisingly, Joffre did not stray from the official Government line. He appeared to be as set on the campaign in Macedonia as he was on the need to hang on to the Peninsula, and had no objection to the exchange of troops so long as the numbers were kept up at Salonika.[28] In truth Joffre intensely disliked both projects. He did not, however, want to weaken the Government's hand by speaking out against the Balkan adventure and in the process invite his own ruin, nor did he think it wise to have it out with Kitchener over the Dardanelles Operation and possibly jeopardize the dispatch of English reinforcements to France.

Kitchener confided in Joffre that the British Government was considering a naval *coup de main* at the Dardanelles. He hoped that the French squadron would be entrusted to Guépratte [29] and that it would join the English in the contemplated maritime operation.[30]

Late in the day Kitchener telegraphed the Admiralty, asking that Commodore Keyes meet him at Marseilles to discuss the plan for a naval attack on the way out to the Dardanelles. Keyes never received the message. The Naval Secretary to the First Lord took it upon himself not to forward the communiqué in the mistaken belief that the Commodore could not reach Marseilles in time. When Keyes failed to turn up, Kitchener concluded that the naval

---

[27] Bertie to Grey, November 6, 1915; F.O. 800/172, Bertie papers. Noted: November 9, 1915, Diary of Henry Wilson.

[28] Kitchener to Balfour, November 6, 1915; 49726, vol. XLIV, Balfour papers; Sir George Arthur, *op. cit.*, vol. III, p. 186.

[29] Recalled from the Dardanelles and promoted Vice-Admiral, Guépratte had been appointed Port-Admiral at Brest.

[30] Raymond Poincaré, *op. cit.*, pp. 227-8.

scheme had fallen through and thus decided to leave without him.[31]

During the voyage the whole subject of evacuation was examined afresh between Kitchener and Girodon. The Secretary of State for War was fundamentally opposed to retirement, regarding this as a 'frightful disaster to be avoided at all costs'. Girodon, on the other hand, was more realistic in his appraisal. In the absence of help, he saw that the Expeditionary Force was in danger of being driven into the sea. He was of the opinion that the Peninsula could be defended even if the Turks should receive considerably more ammunition, but that it could not be held against a strong German or Bulgarian force. Therefore the Allies must clear out when they were certain that the Germans or Bulgarians were about to storm their positions. To do so with the minimum of loss in men and material the 'withdrawal must be started in good time and must be gradual'.[32] Eventually Kitchener would bend towards this point of view.

Meanwhile, on October 10th Keyes took in Paris en route to Italy. Having been authorized to explain his project to the French, Keyes had an interview with Admiral Lacaze, an intimate friend whom he had met in Rome when both served as naval attachés. Lacaze embraced the idea with enthusiasm and promised, subject to Government approval, to send six battleships to assist in the combined attack on the Straits. Keyes ventured to press for the reinstatement of Guépratte as commander of the French squadron but was politely turned down. The present naval commander, Vice-Admiral Gauchet, was experienced and highly qualified and it would have been unfair to replace him.[33]

Keyes hurried off to Italy confident that all was well. When he finally made his way to the Aegean a week later he found that Kitchener had accepted the necessity of abandoning the Peninsula.

[31] Brig.-Gen. C. F. Aspinall-Oglander, *Roger Keyes*, pp. 188–9; Brig.- Gen. C. F. Aspinall-Oglander, *Military Operations : Gallipoli*, vol. II, p. 412.

[32] 'Lord Kitchener's report to the Cabinet on his East Mediterranean Mission in November 1915', December 2, 1915; P.R.O. 30/57/66, Kitchener papers; Girodon to Galliéni, November 11, 1915; *Les armées françaises dans la grande guerre*, tome 8, vol. 1, annexe no. 382.

[33] Keyes to Jackson, November 11, 1915; Pk. 8, Jackson papers (Historical section, Admiralty); Keyes before Dardanelles Commission; Dardanelles Commission Report, p. 1475; CAB 19/33. There is also a brief account of the meeting in Roger Keyes, *op. cit.*, vol. 1, pp. 459–60.

'When you didn't turn up at Marseilles', Kitchener said to him, 'I made up my mind that the naval plan was dead.' [34]

Arriving at Lemnos on the evening of November 9th, Kitchener had at once engaged in conferences with his advisers on the spot. He was made to understand that the situation on the Peninsula was far more menacing than he had envisaged. Kitchener began to have second thoughts. On November 11th he cabled his 'provisional decisions' to Asquith. As yet he could not definitely recommend withdrawal until he had an opportunity to inspect the Peninsula. Nonetheless he had gained the impression that with the possible exception of Cape Helles, Gallipoli should be evacuated. To cushion the impact of retirement upon Moslem opinion and to thwart a Turkish advance on the Suez Canal, Kitchener proposed that the troops released from Anzac and Suvla be used to effect a fresh landing in Ayas Bay, near Alexandretta. [35]

Kitchener's report was, at the same time, forwarded to Paris by Girodon who supported all aspects of it. [36] The French Government brooded about Kitchener's suggestion for an alternative operation. Anticipating a plan to move in this area, the *Section d'études* had only very recently made a study of the possibility of a landing in Ayas Bay, concluding that an 'expedition to Alexandretta, beset with all sorts of difficulties and risky from the point of view of execution, would necessitate a dispersion of our forces which, for the sake of secondary results, would prevent us from operating effectively on the main theatres of operations in the Orient'. [37] Added to the military disadvantages were weighty political considerations. Notwithstanding that Ayas Bay was beyond the French sphere of influence, Paris disliked the thought

[34] Brig.-Gen. C. F. Aspinall-Oglander, *Military Operations: Gallipoli*, vol. II, p. 412 and Brig.-Gen. C. F. Aspinall-Oglander, *Roger Keyes*, p. 189.

[35] Philip Magnus, *op. cit.*, p. 364; Brig.-Gen. C. F. Aspinall-Oglander, *Military Operations: Gallipoli*, vol. II, p. 415; Robert Rhodes James, *op. cit.*, pp. 329–31; Sir George Arthur, *op. cit.*, vol. III, pp. 188–91.

[36] Girodon to Galliéni, November 11, 1915; *Les armées françaises dans la grande guerre*, tome 8, vol. 1, annexe no. 383; 'Report on a project submitted by Lord Kitchener to his Government', November 13, 1915; 3837, G.Q.G. fol. 3, Military archives.

[37] 'Report on a plan of operation at Alexandretta', October 23, 1915; 3837, G.Q.G. fol. 3, Military archives.

of having British troops so close to Syria. Accordingly on November 13th the French Military Attaché was instructed to deliver a formal protest to the British Government. The note advised that before the British disembarked troops in the region of Alexandretta it would be necessary 'to take into consideration not only the economic interests, but also the moral and political situation held by France in these countries'. It went on to say:

> French public opinion could not be indifferent to anything that would be attempted in a country that they consider already as being intended to become a part of the future Syria, and they would require of the French Government that, not only no military operations in this particular country could be undertaken before it has been concerted between the Allies, but even that, in the case of such an action being taken, the greater part of the task would be entrusted to the French troops and the Generals commanding them.[38]

The French note served to buttress the British General Staff's objections to the contemplated landing. Saddled by two fronts in the Near East and with their resources already overextended, it was unthinkable to add a third. And if the Turks intended to attack Egypt it would be wiser to strike against them at the end of their long journey rather than at the outset.[39] On November 14th Asquith informed Kitchener than the French were utterly opposed to his scheme.[40] The next day the War Committee provisionally concluded that the Ayas Bay project should be dropped.

In view of the danger of another military commitment while confusion reigned at Salonika and while the situation in the Dardanelles was so uncertain, the French Government requested a conference to review and co-ordinate Allied policy in the Near East. The English and French delegations [41] met at Calais on

[38] A copy of the letter was appended to the minutes of the War Committee meeting of November 13, 1915; CAB 22/3.

[39] Brig.-Gen. C. F. Aspinall-Oglander, *Military Operations: Gallipoli*, vol. II, pp. 415–16; Julian S. Corbett, *op. cit*, vol. III, p. 208.

[40] Asquith to Kitchener, November 14, 1915, Vol. 121, Asquith papers.

[41] The English group included Asquith, Balfour, Grey and Lloyd George, while the French were represented by Briand, Galliéni, Lacaze and Joffre.

November 17th. Discarding almost immediately the idea of an operation at Ayas Bay, the conversation passed on to other business. The French, as always, resented Britain's procrastination in sending the promised units to Salonika and pointed out the inevitable consequences that defeat in the Balkans would bring. Sitting ill-at-ease around the table the English, none of whom could speak French with any semblance of authority,[42] fared badly in the argument and were more or less coerced into agreeing to divert two British divisions earmarked for the Expeditionary Force to Salonika.

With regard to the Dardanelles nothing was settled. Galliéni considered it imperative that the Anglo-French troops remain on the Peninsula as long as possible. He alluded to recent appreciations by Brulard and Girodon to the effect that the Allied force, even with minimal help, could withstand any Turkish attack. They added, however, that in case the Turks were strengthened by Germans and heavy artillery, their position would be untenable. The upshot of all this was to defer the question of evacuation pending the final reports of Lord Kitchener and Colonel Girodon.[43]

It seemed strange to the English that, while the debate over the Dardanelles was going on, Joffre had not been afforded an opportunity to say a word. Whenever Joffre's opinion was invited, General Galliéni would interject and answer for him. Once the conference was over, Lloyd George asked Joffre in private for his personal feelings on the future of the Dardanelles. The military chief unhesitatingly came out in favour of withdrawal 'in view of the fact that neither the English nor the French had troops available to relieve those now on Gallipoli, also in view of the great sickness, also in view of the possible arrival of more Boche guns, and H.E. and gas . . .'.[44]

[42] Lord Kitchener, the only one in the War Committee who spoke French with idiomatic fluency, was of course absent. Lloyd George, it was alleged, had partial command of the language but when asked if he could make out what the French said replied that 'he could not understand the Frenchmen when they spoke French but that he could understand Grey perfectly when he did'. Lt-Col. C. à Court Repington, *The First World War, 1914–1918* (London, 1920), vol. 1, p. 81.

[43] Anglo-French and Allied Conferences between September 11, 1915–November 16, 1916; CAB 28 /1.

[44] Noted: November 18, 1915, Diary of Henry Wilson.

Entangled as they were in the Dardanelles, the Allies were drifting into an equally critical situation in the Balkans. The British [45] and French units which had pushed up-country had failed to make contact with the Serbs [46] and were now obliged to fall back into Greece. Awed by Teutonic might, the new Government at Athens suddenly announced that it would disarm the Allied troops if they recrossed the frontier. In haste Kitchener, leaving the Gallipoli question unsolved, set off for Salonika to see what could be done. On arrival, General Sarrail came on board to visit him. The French General described the great difficulties that the Anglo-French force faced in a futile bid to rescue the Serbs and then turned on the Greek authorities for denying him the right 'to occupy defensive positions or create defended camps' at Salonika. He warned that should the Greek army become actively hostile, only a fraction of the Allied troops would be able to re-embark.[47]

Returning to Mudros on November 19th Kitchener received the news that the Ayas Bay scheme was dead and was asked if he could now give a considered opinion on the question of 'the evacuation of the Peninsula, in whole or in part'. Kitchener had already made a thorough survey of the Allied fronts and held numerous con-conferences with the chief naval and military officers when he cabled home his final and much-awaited reply on November 22nd.[48] He observed that, as German aid was practically within reach of the Turks, the Allied position could not be maintained. He proposed that Anzac and Suvla should be evacuated but that

[45] Giving way to French pressure, London had ordered Mahon to support Sarrail.

[46] Cut off, the Serbs chose to retreat over the rough mountains in the west. Harassed by Albanian tribesmen, beset by hunger and cold, less than 150,000 men finally reached the Adriatic coast, from where Allied ships transferred them to the island of Corfu. Within eight months they were moved to the Salonika front and played a key role in the later operations against Bulgaria.

[47] Sir George Arthur, *op. cit.*, vol. III, pp. 198–200; Brig.-Gen. C. F. Aspinall-Oglander, *Military Operations: Gallipoli*, vol. II, p. 418; Sarrail to Gallieni, November 17, 1915 (copy); F.O. 800/172, Bertie papers.

[48] Within hours an identical report was transmitted to Paris.

Cape Helles should be retained for the present. The next day the War Committee replied that it favoured total evacuation, including Cape Helles, and that the matter had been referred to the Cabinet for confirmation.[49] Early on the morning of November 24th Kitchener sailed for England.[50]

In Paris, the civilian leaders had not been apprised of the War Committee's stand for total evacuation. Impelled by political necessity the Cabinet had come to a tentative and informal agreement to cling to Cape Helles. To give up Gallipoli completely would be to leave the Germans free to develop their plans in the East and to throw the Arabs into their arms, setting the torch of revolt to North Africa. It was hoped, moreover, that the 60,000 or so troops removed from Anzac and Suvla might be used to improve the fortunes of the Allies in the Balkans.[51] On November 29th the *Section d'études*, equally ignorant of the action of the War Committee, decided to take half a loaf and submitted a memorandum in support of Kitchener's concept of partial withdrawal. This solution, it was seen, would free approximately 60,000 troops from a precarious position while continuing to immobilize the greater part of the Turkish army in the Peninsula. In addition it would threaten the seizure of the Straits, deny the enemy an opportunity to establish a submarine base in that vicinity, facilitate the evacuation of Suvla and Anzac and lessen the blow to Allied prestige in the East. After an appraisal of the merits of staying at Cape Helles, the *Section d'études* advanced three suggestions: that the Senegalese who were wasting away from disease there be replaced by English troops; that the front be fortified and defended until the Turks received important German assistance; and that the troops released from Suvla and Anzac be sent to the

[49] Final Report of the Dardanelles Commission, pp. 56–7; Lord Hankey, *op. cit.*, vol. II, pp. 459; Brig.-Gen. C. F. Aspinall-Oglander, *Military Operations: Gallipoli*, vol. II, pp. 420–2.

[50] Before leaving Mudros Kitchener made another dash across the Aegean on November 20th in order to hold talks with King Constantine. Although the Greek King insisted on remaining neutral, he gave his word that the Allied troops would not be interned or disarmed as they crossed the border.

[51] Briand to Cambon, November 25, 1915; England, Box 70, Military archives.

neighbouring islands where they could still menace Turkish communications and serve as a warning to unfriendly neutrals.[52]

On November 29th Lord Kitchener, on his way back from Gallipoli, stopped at Paris and spent the morning with Briand and Galliéni. He explained the reasons for recommending the abandonment of Anzac and Suvla and added that he had reached a similar conclusion in regard to Salonika. Kitchener absolutely refused to consider Briand's plea that the forces about to be released join in the operations in the Balkans. He reminded the Prime Minister that, with the failure to gain contact with the Serbs, the extent of his commitment had been reached and he was now at liberty to withdraw.[53]

Kitchener had lunch with President Poincaré and went over much the same ground. He dwelt on the dangers to which Egypt would be exposed after the front had been reduced on the Peninsula. He was certain that the only way to ensure the safety of Egypt was to reinforce her garrison or make a diversionary landing in Ayas Bay. For either purpose it was indispensable that the troops be drawn from Salonika. Poincaré ventured to ask if 'the Germans and Turks were to fling themselves on Salonika, are you not afraid of the effect of a Franco-British defeat in Greece and Rumania?' To which Kitchener curtly replied: 'That is a matter of politics, but from the soldier's point of view we cannot remain at Salonika if we want to defend Egypt, and if we lose Egypt, we lose the war.'[54]

Back at the British embassy, Kitchener received the visit of Girodon and Gouraud. The discussion that took place was very frank and cordial. Kitchener admitted that another offensive with a view to opening the Straits involved risks that were unjustifiable since he could no longer see that it would lead to any clear advantage.[55] He was of the opinion that evacuation would be extremely difficult and dangerous but that it could be completed with less loss

[52] 'Report on Kitchener's proposals, relative to the partial evacuation of the Dardanelles', November 26, 1915; 3837, G.Q.G., fol. 3, Military archives.

[53] Reginald Viscount Esher, *op. cit.*, p. 180; Noted, November 29–December 4, 1915; F.O. 800/172, Bertie papers.

[54] Raymond Poincaré, *op. cit.*, vol. VII, pp. 288–9; Philip Magnus, *op. cit.*, p. 367.

[55] Reginald Viscount Esher, *op. cit.*, p. 180.

of life than had hitherto been feared. Both Gouraud and Girodon reflected their acceptance of this view by an occasional nod and then in turn spoke out in favour of the liquidation of the Balkan venture.

In the evening Kitchener left for London. He had tried, without much success, to bring the French politicians to a reasonable frame of mind. While Galliéni had given him a sympathetic hearing, Briand and Poincaré, though in support of the evacuation of Anzac and Suvla, adopted a different attitude toward Salonika. 'They were determined to hazard its retention.'[56]

The position of Briand was clear. He had given birth to the concept of a Balkan front, fought for it and naturally felt some pride when it came into being. Despite the fact that the original object of the expedition was no longer attainable and the Anglo-French forces were falling back to Salonika, he refused to lose heart. The Serbian army had not been destroyed, thus it was capable of resuscitation. The presence of the Allies in Salonika would suffice to keep Greece and Rumania from joining the Central Powers, pose a constant threat to the Austro-Hungarian flank and leave the door open for possible future action in the Balkans. Guided by such considerations it is difficult to know where Briand's logic ended and his wishful thinking began.

Poincaré was not as sanguine as the Prime Minister but his differences were not so great as to push him to lead an opposition group within the Ministry. Weighing heavily upon Poincaré was the fear of French reaction to even a reduction of commitment in the Balkans. A wave of enthusiasm for Serbia had been spread by the press all over the country, arousing in the public an almost passionate desire that her gallant army be rescued. Then, too, the Radical Socialists, on whose loyalty Briand relied in the Chamber, had to be reckoned with. Sarrail's prestige was tied to the destiny of the Army of the Orient. Certain to equate disengagement with defeat, the Radical Socialists would never submit to the humiliation of their idol. Poincaré believed that de-escalation of action or withdrawal from Salonika would bring down the Briand Ministry. The only alternative candidate for the premiership was Georges Clemenceau, a man he hated intensely.[57] Quite aside from personal

[56] *Ibid.*
[57] Gabriel Terrail, *Joffre, la première crise du commandement*, pp. 89–90; Gordon Wright, *op. cit.*, p. 166.

antipathy, Poincaré was frightened that a Government headed by the irascible 'Tiger' might turn out to be so reactionary that, rather than tolerate it, the nation would seek a political settlement to the war. It is comprehensible then that Poincaré would not hesitate to incline gracefully when Briand followed a course that differed somewhat from the one he had in mind.

As far as Galliéni was concerned, he stood with the Premier and the President on the issue but only because political realities outweighed military apprehensions. He was too fine a soldier to think that a puny force of 150,000 men at Salonika would produce the least significant results, and only a deep sense of duty impelled him to uphold the Government's Balkan policy. Although he professed to have no understanding of politics, like any true politician in uncertain circumstances, he lay back in wait, hopeful that the way might yet be cleared for a solution to the Balkan problem. For the next few days Galliéni's attention was distracted by a crisis in which he was personally involved. His simmering feud with Joffre had erupted into the open and he, accordingly, braced himself for the showdown.

Since becoming Minister of War, Galliéni's personal relationship with Joffre, a former subordinate,[58] had been marked by constant uneasiness and occasional bitterness. The root of their quarrel was inherent in the system whereby Galliéni was a Cabinet Minister in control of war strategy and a serving General with greater seniority than that of Joffre. Accustomed to being left alone and to direct the war as he pleased, Joffre felt suffocated by that arrangement and finally threatened to resign unless the Government placed him in control of all the French armies. Nothing would have given Galliéni greater pleasure than to see Joffre go. He was convinced that a thorough shake-up at Chantilly was long overdue and began to tinker with the idea of adding the post of Generalissimo to his existing office in order to formalize his responsibility for the supreme direction of French military strategy. At this point Briand and Poincaré intervened to cut short his reverie. The two men contended that Galliéni, who was 66 years old, could not effectively combine the onerous duties of a Supreme Commander with those of a Minister of War. To force

[58] Joffre had served under Galliéni at Madagascar.

227

Joffre's resignation now would not only shake public confidence in the army, but it would also make Galliéni responsible for operations in the field, exposing him to constant harassment from the Chamber and from Parliamentary Commissions. Moreover, it was unlikely that the French could gain ascendancy in the Coalition without Joffre's prestige and authority. In the face of these arguments, Galliéni grudgingly agreed to defer to Joffre's wishes on condition that he dismiss a number of 'Young Turks' at Chantilly.[59]

On December 2nd Poincaré and Galliéni issued a decree elevating Joffre to the rank of Supreme Commander of the French armies.[60] This arrangement had been carefully conceived and developed by Briand who saw an opportunity to solve a number of problems at one stroke. By enlarging Joffre's command, Briand would increase his standing with the General's coterie of admirers. Furthermore Joffre, who had been lukewarm about denuding the main front to supply men and munitions to sustain his arch-rival, General Sarrail, would now be directly responsible for seeing to the needs of the Army of the Orient. The initial resentment of the leftist groups at the subordination of Sarrail to Joffre would disappear once they learned that the Generalissimo would be personally committed to the success of the Army of the Orient.[61]

What seemed like an ideal political solution had, in fact, extended Joffre's once uncertain chances of survival in the bitter, unresolved power struggle with the Government. Toward the latter part of 1915 there was every indication that Joffre's days as Commander-in-Chief were numbered. Forced to make concessions he had eroded his own position and worked himself into a weaker situation where he could have been removed shortly without a major public outcry. But the year ended with Joffre clearly ahead of the politicians. It is true that Joffre's resuscitated powers were temporary and he could never return to the days immediately following the 'Miracle of the Marne', but for the

---

[59] Charles Bugnet, op. cit., pp. 106–8; Gordon Wright, op. cit., p. 198.

[60] Joffre's powers did not extend over the colonial units in Algeria, Tunis and Morocco. See J. C. King, op. cit., p. 86; Field-Marshal Joffre, op. cit., II, pp. 309–403; Gabriel Terrail, Joffre, la première crise du commandement, pp. 87–8.

[61] J. C. King, op. cit., p. 85; J. M. Bourget, op. cit., p. 145.

time being he would exercise a preponderant influence over the conduct of operations.

Momentarily pushed into the background, the Near East issue emerged once more to recapture the centre of political interest. Galliéni had now reluctantly come to the conclusion that as Cape Helles could not be held long in isolation, total evacuation was preferable to being driven into the sea.[62] In this matter he was seconded by Joffre. The Cabinet could not bring itself to sanction a withdrawal, though it did agree to convey the views of the Minister of War and the Generalissimo to the civil authorities in London. At the same time the Cabinet resolved to remain at Salonika and to ask the English for further reinforcements to being up the Allied force to 300,000 men.[63]

On the other side of the Channel the English were equally divided over the evacuation of the Dardanelles. On November 23rd the War Committee had unanimously voted in favour of complete withdrawal but the opposition in the Cabinet, ably led by Lord Curzon, had blocked its ratification. Curzon's arguments were bolstered by Lt-Col. Hankey whose memorandum underlined the lamentable moral and strategic effects of retirement, not the least of which was the possible signing of a separate peace by Russia. Hankey ended by urging: 'It so happens that good divisions are about to be set free from Salonika, and the main plea of this paper is that the question may be considered from the point of view of their possible use to save the position on the Gallipoli Peninsula, and if possible, to take the offensive.' [64]

When the War Committee convened on December 2nd Lord Kitchener had changed his mind and was again strongly opposed to evacuation. He explained that since his telegram on November 23rd, General Townshend's abortive attack on Baghdad made it imperative that Turkey should not be allowed to claim a victory in the Dardanelles. The War Committee inclined to this view and

---

[62] Part of the problem was a lack of troops to replace the 6,000 Senegalese at Cape Helles, all of whom would have to be evacuated no later than December 15th. See Galliéni to Brulard, December 1, 1915; *Les armées françaises dans la grande guerre*, tome 8, vol. 1, annexe no. 396.

[63] Raymond Poincaré, *op. cit.*, vol. VII, p. 295.

[64] Lord Hankey, *op. cit.*, vol. II, pp. 460–2; Brig.-Gen. C. F. Aspinall-Oglander, *Military Operations: Gallipoli*, vol. II, pp. 428–31.

empowered him to inquire if an offensive could be launched at Suvla with four divisions from Salonika. The following day it was agreed that a final decision could not be reached without consulting the French.[65]

On December 4th, Asquith, Balfour and Kitchener hurried to Calais to confer with Briand, Galliéni, Lacaze and Joffre. Touching on the subject of the Dardanelles in the early dialogue it was evident to everyone that a final decision must await settlement of the Balkan imbroglio. Given the floor, Kitchener pointed out that the conditions of British participation in the Salonika expedition had not been met and as the Allied force was in great danger, the only sensible course was to withdraw. Briand took the opposite side, urging that Salonika be retained. A disengagement now would mean that Rumania and Greece would line up with the Central Powers, the port would become a base for enemy submarines, Russia would lose faith in her Allies, the Serbian Army would be destroyed and Serbia would be driven to sue for peace. Neither 'reproaches nor blandishments' could deflect the English from their purpose. Asquith read a formal statement, declaring that to keep 150,000 men at Salonika was likely to lead to a military disaster and in the name of his Government insisted that preparations be made without delay for evacuation. Joffre interjected to suggest that the Allies could retreat to Salonika, strengthen the defences of the city and, in the spring, break out in a broad sweep with an army of 400,000 to 500,000 men. Evoking sharp rebuttals from Kitchener and Galliéni, Joffre was quickly jarred back into reality. Kitchener eventually broke the deadlock when he suddenly threatened to resign his post unless the French consented to give up Salonika. Startled by the announcement, Briand bowed to the wishes of the war lord.[66]

The abrupt change of attitude in the face of Kitchener's threat to resign illustrated how closely knit the Alliance had become. It

---

[65] Lord Hankey, op. cit., vol. II, p. 462; Brig.-Gen. C. F. Aspinall-Oglander, Military Operations: Gallipoli, vol. II, pp. 436–7; Julian S. Corbett, op. cit., vol. III, pp. 214–15.

[66] Some accounts have maintained that Briand held out against a withdrawal from Salonika. For example, see Field-Marshal Joffre, vol. II pp. 389–90; Marius-Ary Leblond, op. cit., vol. I, p. 272 and (Anonymous), Paul Cambon (Paris, 1937), p. 282. I have examined the proceed-

was no secret the English authorities relied heavily on Kitchener to bring in recruits and that without him they could not possibly hope to inspire popular enthusiasm. The French clearly saw that any break in the English voluntary system was bound to have serious repercussions on the Western front.

No sooner had the meeting broken up than it was learned in Paris that the Bulgarian Army had struck a hard blow against Sarrail's forces in the Balkans. The Chamber of Deputies was in an uproar, the socialists charging the civil leaders with having deliberately left Sarrail in the lurch. When the Prime Minister returned to the capital he ran into more trouble. Several important socialists paid him a visit and warned that failure to reverse the verdict taken at Calais would be fatal to his Ministry. From another quarter came first-hand news of the gravity of the crisis at Salonika. Denys Cochin,[67] back after a diplomatic mission to Greece, reported that the Allied force was in a precarious position and that, in his opinion, no useful purpose could be served by remaining there. He went on to say that even Sarrail had admitted to him that it was futile to persist unless the size of the Army of the Orient was substantially increased. It was, as Poincaré later wrote, 'a summing up which fairly startled us'.[68]

At one o'clock on the morning of December 5th, Philippe

---

ings both in English (Anglo-French and Allied Conferences between September 11, 1915–November 16, 1916; CAB 28/1) and in French (a copy of the full text may be found in the Balfour papers; 49748, vol. LXVII) and there is no doubt in my mind that Briand backed down at Calais. On this view see Julian S. Corbett, *op. cit.*, vol. III, p. 216; Brig.-Gen. C. F. Aspinall-Oglander, *Military Operations: Gallipoli*, vol. II, p. 437; Joseph Galliéni, *Les carnets de Galliéni*, edited by Gaëtan Galliéni, pp. 227–8; Raymond Poincaré, *op. cit.*, vol. VII, pp. 310–11; Georges Suarez, *op. cit.*, vol. III, pp. 209–13; A. Bréal, *Philippe Berthelot* (Paris, 1937), p. 144; Alan Palmer, *op. cit.*, p. 49; Cyril Falls, *Military Operations: Macedonia*, vol. 1, p. 59; Paul Cambon, *Correspondance, 1870–1924*, edited by Henri Cambon (Paris, 1946), vol. III, p. 91; Lord Hankey, *op. cit.*, vol. II pp. 453–4.

[67] Minister without portfolio.

[68] Raymond Poincaré, *op. cit.*, vol. VII, pp. 308–9; Georges Louis, *op. cit.*, vol. II, pp. 231–2; Reginald Viscount Esher, *op. cit.*, p. 182; Paul Cambon, *Correspondance, 1870–1924*, edited by Henri Cambon, vol. III, p. 91.

Berthelot, chief of cabinet at the Quai d'Orsay, submitted a four-page memorandum on the subject of the Balkans to the Prime Minister. According to Berthelot's biographer:

> 'That note, written as it was in the most impassioned terms, underlined the necessity of maintaining the Army of the Orient, the gross error of capitulating before an imaginary danger, as well as the necessity of retaining control of the Mediterranean. In addition, Berthelot showed how infantile was the theory of the English who were concerned only with the north of France and Egypt; he asserted: "This would lead to defeat and would draw us with them".' [69]

The appreciation did little to unite the divergent opinions held by the members of the Ministry. Split almost down the middle, the Cabinet was unable to agree as to what should be done with the Salonika force. Pulling in the direction of evacuation stood Lacaze, Cochin, Galliéni, Freycinet, Ribot and Méline (the latter two being former exponents of the Balkan scheme). Among those arrayed on the other side were Poincaré, Joffre and two powerful socialists, Sembat and Thomas. The evacuationists, led by Freycinet and Cochin, argued that as Serbia could not be saved and as communications with her army could no longer be maintained, it followed that the Allied troops should be withdrawn for urgent service elsewhere. The chief spokesman for the opposition was Sembat who explained that retirement, coming at the end of a long series of defeats for the Entente Powers, would have devastating effects on what remained of their prestige in the Balkans and the Levant. He insisted that retention could still influence the attitude of the Balkan states and permit a resumption of activity at a later date. Briand stood poised between the two groups. He was sensitive to the need to placate the socialists in order to eliminate the peril to his Government, but he could not overlook his promise to the English or the deteriorating situation in the Balkans. Displaying an attitude of frantic indecision, Briand was afforded several days grace when Léon Bourgeois's proposal that a final settlement be deferred was carried in the Cabinet. The English were to be asked that the whole issue be reopened, with the other

[69] A. Bréal, *op. cit.*, p. 144.

interested parties – the Russians and Italians [70] – invited to participate in the discussions.[71] This measure was generally viewed as a stop-gap, an excuse to avoid taking a vital decision. A more vigorous course would probably have broken up the Government.

Few ministers actually believed that the English could be shaken in view of their firm stand at Calais. But to the socialist Albert Thomas the revelation by the English deputation that opinion in London was unanimous in support of the evacuation of Salonika did not jibe with the recent information he had received from Lloyd George,[72] and he rather suspected that there was a division in the Cabinet. In conversation with Briand on December 5th, Thomas obtained permission to go to London to urge in person the case for remaining at Salonika.

The next day an important Allied Military Conference took place at Chantilly to 'define a concerted policy for all theatres of war'. From the outset Joffre dominated the meeting and, as might be surmised, gained acceptance for his view. The Russians, Italians and Serbians supported the Generalissimo in favouring a retention of Salonika,[73] while everyone was in agreement that the Gallipoli Peninsula should be evacuated.[74]

The position of the pro-Salonika party in the Cabinet was greatly reinforced by this verdict. Nevertheless, the evacuationists were not ready to admit defeat. Two old stalwarts, Freycinet and Ribot,

[70] Russia was massing for operations in Bessarabia while Italy was making arrangements to send an expedition to Albania and both countries saw that a continued effort in the Balkans would lessen the pressure on their own fronts.

[71] Georges Louis, *op. cit.* vol. II, p. 232; Paul Cambon, *Correspondance, 1870–1924,* edited by Henri Cambon, vol. III, p. 91; (Anonymous), *Paul Cambon,* p. 282; Raymond Poincaré, *op. cit.,* vol. VII, pp. 311–12; Marius-Ary Leblond, *op. cit.,* vol. 2, p. 195.

[72] Lloyd George admitted that he told Thomas of his opposition to abandoning Salonika. It is not unreasonable to assume that he passed on the names of other colleagues who shared this view. See Lloyd George, *op. cit.,* vol. 1, p. 453.

[73] The British representative, Sir A. Murray, voted against the resolution.

[74] Cyril Falls, *Military Operations: Macedonia,* vol. 1, p. 49; Raymond Poincaré, *op. cit.,* vol. VII, pp. 315–16; Brig.-Gen. C. F. Aspinall-Oglander, *Military Operations: Gallipoli,* vol. 2, p. 437; Julian S. Corbett, *op. cit.,* vol. III, p. 217; Field-Marshal Joffre, *op. cit.,* vol. II, p. 390.

threatened to resign if the Government chose to cling to Salonika without English backing. The fate of the Briand Ministry now appeared to rest on the outcome of Thomas' mission to London.

Accompanied by Lloyd George, Thomas 'attended more than one prolonged meeting' with the English leaders on December 6th. Everywhere he went he advanced the following arguments. The Briand Ministry was deeply committed to the Balkan scheme and would bring about its own demise by consenting to evacuation. If the Government fell, Poincaré would be forced to ask George Clemenceau to move into the Premier's chair. This would mean the end of the 'Sacred Union' as the socialists would rebel against the old tyrant and resume their factious criticism in the Chamber. Would England allow her ally to fall into factional strife, the consequences of which would deal the Allied military effort a crippling blow? [75]

Thomas's visit was not without its effect, but the scale was tipped only upon receipt of the results of the Chantilly conference. It was left to the Russians to seal the matter. At the instigation of the French,[76] Petrograd cabled the Foreign Office to urge that Salonika should on no account be abandoned.[77] Fifty years later Lord Hankey would recall: 'The risks of so serious a quarrel with our Allies were too grave to be run, especially on an issue on which opinion in the Cabinet itself was divided.' [78]

Once it became evident that troops would not be released from the Balkan front the English gave up the idea of reinforcing Suvla and accepted the conclusions of the Allied Military Conference. On December 7th the Cabinet decided to evacuate Anzac and Suvla, retaining Cape Helles for the present to avoid the admission of total failure. Admiral Wemyss, who had replaced de Robeck, made a last-hour appeal to induce the Admiralty to sanction a naval attack on the Straits. But his protests and arguments were to no avail. The die had been cast at last.

The evacuation of Anzac and Suvla began in the second week of

---

[75] Léopold Marcellin, *op. cit.*, vol. 1, p. 164; Lord Hankey, *op. cit.*, vol. II, p. 454; Lloyd George, *op. cit.*, vol. 1, p. 453.

[76] Raymond Poincaré, *op. cit.*, vol. VII, p. 312.

[77] The English of course did not know at the time that the telegram had been sent at the request of Paris.

[78] Lord Hankey, *op. cit.*, vol. II, p. 462.

December. The plan, devised by Captain Aspinall, now on Birdwood's staff, and Lt-Col. White, an Australian at Anzac, called for a gradual and secret withdrawal, leaving only a hand-picked corps behind as a covering force. The sick and wounded, the prisoners of war and finally the infantry began leaving in small boats. The weather was favourable and the Turks, unaware of what was happening, were quiescent. By December 15th the programme was well advanced; by the 18th half the force had been removed; and by the 20th the evacuation was completed. A week later the Cabinet agreed to give up Cape Helles. Again plans were prepared with utmost care and skill. This was to be a three-stage evacuation, with the final withdrawal fixed for January 8th. Here too the entire operation ended without mishap.[79]

The evacuation of Gallipoli was far more competently conducted than any other phase of the campaign and stands out as one of the great retreats of history. It came at a time when hope of removing a sizeable portion of the army had almost disappeared and its success was a fitting epitaph to an enterprise that was brilliant in conception but deplorable in execution.

[79] Robert Rhodes James, *op. cit.*, ch. 13; Brig.-Gen. C. F. Aspinall-Oglander, *Military Operations: Gallipoli*, vol. 2, chs. XXXI–II; Alan Moorehead, *op. cit.*, ch. 17.

RETROSPECT

'Wars cannot be won by indecision.'
Sir Henry Wilson, 1915

'It is not my contention that the force at Gallipoli frustrated the campaign
in France, as in my view the attacks made in the West were not justified
on military grounds, as being without hope of strategic success, even if
undertaken with larger forces. As it was the French, the protagonists of
. . . great offensives in the West, could throw in there their maximum
force with the exception of two weak divisions at Helles. But if better
reinforcements had been sent earlier in rather greater numbers to
Hamilton, it is probable that within three months of the landing a
victory could have been won of very high importance, though not the
shattering decision which might have been attainable in March.'
C. R. M. F. Cruttwell, *A History of the Great War, 1914–1918*

'Abandoned at the moment when victory was still within our grasp, the
campaign of the Dardanelles will remain through all ages to come an
imperishable monument to the heroism of our race, to the courage and
endurance of our soldiers and sailors, to the lack of vision and incapacity
of our politicians.'
Lord Wester-Wemyss, *The Navy in the Dardanelles Campaign*

'The drama of the Dardanelles campaign, by reason of the beauty
of its setting, the grandeur of its theme and the unhappiness of its
ending, will always rank amongst the world's classic tragedies.' [1]
During the period that elapsed between the opening naval bombardment in February 1915 until the final withdrawal in January
1916 the Allies sent half a million men to the Dardanelles. Of these
about half became casualties – British casualties totalled 205,000,
while French losses were computed at 47,000. On the other side,
the Turkish official statement of 86,692 deaths and 164,617
wounded and evacuated sick is probably an underestimate of their

[1] Brig.-Gen. C. F. Aspinall-Oglander, *Military Operations: Gallipoli*,
vol. II, p. 479.

actual losses. Turkish records were loosely kept and some of their authorities place the figure as high as 350,000.

The consequences of Anglo-French retirement resounded ominously throughout Europe and the Moslem world. The Entente suffered a blow to its prestige (though not as serious as had been predicted). Russia remained blockaded and isolated from her allies. Greece and Rumania 'lay frozen in terrorized neutrality'. The Turks, reinforced by twenty divisions set free from the Peninsula, became more active in the Caucasus and the Near East, and intensified their brutal and pitiless campaign to exterminate the Armenians. The Germans claimed another victory and moved a step closer to world domination.

For many years controversy has centred over the merits of attacking Turkey through the Dardanelles and of the plan which was evolved. There was no novelty in the concept of forcing the Dardanelles. The British Admiralty and General Staff had studied such a project on a number of occasions prior to the war and had reached the firm conclusion that the navy alone could not accomplish the task. The Gallipoli Peninsula, on the north side of the Straits, would have to be cleared and that would require an army. When the Russian request for a demonstration was received in London in January 1915, Churchill saw an opportunity to apply Britain's naval supremacy in a different theatre to try to split the Teutonic alliance and pave the way for the encirclement of Germany.

If Churchill understood the far-reaching consequences of the capture of Constantinople, there is little evidence that he fully realized the gigantic odds the ships would first have to overcome. As far as he was concerned the fleet's supreme test was to get through the Narrows and he was confident that this could be done. The Germans had demonstrated the power of mobile guns against fortresses in the destruction of the emplacements at Liège and Namur, and Churchill had mistakenly concluded that there was an analogy between the Belgian experience and the forts at the Dardanelles. Once the fleet broke into the Sea of Marmora, Churchill looked forward to the evacuation of Gallipoli by the Turks, thus negating the necessity of an army, and to the surrender of Constantinople.

It can be seen that too much reliance was placed on chance. In short, at each stage in the development of the plan the means available were insufficient to lead to the consummation of the ultimate objective, the defeat of the enemy. Yet the Government, under Churchill's hypnotic spell, took no notice of the reasoned studies by the joint army and naval staffs and agreed to an unaided maritime attack on the Straits.

The French Minister of Marine was loath to embark upon so uncertain an adventure. It was only after the British abandoned the idea of invading Asia Minor that he consented to join in the naval assault. Paris viewed with fear any action on the part of the English which would imperil its future domination of Syria. Impressed by Churchill's glowing picture of the limitless political and military benefits that lay beyond the Narrows, Augagneur not only committed the French navy to support an operational plan he had not seen, but willingly abdicated his right to choose a naval commander-in-chief. Augagneur was not nearly as sanguine as Churchill about the fleet's prospects of victory but, as was understood from the start, the naval operation could be broken off without reproach if progress was found to be difficult.

The Straits Agreement [2] had the effect of changing the avowed purpose of the naval assault by focusing the attention of the Allies on the dismemberment of Turkey, rather than on forcing her to withdraw from the war. It thus jeopardized whatever chance there was of a successful naval operation by introducing the Imperial ambitions of the Allies, which a purely maritime enterprise did not have the capacity to fulfil. With each Entente Power bent on improving its position, even against its present partner, one vital question was overlooked. Since the three conferees intended to carve out slices of Ottoman territory, it is difficult to imagine how they could have ignored the reaction of the new Turkish regime to such a proposition. It goes without saying that no Turkish Government, regardless of how strong its feelings were for the Entente, would seriously have considered or dared to give up major portions of its territory unless forced to do so. Without troops on hand the Allies would not have been able to press their

---

[2] It will be remembered that England and France acknowledged Russia's eventual right to annex Constantinople and the Straits. In return Russia agreed to recognize the claims England and France intended to stake out in the Near East.

demands on the Turkish authorities. In the end they would have been compelled to leave Turkey alone in exchange for her promise to leave the war. Therefore the naval attack, even if successful, could not have yielded the desired results. If the Powers wanted to satisfy their Imperial ambitions, then they required an undertaking on a broader scale. It was the familiar story of wanting the ends without providing the means.

It was, of course, short-sighted of the three partners to sacrifice Allied interests to their own Imperial goals. By her demand for Constantinople and the Straits, Russia has often been criticized for opening up the entire question of war aims. But besides the realization of her traditional aspirations, Russia stood to gain little from the war beyond an unwelcome increase of Polish malcontents. Her interests were not as deeply engaged as those of France, which was locked in a struggle for survival. Russia, therefore, had a greater temptation to leave the conflict if her desires with regard to Turkey were not satisfied, and in the event that the Ottoman Empire became a negotiable item in a peace conference with the Germans. In the course of the war, Russia had expended enormous human and material resources, and she clearly had the same rights as the other Entente members to her share of the spoils. This makes her opposition to Greek participation in the attack on the Dardanelles quite understandable. What was lacking in all this was the ability of the Powers to co-ordinate military and political ends. The Imperial ambitions of the Allies with regard to Turkey, and the consequent distortion of the naval and military ends of the campaign, is surely a classic example of the way in which secondary goals (namely the dismemberment of the Ottoman Empire) have the tendency to impede the fulfilment of what might have been expected to be the primary aim, namely the defeat of the German Empire.

Apart from the failure to decide on the ultimate political ends of the campaign, the effort in the Dardanelles was further weakened by the absence of harmony in the Anglo-French camp. Throughout the operation disputes were frequent and occasionally bitter. The conflicts were concerned either with rival political claims, with the question of common operational plans or with the problem of command. The bickering showed how little trust or community of outlook existed between the Entente partners and is a sad echo of an observation made by Montluc in the sixteenth century:

'. . . when two princes undertake the conquest of a Kingdom, they never agree; because each one thinks always that his companion wants to cheat him and so they distrust each other. . . . Always there is reproach and two nations do not agree easily.' [3]

War cannot be waged without risks and therefore every operation is to some extent a gamble. But it is only legitimate when the risks are based on exact calculation rather than on haphazard improvisation. Churchill's admirers have insisted to this day that to send old ships which, even if lost, would not weaken in any measure Allied naval strength, was a legitimate gamble, given the profits that would occur in the event that the Straits could be forced. Assuming that their case has validity, as soon as the gamble turned out badly the enterprise should have been abandoned. The element of surprise, so vital for success, was forfeited. Henceforth it would no longer be a gamble with a small stake. But to the politicians the lure of Byzantium overshadowed all other considerations. Thus when the fleet failed, the temptation to try again with the aid of the army became irresistible.

Before the end of the summer the campaign on the Peninsula turned into a terrible nightmare for Kitchener. Initially he had leapt at what seemed to offer a means to fulfil a commitment and to escape from the impasse in France. He was under the impression then that any attack made could be ended at will, but by the middle of February came to accept the view that the effort should continue and that the army should help the navy to get through. It is strange that after he had arrived at the decision to use troops he should carry out the naval attack without them.

The one thing Kitchener feared and fought was to commit the country to an operation which was apt to call for heavy reinforcements. For the sake of national prestige and swept by Churchill's ardent persuasion, Kitchener was drawn, against his better judgment, into an ever-expanding and difficult theatre of war. He learned too late that he had made a fatal error. His confidence and

[3] Alfred Vagts, *A History of Militarism: Romance and Realities of a Profession* (New York, 1959), p. 255.

241

steadiness began to desert him as he seemed no more capable of finding a solution than any of his colleagues. The harder he tried to extricate himself from the Dardanelles miasma, the deeper he became involved. After Hamilton's second offensive foundered, all hope of victory appeared to have vanished. At this crucial moment the French unexpectedly declared their willingness to land an army on the Asiatic shore and advance on Chanak.

French attention had first been directed toward Asia in February by Colonel Maucorp's report, urging that the east shore of the Straits be seized in conjunction with the naval attack. Thereafter the possibility of an undertaking in Asia was revived periodically by Gouraud and Bailloud, both of whom wanted the Turkish batteries on that side silenced. The French Government early in 1915 tended to resist all thoughts of a diversionary operation, preferring to concentrate its resources on the main front. When the futility of further offensives against the German lines became apparent, opinion in political circles, as well as in the country, shifted in favour of an autumn drive in the Eastern Mediterranean.

Along with the military reasons for sending troops to the Dardanelles there was another motive based on internal French politics. At the beginning of 1915 a political movement to supersede Joffre by General Sarrail had got under way and had steadily gained strength as the Allied reverses in the West continued to mount. Joffre decided to put an end to this intrigue by relieving Sarrail of his command at Verdun, citing incompetency as the reason. Sarrail, who was the darling of left-wing groups, refused to consent to his forced retirement. His political friends at once intervened and insisted he be given a new and independent assignment. The Government was desirous that any such command be far removed from Paris and offered the Republican General the French corps already at the Dardanelles, in succession to Gouraud. Sarrail was unwilling to accept a berth which he considered inferior to his rank and dignity. He would take the proffered post but only if the French contingent was increased from two to six divisions and he would not leave the country until he could sail with the reinforcements. It happened that the Government was thinking about augmenting the size of the French force in the Dardanelles, and a compromise satisfactory to Sarrail was reached. Joffre was not in a position to block the

242

appointment of Sarrail but he could delay and possibly prevent the departure of the troops to the new theatre.

The prolonged stalemate in the West had enabled the Government to recover much authority since the period of abdication. Through default, political power was shifting from the army to the civil authorities. As Joffre's fame dimmed with each bloody and inconclusive battle, he became more and more jealous of his authority and autonomy.

Friction between the High Command and the politicians, confined to relatively minor issues in the first half of 1915, took on new dimensions during *l'affaire Sarrail*. While the Government sought to give Sarrail a new assignment and preserve the 'Sacred Union', Joffre was determined to ease his popular rival out of the army or at least out of the political picture. The civil leaders were careful not to push Joffre too far and force his resignation, thinking that he was irreplaceable. Given enough latitude, Joffre continued to throw obstacles in the way of the Government and in the end succeeded in making it a condition that the reinforcing divisions should not leave France until the results of his offensive had been determined. The second week of October was fixed as the earliest possible date when this would be known and by then the lateness of the season would make a landing in Asia inadvisable.

Sarrail and his army never went to the Dardanelles. Towards the end of September the skies darkened rapidly over south-east Europe. Bulgaria mobilized and, in conjunction with Germany and Austria, evidently intended to march against Serbia. To meet this imminent threat the French Government promised to send an army to Salonika.

The new commitment meant that the Expeditionary Force, originally earmarked for the Dardanelles, would be diverted to the Balkan theatre. The change in plans was decided on the spur of the moment and was the result essentially of political rather than of military factors. The French authorities hoped that by acting expeditiously they would avoid Parliamentary censure for the dilatory manner in which they had treated the Serbian question. In addition they thought there was an outside chance of keeping Serbia afloat, thus frustrating Germany's expansionist dreams in the Near East. Finally, there was a feeling that a show of force in the Balkans would change the attitude of Greece and Rumania.

243

Joffre agonized over the problem of aiding Serbia. For weeks he had stood fast against the Government's desire to undertake operations in Asia and he found it no less objectionable to detach divisions from France for an enterprise in the Balkans which he considered was militarily futile. Yet Joffre could not overlook the helpless position the Cabinet would be in unless something definite was done in the Balkans and that even if he tried to resist the Ministers he lacked the strength to do so effectively. All things considered Joffre felt impelled to support the Government's Balkan policy.

If the French proposal to send troops to Salonika had been actuated primarily by political reasons, it was, of course, only on strategic grounds that it could be recommended to the British Government. The authorities in London were reluctant to move but could hardly refuse without rupturing the Alliance, even though they doubted that an adequate force could arrive in time to save Serbia. It was an instance where loyalty for the Alliance was carried to excessive limits.

The Anglo-French force which disembarked at Salonika was too small, too disorganized and arrived too late to assist the Serbs. In October the Austro-German forces entered Belgrade from the north and pushed rapidly toward Nish, driving part of the Serbian army into the centre of the country. From the east, the Bulgarians cut across the rear of the main Serbian armies and drove a wedge between the Serbs and the Allies, moving up from Salonika. Without immediate reinforcements the Anglo-French force had no alternative but to fall back to Salonika. Since the attempt to save Serbia had failed, the British proposed that the Allied troops be removed from Greece. But the French were determined to persevere. Briand was deeply committed to the venture and evacuation could only have been achieved at the cost of wrecking his Ministry. This was not the first time that French politics had governed Allied strategy.

The decision to remain at Salonika marked the beginning of the end of the Dardanelles operation. The increasing needs of Salonika made it impossible to send reinforcements to the Peninsula. Whether or not the projected fall offensive in the Dardanelles could have succeeded will, of course, never be known. One is inclined to believe, however, that if the Allies

244

had been unable to defeat Turkey when she was isolated, it was unlikely they could do so now that she had a direct link with Germany.

As in the case of Gallipoli, the belated effort in the Balkans was a bad compromise. With the repulse of the first attempt to advance inland, the Anglo-French troops retreated to Salonika and dug in for the winter. The reconstituted Serbian army, as well as contingents from Italy and Russia, soon joined the French and the English at Salonika. By the summer of 1916 nearly 250,000 were stationed around the port and by the end of 1917 there were over 600,000. This conglomerate force was relatively quiescent until the autumn of 1918 when it was able to march against Bulgaria. On the other side the Germans could not help but be overjoyed at the immobilization of a strong force which could be used to greater advantage elsewhere. They turned over the new front to the Bulgarians, while they steadily withdrew their own units, and relied on the natural difficulties guarding the approaches to the Balkans to assist their ally in containing the larger Entente force. Well might German commentators refer to Salonika as their 'greatest internment camp'. Beyond checking German influence over Greece and pinning down a considerable part of the Bulgarian army, the Salonika expedition did little to help the Allied cause.

The sense of frustration and disillusionment over the course of events in the West had caused the politicians in both London and Paris to rush headlong into the extreme theatres. No strategic change was destined to occur in France in 1915. But it was a year in which the opposing armies expanded. The British army was raised to 37 divisions, the French to 107 and the Germans to 94 (out of a total of 159). In round figures the Allies had 3,000,000 men on the Western front and the Germans 2,000,000. It was also a year which witnessed great gallantry and grievous death in violent but futile assaults upon a system of fortifications that constantly increased in strength.

The end of open warfare had left the front in the shape of a great salient that bulged westward between Ypres and Verdun, with its apex near Compiègne. The basis of Joffre's plan in 1915 was to attack simultaneously the flanks of the salient, break through and force the Germans to retreat. To this end a sequence of bloody but

245

inconclusive engagements took place. They are listed as follows: the First Battle of Champagne (December 20th–March 7th); the Battle of Soissons (January 8th–14th); the Battle of Neuve-Chapelle (March 10th–13th); the Battle of Festubert (May 15th–25th); the Second Battle of Artois (May 9th–June 18th); the Battle of Loos (September 25th–October 15th); and the Second Battle of Champagne (September 25th–November 6th). All these battles began and ended the same way – gaining a few hundred yards at first, then losing it in a German counter-attack. It was evident that a simple break-in could not be pushed fast enough to prevent new lines of resistance from being established.

The French High Command was confident that a breakthrough followed by the complete collapse of the line would be achieved after the Germans had been so worn down that they would have no reserves left to avert a decisive push. Reduced to simplest terms the strategy of attrition meant that battles were fought only with the object of exchanging lives for lives. Since the Entente Powers were numerically superior to the enemy, their preponderance would be proportionately increased by an equal exchange. Hence if the Allies and the Germans went on killing one another long enough, a time would come when there would be no Germans left and the Allies would win the war. To many figures in the army and in public life during the Great War this 'theory appeared the last resort of unimaginative generalship'.

Joffre showed a criminal disinclination to learn from the experience of repeated failures and persisted in directing his offensives at the enemy's most formidable front. A superiority of no less than two to one was laid down as necessary for the attack and the Allies in the West held a mere three to two advantage over the Germans. Now assuming that German losses were greater than or equal to Allied losses one could see the logic in this strategy, inhuman as it may seem. But in fact, and this was well known in Paris and London at the time, Allied casualties as against those of the enemy were between two and three to one.[4] At the current rate of exchange in human lives, the result would be precisely the reverse of the one the Allies anticipated.

The principle of concentration at the 'decisive point' at the

---

[4] Winston S. Churchill, *op. cit.*, vol. 3. See charts facing p. 38.

'decisive time' is undoubtedly sound strategy. To be sure, the direct method of fighting and defeating the enemy's principal armies is preferable to the indirect effects of a victory in a secondary theatre. But the decisive time in France could not have been in 1915. An entirely new set of tactics had to be evolved first.

The main problem, in terms of grand strategy during the First World War, was always the disassociation of military from political ends. In the West the politicians had no ends and, therefore, they allowed the military commanders to impose military ends upon them. In this context Joffre was justified in trying to evolve plans that would conform to his military ends; but he erred in repeatedly pursuing ends that his plans had not made possible. In other words Joffre is to blame, not so much because he failed to break through the German lines as because he went on trying to do it, wasting thousands of lives in each attempt, long after it should have been apparent that he could not succeed with old methods. No conceivable argument can erase the guilt that must be borne by this man whose inhuman obstinacy destroyed the flower of the French army and drove France to the brink of ruin.

It is difficult but not impossible to rewrite tactical doctrine in the midst of a conflict. It was obviously too much for Joffre not because, as his apologists have maintained, he was a prisoner of pre-war views but simply because he was incompetent. At the turn of 1915 a number of senior French generals such as Galliéni and d'Espèrey, trained under the same system that produced Joffre, had concluded that the German line was strong enough to withstand any attack and that it would be necessary to force a decision elsewhere. If the Allies had adopted a strategic defensive position in the West, a joint naval and military offensive at the Dardanelles, launched in the spring of 1915 and carried with resolution by the French and the English, would probably have succeeded. It is true that the opening of the Dardanelles would not have ended the war. As the British Official Historian wrote: 'Germany, with all the advantages of her central position, would still have had to be beaten. But it is hard to resist the opinion that such a success in the East would have shortened the war and averted incalculable suffering.' [5]

[5] Brig.-Gen. C. F. Aspinall-Oglander, *Military Operations: Gallipoli*, vol. II, pp. 380–1.

Dedicated to the dream of an early victory in the West, Joffre was hostile to any plan which might take away a fraction of his forces. There is no reason to believe that the demands of a major Eastern campaign in the spring would have been sufficient to imperil the existing Allied position against any possible German attack, or influence the outcome of any of Joffre's offensives, except by reducing the number of casualties. On the other hand a modest force sent to the Dardanelles at this time might have made all the difference. But Joffre's vision never went beyond the Western front. From the very start he gave indications that he was out to destroy the Dardanelles project. It was at his insistence that Lord Kitchener delayed sending the 29th Division to the Dardanelles. During the summer Joffre grudgingly agreed to postpone any further offensives in France until 1916 in order to permit a greater effort on the Peninsula. However, he revoked his pledge and proceeded to draw up plans for an autumn drive in Champagne, concealing these designs from his own Government. When the French civil authorities decided on a landing in Asia, it was Joffre's obstructionism that prevented the expedition from being set in motion. It was Joffre who eliminated whatever chance there was of Italian participation. It was Joffre who threw his weight behind the Salonika project to the detriment of the Dardanelles operation. Finally, it was at Chantilly under Joffre's guidance that the decision was taken to evacuate Gallipoli. Even if the Dardanelles expedition had only a slight chance of succeeding after the failure of the naval attack, Joffre made certain that it never would.

The Dardanelles Operation was, perhaps, the most profitable sideshow that the Allies could have undertaken in 1915. But to achieve success in this theatre it was vital that, at the outset, the Allies co-ordinate their political and military aims. Instead, the political aims of the Entente Powers prevented them from using adequate military forces for their military ends. In their drive to satisfy their Imperial ambitions, the Allies sought aims for a military operation which had no political ends in relation to the war against Germany. So that, in essence, it became a military operation to defeat Germany (no one knew how) with political goals which were designed to dismember the Turkish Empire (no one knew how militarily).

There is no guarantee that the capture of Constantinople would have yielded all, if any, of the expected results. Turkey, though condemned to a hopeless resistance, could still have continued the war. In addition, there is no evidence that the Balkans would have united in a common front against Austria-Hungary. While the reopening of the most practical route to Russia might have affected the situation on the Eastern front, it is not known if Russia could have averted a Bolshevik revolution. Taking every-thing into consideration, all that can be said in favour of the Dardanelles operation is that its success might have made possible any or all of the above changes in the history of the First World War.

APPENDIX

27 janvier 1915

Mon Cher Ministre,

Je viens d'avoir l'occasion de discuter avec Sir Edward Grey et Lord Kitchener. Je trouve que, vu la nouvelle pression de la Turquie sur l'Egypte, l'occupation d'Alexandrette n'est pas à envisager dans un avenir immédiat. Si cette opération devenait nécessaire à une date ultérieure, nous nous consulterions auparavant avec le Gouvernement français par les voies régulières (employées jusqu'ici) sur les considérations non seulement militaires, mais aussi politiques de l'expédition. Il n'y a certainement aucuune objection de principe de notre part à une entreprise faite en commun, à la fois par mer et par terre.

Nous désirons conserver le commandement aux Dardanelles à cause de l'effort très sérieux que nous comptons faire là dans l'intérêt général des Alliés. Nous ne demandons aucun concours, sauf en ce qui concerne un certain nombre de petits bâtiments appropriés au dragage des mines et quelques détails qui ont déjà été promis, les arrangements nécessaires étant réglés dans la forme habituelle. Mais nous saluerions cordialement la coopération de l'Escadre française actuellement aux Dardanelles à l'action générale de bombardement des forts. Nous pensons que ce serait dans l'intérêt de la France et des Alliés en général qu'il se produisit une telle coopération. Si elle avait votre agrément en principe les arrangements de détail en seraient élaborés entre le Vice-Amiral Carden qui commande aux Dardanelles et le Contre-Amiral de l'Escadre française, et les résultats de cette entente pourraient vous être transmis télégraphiquement avant le commencement de l'opération. Je ne doute pas que ces deux officiers généraux n'en aient déjà fait sur place l'objet de leurs entretiens dans un parfait esprit de camaraderie militaire. L'étendue et la forme de la coopération française pourraient alors être définitivement fixées.

En ce qui regarde la côte de Syrie, il nous serait agréable qu'un

Vice-Amiral français fût chargé du commandement des forces navales dans cette zone, tous les navires anglais employés dans le Levant passant sous son autorité. En cas d'action contre Alexandrette, nous désirerions que l'opération même de débarquement des troupes britanniques fût conduite par nos propres bâtiments. Mais ceci ne viendrait pas en travers de l'autorité du commandement français. Nous espérons néanmoins que toutes les mesures que l'Escadre française pourrait recevoir l'ordre de prendre, sur la côte de Syrie (sauf celles d'urgence) pourront faire l'objet d'une conversation préalable entre les deux Gouvernements, en raison de ce que l'état d'esprit des populations de ces régions est en relations étroites avec le problème de la défense de l'Egypte.

La conduite effective des opérations dans les eaux égyptiennes restera, comme vous l'avez suggéré, entre les mains du Vice-Amiral anglais qui s'y trouve actuellement.

Cette lettre constitue, dans son esprit, le développement et les modifications nécessaires à la convention du 6 août. Mais il ne serait peut-être pas inutile de faire observer que cette convention, aussi bien que les développements que comporte la présente lettre, sont l'un et l'autre dépourvus de tout caractère de permanence et de toute signification politique; que ce sont des arrangements pratiques concertés entre les autorités navales poul ra conduite de la guerre au jour le jour, et susceptibles d'être revisés au gré des circonstances, par une discussion amicale entre les parties en cause.

L'entrée de la Turquie dans le conflit a évidemment soulevé de nombreux problèmes et elle a nécessité de nouveaux efforts de notre part, mais nous désirons toujours que le Commandant en chef français ait la direction générale des opérations navales en Méditeranée.

Nous comptons sur la Marine française, notamment pendant l'opération contre les Dardanelles, pour maintenir la surveillance effective de la flotte autrichienne, et nous avons l'impression profonde des grands avantages pour la situation politique générale du Sud-Est de l'Europe, qui, sans aucun doute, apparaîtraient si une offensive plus prononcée était trouvée possible dans l'Adriatique.

Sincèrement vôtre

WINSTON CHURCHILL.

LETTRE DE M. AUGAGNEUR À MR CHURCHILL

Paris, le 31 janvier 1915

Excellence,

Après avoir conféré avec MM. Viviani, Président du Conseil, et Delcassé, Ministre des Affaires Etrangères, je suis heureux de vous faire savoir que j'adhère entièrement aux propositions contenues dans votre lettre du 27 janvier.

En ce qui concerne une action sur terre à Alexandrette, ou sur tout autre point de la côte asiatique méditérranéenne, il est convenu que, le jour où cette action paraîtrait opportune, elle ne serait engagée qu'après entente entre les deux Gouvernements, ayant à considérer l'entreprise tant au point de vue militaire qu'au point de vue politique. Les opérations à terre, auxquelles la France serait heureuse de prendre part aux côtés des troupes britanniques, seraient réglées par les Ministres de la Guerre de France et d'Angleterre, ou leurs représentants.

L'action que vous avez décidé d'entreprendre et de poursuivre aux Dardanelles jusqu'au point que les circonstances permettront sera dirigée par le Vice-Amiral commandant votre flotte dans cette région. Notre coopération s'y manifestera par le concours de quatre cuirassés, de torpilleurs, de sous-marins, de dragueurs de mines et du port-avions *Foudre*. Ces divers bâtiments seront placés sous le commandement d'un Contre-Amiral étant lui-même, pour tout ce qui se rattachera à l'expédition des Dardanelles, sous les ordres du Vice-Amiral Carden. Je lui envoie des instructions dans ce sens et lui demande un rapport sur les plans élaborés par entente avec l'Amiral Carden. L'opération sur les Dardanelles est une entreprise spéciale, distincte de celles dépendant, pour tout le reste de la Méditerranée, du Vice-Amiral Boué de Lapeyrère, Commandant en chef des Escadres alliées dans cette mer.

En ce qui concerne la côte de Syrie, conformément à vos suggestions, le commandement appartiendra, sur mer, à un Vice-Amiral français étendant son autorité sur les forces françaises et sur les vaisseaux anglais croisant sur la côte syrienne. Aucune opération ne sera entreprise (sauf les cas d'urgence), sans que les deux Gouvernements soient d'accord préalablement. Si une expédition était décidée sur Alexandrette, le débarquement des troupes anglaises serait exécuté par des bateaux anglais, celui des troupes françaises par des bateaux français sans que ces dispositions portent atteinte aux droits du Commandant en chef des flottes alliées.

En ce qui concerne la flotte autrichienne, vous pouvez être assuré que nous n'en laisserons aucune unité sortie de l'Adriatique et que, dès que la possibilité s'en présentera, nous prendrons contre cette flotte ennemie l'offensive la plus énergique, convaincus de l'importance de cette offensive sur la situation politique générale.

Sincèrement vôtre,

VICTOR AUGAGNEUR.

LETTRE DE M. AUGAGNEUR AU MINISTRE DE LA MARINE

Chambre des Députés   *Paris le 26 février 1917*

Monsieur le Ministre,

Après avoir pris connaissance de la communication de son Excellence l'Ambassadeur d'Angleterre, que vous m'avez transmise au nom du Gouvernement par lettre du 24 février, je crois devoir formuler les observations suivantes :

Il me parait nécessaire que la note transmise ne contienne pas une citation litterale de ma réponse au memorandum de Mr. Churchill daté du 2 février 1915, mais se borne à en constater l'acceptation par le Ministre de la Marine française.

Le texte destiné à une commission d'enquête de la Chambre des Communes est rédigé de point de vue anglais, ce qui est tout naturel et, par suite sans préoccupation des effets qu'il serait susceptible de produire chez nous, du point de vue français.

Dans l'affaire, telle qu'elle est présentée, apparaît la seule action, la seule responsabilité du Ministre de la Marine. Or le Président du Conseil et le Ministre des Affaires Etrangères ont connu, dans leur détail les pourparlers que j'avais engagés à Londres au nom du governement et j'ai soumis à leur agrément le résultat de ces pourparlers.

Diverses correspondances que je n'ai pas en ma possession et qu'on trouverait au Ministère de la Marine ont précisé l'envoie et l'acceptation du memorandum qui n'était que l'exposé d'un plan d'exécution.

Dans une lettre de Mr Churchill, du 27 janvier, je crois, on verrait qu'il ne sollicitait pas, contrairement à ce que rapporte la note communiquée, mais se bornait à *accepter*, le concours de la flotte française.

Mon voyage en Angleterre, sur la demande de notre ambassadeur à Londres, avait été déterminé par deux raisons: mon refus de mettre aux ordres de l'Angleterre, les drageurs pour une entreprise militaire (le forcement des Détroits) qui l'Amirauté avait décidée sans nous en faire part et les empiétements de l'Amiral anglais commandant en Egypte, sur la côte Syrie, où, aux termes de la Convention du 6 août 1914, la direction des opérations, nous revenait.

Tous ces préliminaires, importants pour l'opinion française sont passés nécessairement sous silence dans la note anglaise, qui ne parle que du rôle du Ministre de la Marine.

Au point de vue anglais, même, la citation littérale de mon texte, n'est pas sans inconvénient. Je pourrais être appelé à m'expliquer sur ce passage: 'elles [les dispositions] me paraissent conçues avec prudence et prévoyance permettant à chaque étape de s'arrêter, sans dommage moral, si la continuations des opérations rencontrait d'insurmontables difficultés'.

Sentant les difficultés et les périls de l'entreprise engagée par la flotte seule, j'avais insisté, au cours de mes conversations avec Mr Churchill, sur les conséquences morales d'un échec et sur la nécessité pour éviter, de pouvoir rompre, comme après une simple démonstration, si le succès semblait impossible.

Dans ma réponse au memorandum, la phrase ci-dessus, était un rappel formel de cette préoccupation que le premier lord de l'Amirauté semblait avoir comprise et partagée.

Or l'attaque inconsidérée des passes des Dardanelles, le 18 février, fut exécutée en opposition avec la réserve que j'avais formulée. Alors que les renseignements montraient l'impuissance des bombardements poursuivis violemment, pendant des semaines, au lieu de 'd'arrêter', le commandement anglais, sans tenir compte des conditions jointes à l'acceptation du memorandum, a persisté dans la voie qui nous a conduite à l'échec moral, d'abord, matériel ensuite.

Je considère donc que l'insertion du texte même de ma réponse au memorandum est dangereuse pour l'opinion française, par les détails qu'elle laisse ignorer, pour l'opinion anglaise par la révélation des divergences qu'elle pourrait soupçonner.

Veuillez agréer, Monsieur le Ministre, l'assurance de ma haute considération.

VICTOR AUGAGNEUR.

BIBLIOGRAPHY

Considerations of cost, regrettably, compel me to list only those works which have been of material assistance. Nor has it been possible, for the reasons indicated in the preface, to include all the private collections which I have consulted. It has seemed desirable to classify the bibliography under the following six headings: (1) Unpublished Collections; (2) Unpublished Manuscripts and Diaries; (3) Published Government Sources and Official Histories; (4) Primary Works; (5) Secondary Works; (6) Articles.

1. *Unpublished Collections* [1]

Admiralty archives, Public Record Office.

Army Commission Report, National archives, Paris.

Asquith papers, The Bodleian Library, Oxford.

Balfour papers, The British Museum.

Bertie papers, Public Record Office.

Budget Commission Report, National archives, Paris.

Cabinet papers, Public Record Office.

Dardanelles Commission Report, Public Record Office.

Delcassé papers, Ministry of Foreign Affairs, Paris.

Diplomatic archives, Ministry of Foreign Affairs, Paris.

Esher papers, in the possession of his grandson, Hon. Christopher Brett.

Foreign Affairs Commission Report, National archives, Paris.

Foreign Office archives, Public Record Office.

Grey papers, Public Record Office.

Jackson papers, Historical section, Admiralty.

Kitchener papers, Public Record Office.

Marine archives, Ministry of Marine, Paris.

Marine Commission Report, National archives, Paris.

War archives, Vincennes, Paris.

[1] The location is London unless otherwise indicated.

BIBLIOGRAPHY

War Committee: Anglo-French and Allied Conferences between September 11, 1915–November 16, 1916, Public Record Office.

War Office archives, Public Record Office.

I also obtained invaluable information through correspondence and personal interviews with, among others, Mr Ian Hamilton and Dean Pierre Renouvin.

2. Unpublished Manuscripts and Diaries

Brohan, Capitaine, 'Le Commandement naval aux Dardanelles', Ministère de la Marine, Paris, 1921.

Desmazes, Commandant, 'L'Expédition des Dardanelles', Ecole de guerre, 1925.

Diary of Henry Morgenthau, Division of Manuscripts, The Library of Congress, Washington, D.C.

Diary of Sir Henry Wilson, in the possession of his nephew Major C. J. Wilson.

Martin, William, 'Notes de guerre', Stanford University Library, Stanford, California.

Rivoyne, Lieutenant de vaisseau de, 'L'Expédition des Dardanelles, 1914–1915', Ministère de la Marine, Paris, 1923.

3. Published Government Sources and Official Histories

Aspinall-Oglander, Brig.-Gen. C. F., *Military Operations: Gallipoli*, vols. I–II, London, Wm Heinemann, 1929, 1932.

Bean, C. E. W., *Official History of Australia in the War of 1914–1918: The Story of Anzac*, vols. I–II, Sydney, Angus and Robertson, 1921, 1924.

Corbett, Julian S., *Naval Operations*, vols. I–III, London, Longmans and Green, 1920–3.

Dardanelles Commission, *First Report* and *Supplement*, and *Final Report*, London, H.M.S.O., 1917, 1919.

Edmonds, Sir James E., *Military Operations: France and Belgium*, vols. I–II, London, Macmillan, 1927, 1936.

Falls, Cyril, *Military Operations: Macedonia*, vol. 1, London, H.M.S.O., 1933.

258

France, Assemblée nationale, *Annales de la chambre des députés, débats parlementaires, sessions ordinaires et extraordinaires de 1915*, Paris, 1918.

France, Assemblée nationale, *Journal officiel de la république française. Comité secret, juin 1916–octobre 1917*, Paris, 1919.

France, Ministère de la guerre, Etat Major de l'armée. Service historique. *Les Armées françaises dans la grande guerre*, tome 8, vols. 1–2, annexes, Paris, 1924.

Mühlmann, C., *Der Kampf um die Dardanellen*, Oldenburg, Stalling, 1927.

Russia, *Constantinople et les détroits*, 2 vols., translated by S. Volski, G. Gaussel and V. Paris; edited and annotated by G. Chklaver, Paris, Les éditions internationales, 1930, 1932.

Russia, *Documents diplomatiques secrets russes, 1914–1917*, translated by J. Polonsky, Paris, Payot, 1928.

Turkish General Staff, *The Turkish War in the World War*, translated by Major M. Larcher, Washington, U.S. Army College, 1931.

4. *Primary Works*

Alexandre, G. R., *Avec Joffre d'Agadir à Verdun*, Paris, Berger-Levrault, 1932.

Asquith, H. H., *Memories and Reflections*, vol. 2, London, Cassell, 1928.

Benoist, Charles, *Souvenirs*, vol. III, Paris, Plon, 1934.

Birdwood, Lt.-Gen. W. R., *Khaki and Gown*, London, Ward and Locke, 1942.

Cambon, Paul, *Correspondance, 1870–1924*, vol. III, Henri Cambon (ed.), Paris, Bernard Grasset, 1946.

Charteris, Brig.-Gen. John, *At G.Q.G.*, London, Cassell, 1931.

Corday, Michel, *The Paris Front*, New York, Dutton, 1934.

Djemal Pasha, *Memoirs of a Turkish Statesman, 1913–1919*, London, Hutchinson, 1922.

Einstein, Lewis, *Inside Constantinople*, London, John Murray, 1917.

Falkenhayn, Gen. Erich von, *General Headquarters 1914–1916 and Its Critical Decisions*, London, Hutchinson, 1919.

Ferry, Abel, *Les carnets secrets, 1914–1918*, Paris, Bernard Grasset, 1957.

Fisher, Lord, *Memories and Records*, vol. I, New York, George Doran, 1920.

Frappa, Jean José, *Makédonia: Souvenirs d'un officier de liaison en Orient*, Paris, Ernest Flammarion, 1921.

Galliéni, Joseph, *Mémoires*, Paris, Payot, 1920.

Galliéni, Joseph, *Les carnets de Galliéni*, Gaëtan Galliéni (ed.), Paris, Albin Michel, 1932.

Gheusi, P. B., *Guerre et théâtre, 1914–1918*, Paris, Berger-Levrault, 1919.

Grey of Fallodon, Viscount, *Twenty-Five Years, 1892–1916*, vol. 2, London, Hodder and Stoughton, 1925.

Guépratte, P. E., *L'Expédition des Dardanelles, 1914–1915*, Paris, Payot, 1935.

Haig, Field-Marshal Sir Douglas, *The Private Papers of Douglas Haig, 1914–1919*, Robert Blake (ed.), London, Eyre and Spottiswoode, 1952.

Hamilton, Sir Ian, *Gallipoli Diary*, 2 vols., London, Edward Arnold, 1920.

Hankey, Lord, *The Supreme Command, 1914–1918*, vols. I–II, London, Allen and Unwin, 1961.

Herbillon, Emile, *Souvenirs d'un officier de liaison pendant la guerre mondiale*, 2 vols., Paris, Jules Tallandier, 1930.

Jobert, Aristide, *Souvenirs d'un ex-parlementaire, 1914–1919*, Paris, Figuière, 1933.

Joffre, Field-Marshal, *Personal Memoirs*, vols. I–II, translated by Col. T. Bentley Mott, New York, Harper, 1932.

Kannengiesser, Hans, *Campaign in Gallipoli*, London, Hutchinson, 1928.

Keyes, Sir Roger, *Naval Memoirs of Admiral of the Fleet, 1905–1915*, vol. 1, New York, Dutton, 1934.

Leblond, Marius-Ary, *Galliéni parle*, 2 vols., Paris, Albin Michel, 1920.

Lloyd George, David, *War Memoirs*, vol. I, Boston, Little and Brown, 1933.

Louis, Georges, *Les carnets des Georges Louis*, vol. II, Paris, Rieder, 1926.

Mackenzie, Sir Compton, *First Athenian Memories*, vol. II, London, Cassell, 1931.

Morgenthau, Henry, *An Ambassador's Memoirs*, New York, Doubleday, 1919.

Paléologue, Maurice, *An Ambassador's Memoirs*, 2 vols., London, Hutchinson, 1924.

Pierrefeu, Jean de, *French Headquarters, 1915–1918*, translated by Maj. C. J. C. Street, London, Geoffrey Bles, 1924.

Poincaré, Raymond, *Au service de la France*, vols. VI, VII, Paris, Plon, 1930–1: English version translated by Sir George Arthur, *The Memoirs of Raymond Poincaré*, vol. IV, New York, Doubleday & Doran, 1931.

Repington, Lt.-Col. C. à Court, *The First World War, 1914–1918*, vol. 1, Boston, Houghton Mifflin, 1920.

Ribot, Alexandre, *Lettres à un ami: souvenirs de ma vie politique*, Paris, Bossard, 1924.

Ribot, Alexandre, *Journal d'Alexandre Ribot et correspondance inédites, 1914–1922*, A. Ribot ed., Paris, Plon, 1936.

Herbert, Admiral Sir Herbert, *Portrait of An Admiral: The Life and Letters of Sir Herbert Richmond*, A. J. Marder (ed.), London, Jonathan Cape, 1952.

Robertson, Field-Marshal Sir William, *Soldiers and Statesmen*, 2 vols., London, Cassell, 1926.

Sanders, Liman von, *Five Years in Turkey*, Annapolis, United States Naval Institute, 1929.

Sarrail, M. P., *Mon commandement en Orient*, Paris, Ernest Flammarion, 1920.

Sazanov, Serge, *Fateful Years, 1906–1916*, London, Butler and Tanner, 1927.

Scott, Admiral Sir Percy, *Fifty Years in the Royal Navy*, London, John Murray, 1919.

Stuermer, H., *Two Years in Constantinople*, London, Hodder and Stoughton, 1917.

Swing, Raymond, *'Good Evening!'*, New York, Harcourt, Brace & World, 1964.

Tirpitz, Grand Admiral von, *My Memoirs*, vol. 2, London, Hurst and Blackett, 1919.

Wester-Wemyss, Lord, *The Navy in the Dardanelles Campaign*, London, Hodder and Stoughton, 1924.

5. Secondary Works

Abbot, G. F., *Greece and the Allies*, London, Methuen, 1922.

Albrecht-Carrié, René, *France, Europe and the Two World Wars*, New York, Harpers, 1961.

Ardant du Picq, Charles, *Battle Studies*, New York, Macmillan, 1921.

Arthur, Sir George, *Life of Lord Kitchener*, vol. III, London, Macmillan, 1920.

Ash, Bernard, *The Lost Dictator: A Biography of Field-Marshal Sir Henry Wilson*, London, Cassell, 1968.

Ashmead-Bartlett, E., *The Uncensored Dardanelles*, London, Hutchinson, 1928.

Aspinall-Oglander, Brig.-Gen. C. F., *Roger Keyes*, London, The Hogarth Press, 1951.

Aulard, A. (avec E. Bouvier et A. Ganem), *Histoire politique de la grande guerre*, Paris, Quillot, 1922.

Azan, Paul, *Franchet d'Espèrey*, Paris, Flammarion, 1949.

Ballard, Gen. C. R., *Kitchener*, New York, Dodd and Mean, 1930.

Beaverbrook, Lord, *Politicians and the War, 1914–1916*, London, Olbourne, 1950.

Bienaimé, A. P., *La guerre navale, 1914–1915: fautes et responsabilités*, Paris, Jules Tallendier, 1920.

Blake, Robert, *The Unknown Prime Minister*, London, Eyre and Spottiswoode, 1955.

Bonham-Carter, Violet, *Winston Churchill As I Knew Him*, London, Eyre, Spottiswoode and Collins, 1965.

Bonnefous, Georges, *Histoire politique de la troisième république: la grande guerre 1914–1918*, tome II, Paris, Presses Universitaires de France, 1957.

Bourget, J. M., *Gouvernement et commandement: les leçons de la guerre mondiale*, Paris, Payot, 1930.

Bourne, K. and Watt, D. C. (eds.), *Studies in International History*, London, Longmans, 1967.

Bréal, A., *Philippe Berthelot*, Paris, Gallimard, 1937.

Callwell, Maj.-Gen. Sir C. E., *The Dardanelles*, New York, Houghton Mifflin, 1919.

Carrias, Eugène, *La pensée militaire française*, Paris, Presses Universitaires de France, 1948.

Challener, Richard D., *The French Theory of the Nation in Arms, 1866–1939*, New York, Russel, 1965.

Chambers, F. P., *The War Behind the War, 1914–1918*, New York, Harcourt & Brace, 1939.

Chatterton, E. K., *Dardanelles Dilemma: the Story of the Naval Operations*, London, Rich and Cowan, 1936.

Churchill, Winston S., *The World Crisis*, vols. 2–3, London, Mentor (New English Library), 1968.

Coblentz, Paul, *The Silence of Sarrail*, London, Hutchinson, 1930.

Collier, Basil, *Brasshat: A Biography of Field-Marshal Sir Henry Wilson*, London, Secker and Warburg, 1961.

Contamine, Henri, *La Revanche, 1871–1914*, Paris, Berger-Levrault, 1957.

Cosmin, S., *L'Entente et la Grèce pendant la grande guerre, 1914–1915*, vol. I, Paris, Société Mutuelle d'Editions, 1926.

Cummings, H. H., *Franco-British Rivalry in the Post-War Near East*, London, Oxford University Press, 1938.

Delage, Edmond, *The Tragedy of the Dardanelles*, translated by Winifred Ray, London, John Lane, 1932.

Deygas, F. J., *L'Armée d'Orient dans la guerre mondiale, 1915–1919*, Paris, Payot, 1932.

Earle, Edward M. (ed.), *Makers of Modern Strategy*, Princeton University Press, 1943.

Ellison, Sir Gerald, *The Perils of Amateur Strategy*, London, Longmans and Green, 1926.

Esher, Reginald Viscount, *The Tragedy of Lord Kitchener*, London, John Murray, 1921.

Falls, Cyril, *The First World War*, London, Longmans, 1960.

Foch, Marshal, *The Principles of War*, New York, Holt, 1920.

French, Maj. Gerald, *Life of Field-Marshal Sir John French*, London, Cassell, 1931.

Fuller, Maj.-Gen. J. F. C., *The Conduct of War, 1789–1961*, London, Eyre and Spottiswoode, 1961.

Fuller, Maj.-Gen. J. F. C., *The Decisive Battles of the Western World*, vol. III, London, Eyre and Spottiswoode, 1956.

Gheusi, P. B., *La Vie prodigieuse du maréchal Galliéni*, Paris, Plon, 1939.

Goguel, François, *La Politique des partis sous la IIIᵉ république, 1871–1931*, vol. I, Paris, Seuil, 1946.

Gorce, Paul Marie de la, *The French Army: A Military-Political History*, New York, George Braziller, 1963.

Guinn, Paul, *British Strategy and Politics, 1914 to 1918*, Oxford at the Clarendon Press, 1965.

Hamilton, Ian, *The Happy Warrior: A Life of General Sir Ian Hamilton*, London, Cassell, 1966.

Higgins, Trumbull, *Winston Churchill and the Dardanelles*, London, Wm Heinemann, 1963.

Howard, Harry, *The Partition of Turkey, 1913–1923*, Norman, University of Oklahoma Press, 1931.

Howard, Michael, ed., *Soldiers and Governments*, Bloomington, Indiana University, 1959.

James, Robert Rhodes, *Gallipoli*, London, Batsford, 1965.

James, Admiral Sir William, *The Eyes of the Navy: A Biographical Study of Admiral Sir Reginald Hall*, London, Methuen, 1955.

Jenkins, Roy, *Asquith*, London, Collins, 1964.

King, J. C., *Generals and Politicians*, Berkeley, University of California Press, 1951.

Laurens, Adolphe, *Le Commandement naval en Mediterranée, 1914–1918*, Paris, Payot, 1931.

Laurent, Marcel, *Nos gouvernements de guerre*, Paris, Félix Alcan, 1920.

Liddell-Hart, B. H., *A History of the World War, 1914–1918*, Boston, Little & Brown, 1935.

Liddell-Hart, B. H., *Foch: The Man of Orleans*, London, Eyre and Spottiswoode, 1931.

Liddell-Hart, B. H., *Reputations: Ten Years After*, Boston, Little and Brown, 1928.

Liddell-Hart, B. H., *Through the Fog of War*, London, Faber, 1938.

Lyautey, Pierre, *Galliéni*, Paris, Gallimard, 1959.

Lyautey, Pierre, *Gouraud*, Paris, Julliard, 1949.

Magnus, Philip, *Kitchener: Portrait of an Imperialist*, London, John Murray, 1958.

Marcellin, Léopold, *Politique et politiciens pendant la guerre*, vol. I, Paris, La Renaissance du Libre, 1932.

Marder, A. J., *From the Dreadnought to Scapa Flow*, vols. I–II, London, Oxford University Press, 1961, 1965.

Maurice, Sir Frederick, *Lessons of Allied Co-Operation: Naval, Military and Air*, London, Oxford University Press, 1942.

Mayer, Emile, *Nos chefs de 1914*, Paris, Stock, Delamain et Boutelleau, 1930.

Michon, Georges, *The Franco-Russian Alliance, 1891–1917*, translated by Norman Thomas, New York, Howard Fertig, 1969.

Moorehead, Alan, *Gallipoli*, London, Hamish Hamilton, 1956.

Neton, A., *Delcassé*, Paris, Académie Diplomatique Internationale, 1952.

Nevinson, H. W., *The Dardanelles Campaign*, London, Nisbet, 1928.

Nickerson, Hoffman, *The Armed Horde, 1793–1939*, New York, Putnam, 1942.

North, John, *Gallipoli: The Fading Vision*, London, Faber, 1936.

Oehmichen, J. F., *Essai sur la doctrine de guerre des coalitions: la direction de la guerre*, Paris, Berger-Levrault, 1927.

Palmer, Alan, *The Gardeners of Salonika*, London, Deutsch, 1965.

Persin, A., *Deux hommes de guerre: Sarrail et Galliéni*, Paris, Fournier, 1919.

Pingaud, A., *Histoire diplomatique de la France pendant la guerre*, vol. I, Paris, Alsatia, 1938.

Porter, C. W., *The Career of Théophile Delcassé*, University of Pennsylvania, 1936.

Puleston, W. D., *High Command in the War*, New York, Scribner, 1934.

Renouvin, Pierre, *La Crise européenne et la grande guerre, 1914–1918*, Paris, Félix Alcan, 1934.

Renouvin, Pierre, *The Forms of War Government in France*, New Haven, Yale University Press, 1927.

Roberts, Stephen H., *The History of French Colonial Policy, 1870–1925*, Hamden, Archon, 1963.

Smith, C. J., *The Russian Struggle For Power, 1914–1917*, New York, Philosophical Library, 1956.

Soltan, R., *French Parties and Politics*, London, Oxford University Press, 1930.

Spender, J. A. and Asquith, Cyril, *Life of Herbert Asquith, Lord Oxford and Asquith*, vol. II, London, Hutchinson, 1932.

Suarez, Georges, *Briand; sa vie – son œuvre*, vol. III, Paris, Plon, 1939.

Tabouis, G., *The Life of Jules Cambon*, London, Jonathan Cape, 1938.

Taylor, A. J. P., *Politics in Wartime*, London, Hamish Hamilton, 1964.

Taylor, A. J. P., *The Struggle For Mastery In Europe, 1848–1918*, London, Oxford at the Clarendon Press, 1957.

Terrail, Gabriel, *Joffre: la première crise du commandement*, Paris, Ollendorff, 1919.

Terrail, Gabriel, *Sarrail et les armées d'Orient*, Paris, Ollendorff, 1920.

Vagts, Alfred, *A History of Militarism: Romance and Realities of a Profession*, New York, Meridian, 1959.

Watt, Richard M., *Dare Call It Treason*, New York, Simon and Schuster, 1963.

Wright, Gordon, *Raymond Poincaré and the French Presidency*, Stanford University Press, 1942.

6. *Articles*

Allen, Captain G. R. G., 'A Ghost from Gallipoli', *Journal of the Royal United Service Institution*, May, 1963.

Ancel, Jacques, 'La Croisade de Salonique', *Revue des deux mondes*, tome 55, février, 1920.

Colin, H., 'Gouraud', *Revue historique de l'armée*, juillet– septembre, 1947.

D'Amade, Albert, 'Constantinople et les détroits', *Revue des questions historiques*, janvier et février, 1923.

Edmonds, Brig.-Gen., J. E., 'Generals and the Government', *The Army Quarterly*, vol. v, January, 1923.

French General Staff, 'The French Official Account of the Dardanelles Campaign', *The Army Quarterly*, January, 1919.

Leyret, Henri, 'Delcassé parle', *Revue des deux mondes*, tome 41, septembre, 1937.

Oehmichen, J. F., 'L'Engagement de la coalition en Orient, 1914–1916', *Revue militaire française*, juillet, 1923.

Pingaud, A., 'Les Origines de l'expédition de Salonique', *Revue historique*, tome 176, juillet-decembre, 1935.

Pingaud, A., 'Le Second Ministère Venizelos (24 août–5 octobre) et les origines de l'expédition de Salonique', *Revue d'histoire de la guerre mondiale*, vol. 12, 1934.

Pingaud, A., 'Le Ministère Zaimis (7 octobre–4 novembre) et les débuts de l'expédition de Salonique', *Revue d'histoire de la guerre mondiale*, vol. 12, 1934.

Pingaud, A., 'L'Entente et la conduite de la guerre', *Revue d'histoire de la guerre mondiale*, vol. 13, 1935.

Torau-Bayle, X., 'Deux ans de politique militaire en Grèce', *Archives de la grande guerre*, vols. 5–6, 1920.

Vidal, C., 'En marge de la grande guerre: L'Italie et l'Albanie (1914–1916)', *Revue d'histoire de la guerre mondiale*, vol. 16, 1938.

Index

Achi Baba, 136
Adalia, 184, 186
Adramyti, Bay of, 89, 116, 169
Alexandre, Col. Georges, 187
Alexandretta, 46, 49, 52, 54–5, 59, 73, 119, 169–70, 220–1
Alexandria, 115, 119
André, Gen. Louis, 9, 152
Anzac Cove, 136, 149, 220, 223–4, 226, 234–5
Ardant du Picq, Col. Charles, 17–18
Argonne, 123, 154–6
Army Commission, 74, 170, 175
Arras, 156
Artois, Second Battle of, 141, 160, 246
Asia, 42, 86, 176, 189–92, 193
  on a landing in, 82–3, 89, 115–17, 147–9, 159–60, 169, 174, 177–178, 187–8, 195, 242
Asquith, Herbert H., 43, 44, 52, 85, 109, 131, 140, 143, 206–7, 214, 220–1, 230
Aubers Ridge, 130
Aubert, Vice-Admiral Marie-Jacques-Charles, 58
  opposes purely naval operation, 66–7
  has a low opinion of Carden's plan of attack, 67–8
Augagneur, Victor, 14, 110, 135, 167, 176
  concern over French rights in the Mediterranean, 50–6
  meets with Churchill, 56–60
  discusses his naval arrangements with Viviani and Delcassé, 61
  shows Churchill's memorandum to Poincaré, 62

ignores the opinion of French naval authorities, 63
attempts to mollify naval commander, 64–5
asks Guépratte for the naval plan of operation, 65
his lack of technical knowledge, 65
is swept by Churchill's glowing enthusiasm, 69, 239
on the naval attack, 106–8
insists on taking the initiative at Budrum, 118–19
opposes resumption of independent naval action, 125–6
replaces Guépratte, 127
attempts to wrest naval command from the English, 128–9
gives Nicol his instructions, 129
at Calais, 143–4
at official meetings, 177, 183
is excluded from new ministry, 212
Ayas Bay, on sending an expedition to, 220–3, 225

Baghdad–Bahn, 170
Bailloud, Gen. Maurice, 121, 140, 161, 171, 178, 183, 188, 204, 242
  succeeds Gouraud, 139
  on plans for an offensive in Asia, 149, 159–60
  is instructed to prepare one of his divisions for service elsewhere, 201–2
  his relations with Hamilton, 202–203
Balfour, A. J., 43, 131, 132, 143, 206, 214, 221, 230
Baumann, Gen., 193

72487